K

OKANAGAN UNIV/COLLEGE LIBRARY

02312189

D0392108

D 1065 .U5 H65 1997
The United States and Europe
Holmes, John W
                            231218

DATE DUE

SEP 26 1997	
OCT 10 1997	
Nov 1	
NOV 1 5 1997	
NOV 27 1997	
JAN - 2 1998	
NOV - 2 1998	
NOV - 2 1998	
FEB 1 4 2001	
NOV 2 0 2002	
MAR 0 4 2003	
BRODART	Cat. No. 23-221

OKANAGAN UNIVERSITY COLLEGE
LIBRARY
BRITISH COLUMBIA

THE UNITED STATES
AND EUROPE
AFTER THE COLD WAR

A NEW ALLIANCE?

John W. Holmes

University of South Carolina Press

Copyright © 1997 University of South Carolina

Published in Columbia, South Carolina, by the
University of South Carolina Press

Manufactured in the United States of America

01 00 99 98 97 5 4 3 2 1

*The author gratefully acknowledges
the World Peace Foundation for its
generous support of his research.*

Library of Congress Cataloging-in-Publication Data

Holmes, John W. (John William), 1935–
    The United States and Europe after the Cold War: a new alliance?
/ John W. Holmes.
        p. cm.
    ISBN 1–57003–107–X
    1. Europe—Foreign relations—United States. 2.Europe—
History—1945– 3. United States—Foreign relations—Europe.
4. United States—History—1945– I. Title.
    D1065.U5H65 1997
    327.4073'09'049—dc20   95–50216

For Jill

CONTENTS

PREFACE

This book is the product of two experiences. For more than twenty years, as an American diplomat, I was directly involved in U.S. relations with Europe. More recently, I looked at the same issues from the outside, as senior associate of the World Peace Foundation.

The text essentially reflects the period from the breakup of Soviet dominion in Eastern Europe, and the end of the Cold War, through May 1995—fifty years after the end of World War II in Europe. I have, however, taken note of events in the first part of June 1995 that related significantly to the story of the previous years.

Describing and analyzing this period of profound change, and attempting to predict and prescribe for the future, has been complicated by the change in name of two of the main protagonists of the drama. What had been the European Community was renamed the European Union on 1 November 1993. I have used both names, depending on whether the material being discussed relates to the period before or after its rebaptism. I have followed the same procedure with the Conference on Security and Cooperation in Europe, which renamed itself the Organization for Security and Cooperation in Europe at its summit meeting of 5–6 December 1994.

I wish to express my gratitude to the World Peace Foundation for the opportunity to reflect and to write on a subject that is central to our foreign policy, as it has been to my life.

◆ ◆ ◆

THE UNITED STATES AND EUROPE
AFTER THE COLD WAR

INTRODUCTION

For more than forty years the Atlantic Alliance simultaneously solved three problems: how to contain the USSR; how to tie "Germany organically into the Western Community so as to diminish [the] danger [of] resurgent German nationalism";[1] and how to give the United States a leading role in Europe.

The end of the Cold War, the withdrawal of Soviet forces, and, finally, the disintegration of the Soviet Union itself have removed the original raison d'être for the Atlantic Alliance. Can the old alliance survive, based on the other two legs of its usefulness?

Probably not. The reunification of Germany reawakened long dormant, or at least decently concealed, fears of German dominance. While the Germany of Helmut Kohl is not the Germany of Adolf Hitler, or of Kaiser Wilhelm II, the size, vigor, and geographical location of Germany make it—as it was in the three-quarters of a century from 1870 to 1945—uncomfortably large for its neighbors.[2] But even when John Foster Dulles discussed this problem nearly forty years ago, it was European, not Atlantic, integration that was seen as essential to bind Germany into the West.

The old alliance is also a rusting machine for converting into reality the American will to lead in Europe. The elements of the old bargain have changed. Europe accepted the American presence and leadership because it received, as counterpart, U.S. protection against the threat from the East; or, as Europeans preferred to see it, the extension of U.S. deterrence to Western Europe. The threat from the East has ceased to exist, although with time Russia may both recover its strength and adopt an aggressive foreign policy.

If the Atlantic Alliance had really created an Atlantic Community, the story might be different. But the alliance has remained an alliance, a convenience rather than an emotional reality. On the other hand, the idea of Europe as a community has flourished, and the cohabitation of the Western European nations within the European Union (EU) has reached the point that separation, much less divorce, seems impossible.

In contrast, could the fifty-year-old relationship between Europe and the United States come to an end? Yes, though not immediately, and not inevitably.

The confusion that has reigned in the East of Europe since the annus mirabilis of 1989; the fear of Germany that lurks beneath the surface, especially among the political elites of other European countries; Europe's confusion and inexperience in providing its own leadership; and sheer nostalgia—all have contributed in the short term to an unwillingness to send us on our way.

In the longer term, there is something to be gained by both sides from a close relationship—though not the same relationship as we have enjoyed. While the traditional threat from the USSR is gone, Europe has not developed a new concert of nations; and the U.S. might play a useful political role in whatever new order replaces the old bipolar system. Europe faces threats from outside—the Middle East is the most obvious source—that could best be faced in alliance with the United States. There are, furthermore, strong economic arguments for cooperation: our economies are highly interdependent, and both Europe and America face, and fear, competition from Japan and the emergent economies of East Asia.

Most important, in a world which the United States cannot by itself hope to dominate, we need an ally; and Western Europe is both the most congenial and the most valuable ally on offer. Such a new relationship could take many forms; indeed, even the old relationship had different aspects, though it was shaped and supported by the military alliance.

Three things can be said of the new relationship:

1. It will have to be founded on a basis other than the continued presence of substantial U.S. military contingents in Europe, which, absent the Soviet threat, neither the American public nor the European nations will support.

2. It will have to take account of the changing nature of Europe and, in particular, the increasing integration of the countries of the European Union (nee European Community). We long ago became accustomed to dealing with the European Community (EC) on trade.

2

Despite the bumpy stretch the European Union has traversed since the Maastricht Summit of December 1991, the probability is still that its development will, by the year 2000, make it our necessary interlocutor on monetary issues—and possibly on politics and security.

3. The relationship will have to be a much more equal one than we enjoyed as leader of the North Atlantic Treaty Organization (NATO); we are weaker, and less willing to expend our resources abroad, than we once were. The European nations have become not only stronger but increasingly more united with one another.

The important ties between the United States and Europe—even if they fall short of those which constitute a community—make an effort to preserve close relations a natural objective. At a minimum we shall not want to lose the benefits, economic and cultural, of the intercourse we now enjoy.

That said, the relationship could take many forms, from the most distant but cordial friendship to the more organic. The failure of our relationship with Europe during the 1920s—a combination of political standoffishness and a deep involvement in the transnational world economy of the period—suggests the danger that lurks at one end of this spectrum.[3] Our own experience in NATO and, even more, the experience of the Europeans in the EC and the EU indicate the values, in terms of efficiency and stability, of a close relationship.

Despite its ambivalence about Europe—hoping against hope not just to preserve but to revive and expand NATO—the Bush administration clearly signaled a desire for a broader and deeper relationship between the U.S. and the EC; the Declaration on U.S.-EC Relations of 23 November 1990 embodied that desire. The Clinton administration, which initially seemed tempted to smash the icons of Atlanticism, was by June 1995 responding positively to European proposals for a transatlantic free trade area.

A new alliance with the European Union can build on the de facto integration of our economies and the cultural compatibility between the two sides of the Atlantic. A solid foundation should be laid: something approaching a formal economic union. On that foundation should rest an alliance that also encompasses politics and security.

This may not seem the moment to make such a proposal. For a generation, Western Europe and the United States have been drawing apart, not together. Our leaders have become as inward looking as our peoples.

But the European Union has been chastened by the problems it has encountered since what was seen as the rosy dawn of the Maastricht Treaty. Europe's doubts about the need for a firm connection with the United States have been quenched by a cold shower of reality.

The United States has found the "new world order" to be elusive, if not chimerical. We too need allies, and—given the cultural and political gaps between us on the one hand and Russia, China, and Japan on the other—the old object of our affection, Western Europe, may recover its attraction, even if the nature of the transatlantic relationship has changed, and must change still more.

This book explores the possibilities for U.S. relations with Europe and suggests an outcome—a new alliance—that may, in changed circumstance, be as long-lasting and profitable as the relationship that is now drawing to a close.

CHAPTER 1

THE OLD ORDER PASSES

The European arrangements with which we have lived for more than a generation began to take definitive shape in the summer of 1947. After George Marshall's speech of 5 June offering U.S. assistance to the recovery of Europe, the foreign ministers of the European Big Three met in Paris. On 2 July, Soviet Minister of Foreign Affairs Vyacheslav Molotov rejected the Western ideas. He accused the West of a "line of action directed toward a still greater separation of western German territories from the rest of Germany." Accepting the Franco-British proposal for a response to Marshall's offer, Molotov argued, "would lead to no good results. It would lead to Great Britain, France, and that group of countries, which follows them separating themselves from the other European states and thus dividing Europe into two groups of States."[1]

Self-interested though Molotov's remarks were, they were prophetic. Europe came to be divided between East and West, with the dividing line running through Germany. Quite obviously, the West was reconstructed and then prospered, and it enjoyed democratic freedoms.[2] The East had a warped development, and neither individual nor national freedom existed. Europe, a psychological and cultural reality (though with indeterminate boundaries) was torn apart. Less obviously, this division, despite its costs for all Europeans but especially for East Europeans, had distinct and on balance positive effects on international politics.

The unity of the West quenched whatever temptation the USSR may have had to extend its European dominion. That unity required, for military credibility and the reassurance of the peoples of Western Europe, a strong American commitment to and military presence in Europe. Western Europe's support was, in turn, of assistance to the United States in pursuing its aims in world politics and economics—Western Europeans, however grudgingly, accepted U.S. leadership outside the narrow bounds of defense against the East because they wanted to be defended and were willing to pay a certain price for the insurance provided by the United States.

The division of Germany ended what had been for many years—from well back into the nineteenth century—the nightmare of European and then of world politics. Germany, which even in its more rational moments had been too big and too aggressive to be coped with by its European neighbors, was cut in two pieces, neither of which was fully sovereign and neither of which had independent access to weapons of mass destruction. Thus reduced, Germany became a good neighbor.

The European order which developed in the late 1940s came to be accepted as nearly immutable. One of the most perceptive analysts of that order prophesied, as late as 1986, that it might survive indefinitely.[3] The growing economic stagnation and separateness of the East, in contrast with the increasing interdependence of the West; the barriers to the movement of people and of ideas between the two halves of Europe; the general satisfaction with the status quo of those who counted in the very different political elites of East and West—all of these added strength to the feeling that the post-World War II ordering of Europe would be long-lasting, if not perpetual.

And yet it came to an end, and with surprising speed. If we date the birth of the postwar order from mid-1947, we can date its end in December 1989, when the Berlin Wall was opened, when George Bush and Mikhail Gorbachev met in Malta, when the old Communist governments of Eastern Europe had either been replaced or had yielded so much power that the end of their rule was in prospect.

Forty-two years—a number that reminds one of the metric distance of a marathon, forty-two kilometers. At the end of this race one of the runners, the USSR, dropped out. The United States was the winner—but like the winners of most marathons, it was not in good shape to begin another race immediately. And now, with the race suddenly over, the skills required to win it seemed less important than other abilities.

In the latter years of the race, the fundamental division of the world had remained as it was. But in the fifteen years or so from 1973 to 1988—from the year of the Yom Kippur War and Henry

Kissinger's year of Europe, through the year that ended with Gorbachev's December speech to the United Nations announcing a sizeable cut in Soviet armed strength and revealing a substantially changed view of the world—the United States and Western Europe had drifted apart. The Western Europeans continued to pursue and practice détente on the old Continent, while the United States saw détente as a snare and a delusion. Economic differences arose. Views of the world outside the alliance, never identical, diverged still further, especially regarding the Middle East and (to a lesser extent) Central America. Even the Intermediate-range Nuclear Forces (INF) treaty—in many ways a milestone of military détente—got a troubled reading in Western Europe, which could see in it both disregard for consultations and the potential decoupling of the defense of Europe from the American strategic nuclear deterrent.[4] But while an indefinite continuance of the divergent policy directions—the U.S. on a confrontational-containment track, Western Europe pursuing détente—would have had an impact on the alliance,[5] the historic division of Europe and of the world continued intact until 1989.

With the end of the Cold War, the division of Europe and the world which it engendered also came to an end. Suddenly "Europe" no longer ended at the inner-German frontier. Long divided along a north-south axis, Europe began to be united along an east-west axis.[6] The geographer's, and Charles de Gaulle's, concept of Europe as extending from the Atlantic to the Urals became a possibility if not yet a reality.

As with most historical processes, this change did not happen like a light being turned on. Perhaps the most important fruit of East-West détente in Europe had been "the revival of a conception of Europe rather than the distinction between Western and Eastern Europe," a change in perception not shared in the United States.[7]

With the end of the division of Europe in 1989, the states of Central and Eastern Europe have to be taken into account in a way they have not since the late 1940s—if not since the Versailles peace conference. And, in contrast to the years of divergence over détente, this was perceived to be the new reality both in the United States and in Western Europe.

One can argue about where a line can or should be drawn between that part of Eastern Europe which is associated with Western

Europe culturally and traditionally, and the other part. Most plausibly, the line is more or less the one between Latin (Catholic or Protestant) and Orthodox Christianity—a demarcation which coincides with Emmanuel Todd's dividing line between the authoritarian and egalitarian East and the West with its variety of social value systems.[8]

The United States—which in its post-1947 (and, arguably, post-Yalta) policies toward Europe had emphasized the conflict with the USSR and thus, in connection with that conflict, the creation and preservation of allies in Western Europe—has had to recognize that the long-ignored countries of Central and Eastern Europe are now part of the Europe to which we must relate. This expansion of Europe has been one of the most difficult facts for the United States to cope with. The liberation of Central and Eastern Europe came at a moment when the victorious United States felt too weak to extend itself very much in assisting the liberated countries. Not even domestic ethnic politics could push us very far.

Instead, and rather remarkably, we opted out of leadership, agreeing that the European Community take the leading role in dealing with these countries. American private investors led the world in taking a stake in East Europe, but this financial involvement was not matched by the U.S. government.[9] And Bill Clinton disappointed Central Europeans who had hoped for more commitment from him than Bush had displayed.[10]

We were, and are, fiscally stretched. For a while, there also reigned an understandable fear that too quick and too vigorous an extension of close U.S. ties to the ex-satellites might provoke the Soviet Union—the same fear that initially led NATO, under our tutelage, to be unresponsive to gestures from the East-Central Europeans.

Our private investors were bolder, but their efforts were not a perfect substitute for government policy and action.[11] America missed an important opportunity to develop a new basis for a strong relationship with Europe.

The liberated nations—especially Poland—emerged from their captivity with a touching esteem for the United States, an almost outdated sense of us as a powerful model. They also felt adrift. Having got rid of their Soviet masters, they found themselves without an alliance, without guidance, without even suggestions for behavior. For what were in a sense new countries, with politicians and officials who were totally unused to the responsibilities of conducting independent foreign policies, it was like a birth followed by a total lack of postnatal care. And their memories of pre-Soviet items were of German efforts to create and dominate *Mitteleuropa*. These memories made them want a strong connection to a relatively altruistic, or at least distant, United States.

This was the first test of the United States' ability to forge a new alliance, and we failed it. Energy and imagination were not available, or not expended, even to the extent of active political diplomacy. By default, we left the Eastern countries with only one choice—to seek a close relationship with the European Community.

Evidence that this reality had been accepted came when President Bush, in a September 1992 campaign speech, offered to establish a free trade area with Czechoslovakia, Hungary, and Poland. The cool Central European reaction probably owed something to doubts about the seriousness of the offer, especially as their governments had not been consulted before it was made. But the major factor was a feeling that this proposal was a distraction from Central Europe's urgent need to achieve economic integration with the European Community.[12]

It is probably too late to retrieve our decision to opt out, though, ironically, there could be pressures to reopen it in the sense of active American political and even military involvement should Yugoslavia's troubles be replicated elsewhere in Eastern Europe. On the other hand, the U.S. finds it difficult to accept subordination to other powers, even in a region of limited size and importance. Probably the best we can do at this stage is encourage organized Western Europe—the European Union—to fill the vacuum in Eastern Europe. This is true even though the EU has proved itself unequal, at this stage in its development, to coping with the exceptionally difficult case of the former Yugoslavia, and less excusably, has been grudging in opening its markets to the Eastern Europeans.

This is a prescription with multiple side-effects, starting with the effect on Western European integration; and the question of just who should extend what security guarantees to whom is not easily answered. But having avoided taking responsibility for Eastern Europe, and having at least tentatively assigned that responsibility to Western Europe, we should act consistently. With some luck, Eastern Europe could still be a test ground for a truly cooperative relationship between the U.S. and Western Europe, in which we divide the labor of seeking shared objectives.

CHAPTER 2

THE TRANSFORMATION
OF OLD RELATIONSHIPS

The end of the Cold War not only liberated Central and Eastern Europe; it put the purpose of the North Atlantic Alliance in doubt, and it reopened the question of Germany. In terms of Lord Ismay's famous dictum, with the Russians out, it may be more difficult to keep the Americans in and the Germans down in Europe.

NATO

Since the 1960s, there have been intermittent efforts by the United States to make NATO into something different, something more than a military alliance. This effort dates from the development of the European Community as a significant entity; it also is coterminous with the decline in America's relative economic strength and with the end of the era of great American nuclear superiority. In an effort which is humanly understandable though verging on illogicality, the United States tried because of its developing weakness and sense of competition with Europe to play a larger—not a smaller—role in leading Europe.

This effort took two forms. The United States sought to engage NATO in military ventures outside the North Atlantic treaty area. Too often the United States determined what should be done and then abruptly sought support and assistance from other NATO members. The style of "consultation" was hardly designed to please. But even if a more diplomatic approach had been used, it is unlikely that the response would have been very favorable. The European members of the alliance frequently found the U.S. ideas unacceptable from the standpoints of their own national interests, and they did not buy the argument that the alliance was geographically unlimited. (When some of them had earlier advanced this very argument, the United States itself had rejected it, as in the case of Suez.)

In the latter view they had the text of the NATO treaty on their side.

In the final analysis, the American interest in what NATO offered in terms of the common defense within Europe was always strong enough to force the U.S. to accept the reality of its geographic limits—at least until the next crisis.

The United States also sought to engage NATO in nonmilitary areas—the economy, the environment, etc. The Committee on Challenges of the Modern Society—which has existed, if not functioned, for many years—is such a case. Other NATO members were sometimes willing to play our game—up to a point. But the European members of NATO pointed out, with justice, that existing organizations had the experience and competence to handle, say, economic issues, and that NATO had nothing better to offer.[1]

An example of this clash was the effort to settle the intra-alliance controversy in 1982 over the American attempt to impede Western European cooperation in the construction of a gas pipeline from Western Siberia to Western Europe. The United States pressed repeatedly to use NATO as the forum for negotiation, but the real action took place in the Organization for Economic Cooperation and Development (OECD) and in direct negotiations with the EC states and the EC Commission.

If the United States had so little success in expanding NATO during the period when the Soviet threat was real—and when there was at least a little fear on the part of our European allies that lack of overall cooperation would reduce U.S. willingness to extend its deterrent umbrella over Europe—can we expect to expand NATO's scope when the Soviet threat has vanished? The effort, which has been made and is still being made, may be an attempt to fill an old wine bottle, NATO, with new wine. European members of NATO, by and large, like it as it is and has been. They favor only relatively modest reforms. This position contrasts sharply with the sentiment summed up in Senator Richard Lugar's line that NATO must go out of area or out of business.[2]

Europe might have been less reluctant to be pulled along by the United States in geographic and functional expansion of NATO had the North Atlantic Alliance produced a sense of community. But it did not. The alliance was important, but the relationship between its members and the citizens of its countries was one of convenience.

Unfortunately for NATO, and for a United States that wants to continue to use that alliance as its lever on Europe, NATO suffers by comparison with the European Union, which has created a sense of community among its citizens (though this sense is not, so far, equal to that found within individual states). The economic interchanges between Western Europeans permitted and stimulated by the EU have added force to a sense of Europeanness based on history and culture. Whenever the competition is between European links and Atlantic links, the European, given equal effectiveness, will win.

Effectiveness is the key to what has made NATO endure despite its political-cultural weakness. In the past, Europe could not defend itself. It did not, in fact, want to be defended; it wanted war to be deterred, and only the United States' nuclear capacity provided that deterrence.

Given the end of the Soviet threat, it is conceivable that some Europeans will no longer feel a need for U.S. protection. It is also conceivable that the American public will not support a military presence in Europe without there being a clear and present danger of large-scale war. Several American foreign policy experts argue that the U.S. will not for long pay the costs involved in maintaining forces in Europe simply as a contribution to a Western European stability that is not in jeopardy.[3]

Both of these hypotheses could prove wrong. In the first five years of the post-Cold War era, there was in fact little evidence of a desire for total disengagement on either side of the Atlantic.[4] But as strains developed over what to do about Yugoslavia and about NATO expansion, it still seemed quite possible that such sentiment would develop. Taken together with the difficulty of extending NATO's scope from Europe to the world as a whole, this possibility should mean that the alliance will come to an end.

But this is too quick a judgment. Perhaps it is wrong. In chapter 4, below, the prospects for a second life for NATO—or perhaps more accurately, a prolonged senescence—will be discussed.

GERMANY

The reunification of Germany took the lid off fears of German aggressiveness, or at least dominance, that had been decently concealed for a generation. (Occasionally, during that generation, the truth would slip out—as when, in the mid-1980s, Italy's perennial prime minister, Giulio Andreotti, told a crowd at an Italian Communist summer fair that "everyone" wanted Germany to remain divided.)[5]

Two forces worked to keep fears and accusations from being expressed even more loudly. The American government took an uncompromisingly positive view of German reunification, and public opinion in the United States did not manifest any strong contrary position. Germany itself, for the most part, played a quiet—and responsible—game.

Yet underlying fears of a repetition of Europe's recent past, when Germany was the troublemaker of the Continent, remain strong, even though most politicians and officials have stopped short of emulating the 1990 tirade by Nicholas Ridley, a British cabinet minister. Ridley accused Germany of pushing monetary union as a tool to dominate Europe and declared that surrendering British sovereignty to the European Community would be like surrendering to Hitler.[6]

The Germans themselves fed these fears in three notable episodes. The first was the Kohl-Gorbachev pact of November 1990, in which Germany agreed not to join in any attack on the Soviet Union. It could be and was argued that, since NATO is a defensive alliance, this agreement did not contravene Germany's commitments to the West. Nevertheless, taken together with the fears created by the simple fact of direct German-Soviet negotiations, the Kohl-Gorbachev pact evoked memories of the Rapallo Treaty of 1922 and the Russo-German Reinsurance Treaty of 1887. The idea that the Germans might turn away from the West and form an alliance with the Soviets flew in the face of Germany's economic interdependence with the West, and particularly with the other countries of the European Community. But only the disintegration of the Soviet Union put the fear to rest—at least provisionally.

The second instance was Germany's putting pressure on the European Community to recognize Slovenia and Croatia. It can, of course, be argued that the EC would have come to this position eventually even without German pressure. While much has been made of historic German ties with Slovenia and Croatia, with the suggestion that Germany might be re-creating its hegemony in *Mitteleuropa*, it seems at least as likely that Germany was acting out of the strong popular sentiment in favor of self-determination that was invigorated by Germany's own recent history and example.[7] And, once having succeeded in forcing recognition of Slovenia and Croatia, Germany did not, as Bismarck might have, try to play the role of prime mediator in the Balkan conflict, nor did it take the lead in creating a military coalition against Serbia.[8] But, even drained of any negative connotation, the German pressure was a new experience for a Europe which had come to expect that nation to adopt a low profile on most international issues.

While notions of German aggression seemed absurd, and a reversal of Germany's fundamental alliance improbable, German dominance within the European Community appeared more plausible. In the same month, December 1991, when Germany forced the other members of the EC to follow its lead regarding Croatia and Slovenia, it played the key role at the EC's Maastricht Summit—not as *demandeur* but as the arbiter and benefactor without whose consent little or nothing was possible. And, rejecting pressure from other European states, Germany increased interest rates.[9]

This was a foreshadowing of the third significant episode, the financial crisis of September 1992. At a time when the EC's future was at stake, with the French referendum on the Maastricht Treaty scheduled for 20 September, Germany pursued a monetary policy line that seemed to ignore both the economic situation in the European nations that were bound monetarily to Germany by the European Monetary System's exchange rate mechanism, and the impact that financial turbulence would have on attitudes toward yet tighter links within the EC.

Germany's growing willingness to use its strength within the European Union (a very different thing from using it independently) was shown in the choice of a new president to succeed Jacques Delors at the EU Commission in 1995. Germany's Chancellor Kohl blocked the candidacy of Dutch Prime Minister Ruud Lubbers (because of Lubbers's previous opposition to German unification). The eventual choice, Jacques Santer (the Luxembourg prime minister), was selected by Kohl, who then arranged for approval by the other EU member-states.[10]

At least initially, nowhere was the revival of a great, united Germany more a cause for worry than in France. While Germany was divided, France could aspire to at least a condominium in the European Community. While there was more rhetoric than reality in the Bonn-Paris relationship from the Elysée Treaty of 1963 through early 1989, France at least gained thereby in self-esteem.

With unification, with the removal of some of the self-imposed restraints on German foreign policy, France had to face the fact that in terms of power, it now counts for much less than its neighbor to the east. True, France is a nuclear power, but what this fact means after the Cold War and within a West European context is unclear. What is clear is the divergence in economic power between the two states. And German policy—while intent on pursuing objectives peacefully, rather than by reversion to Germany's militarist traditions—is not bashful about the power, indeed the priority, of economics.[11]

On the other hand, Germany usually seems to be trying to please everyone. At the same time, late 1991, as it was flexing its muscles in Europe, it joined with France in pressing the cause of building a European defense identity on the foundation of the expansion of the Franco-German brigade (while at the same time seeking to maintain NATO and, above all, the American security tie.)[12]

American diplomacy, throughout the turbulent period that began in 1988, has clearly recognized Germany's priority in a way that must be especially galling for the French. France is left with no better choice than to continue to seek to bind Germany to France and into the European Community. Though German dominance is in that case very likely, this is better than the alternative of a Germany that is freed from the restraints of a fixed relationship and orientation.

No likely substitute will equal the restrictions imposed by the Cold War and the division of Germany. The combination of a more powerful Germany with the weakening of the framework surrounding it is legitimate cause for reflection—but not for reflexive action. Germany continues to insist on the avoidance of military involvement except under restrictive conditions, even after the 12 July 1994 decision of the German Constitutional Court permitting use of German troops outside the NATO area.[13] Germany's disinclination to act militarily—together with its evident belief that an approach to international politics which stresses the use of economic power, the efficacy of collective norms and, perhaps, collective security, is the "realistic" course in our new world—should, at the least, reduce short-term fears about its aggressiveness. The U.S. should bend with this wind and encourage Germany in its proclaimed desire to function as a member of the European Union rather than as an independent entity.[14]

Two extremely well placed European commentators write that "Germany's political class is prepared to give up some of the sovereignty it has acquired through unification, believing almost unanimously that it is the only way to escape the foreign policy traps of the past. Such an opportunity should be seized by Germany's European partners while it is available."[15] And it should be seized, as well, by German's transatlantic partner.

In any event, however useful our role of guardian over Germany was to the world order of the past, it cannot be perpetuated. We shall have to seek to persuade an independent Germany rather than constrain a dependent Germany. And we shall only reduce our chances of success by indiscreetly suggesting, as did a paper leaked from the Defense Department in March 1992, that our policy is designed to maintain Germany in perpetuity in a state of dependence.[16]

Almost as indiscreet, and certainly tone-deaf, have been the attempts by the Clinton administration to single out Germany for special consideration, as when President Clinton spoke of a "truly unique relationship" between the United States and Germany during his visit to Bonn and Berlin in July 1994. This remark created dyspepsia in France and Great Britain (the latter has been dining out for more than a generation on the "special relationship"). But it also caused discomfort in Germany itself. Germany is aware of its power and influence; it has its own interests and pursues them. However, it prefers to deal with the United States through multilateral institutional channels.[17] Given the history of Germany's autonomous use of power, this is a predilection that should be welcomed and honored, even if it puts a strain on U.S. diplomatic style.

CHAPTER 3

WESTERN EUROPE ON THE
ROAD TO INTEGRATION

The European Community—rebaptized the European Union on 1 November 1993—has existed for nearly forty years. Taking into account its period of gestation in the early 1950s, it has existed as a powerful idea for even longer. But during a remarkable period of institutional development and renewed enthusiasm, running from the negotiation of the Single European Act in 1985 through the Maastricht Summit of December 1991, the EC seemed on the verge of becoming something more than the "common market" we once called it. If the developments of the last few years continue—and there is a fair chance they will despite the problems Western Europe has had digesting the Maastricht accords—the European Union will acquire some of the traditional core aspects of statehood: a single currency and monetary policy, and a common foreign policy, possibly including an approach to a common defense. This degree of unity may well, however, take longer to achieve than was foreseen by the Maastricht timetable.

It is tempting to think that the rumblings from Europe about security cooperation and defense integration date from the end of the Cold War, but, in fact, they began much earlier. The conception of a European Defense Community (EDC) long predates the Treaty of Rome, much less the end of the threat to which the EDC responded. Kennedy's later idea of a European Pillar was enunciated a quarter-century before the beginning of the end of Soviet domination in Eastern Europe.

Most of the current agenda of the EU can, indeed, be seen as a revision of ideas long ago ventilated but not effectively adopted, usually because Europeanist proposals suffered from competition with the transatlantic connection.

General de Gaulle's ideas, advanced in 1959–1961, for a form of political union and a common foreign policy, embodied in the Fouchet Plan, were rejected for a number of reasons. Some rejected them because they favored supranationalism as opposed to de Gaulle's *Europe des patries*. But de Gaulle's ideas were also threatening to those who feared an impact on the American connection.

In the monetary area, there was an even clearer tug of interests between an Atlantic/global approach and doing things on a regional basis.

Europe was ready for currency convertibility in the same year, 1958, that the Common Market came into being. Ironically, at the same time that the core countries of Western Europe began to distinguish themselves from the rest of the countries of the international trading system by forming a customs union, the West European currencies for the first time "became fully integrated into the dollar area," that is, the Bretton Woods system. While the Treaty of Rome, in ARTICLES 103–5, includes principles for macro-economic and international monetary behavior and exhorts the member-states to coordinate policy, the EC accepted the Bretton Woods system as providing its monetary order.[1]

While a Monetary Committee was set up in 1958, little was done by way of coordination until, in early 1964, Italy, in the midst of a financial crisis, turned to the United States for emergency credits. Italy was moved to do this because of the unsympathetic response of its Common Market partners to the fate of the lira. The United States not only provided bilateral assistance but also helped arrange for the Bank of England and the Bundesbank to contribute to the package of credits.[2]

Italy's recourse to the United States drew a "snooty note" to Rome from Brussels, and Italy then held discussions with the EC Commission, which produced a "Letter of Expectations" to the Italian government regarding the corrective economic actions it should take. A byproduct was the reactivation of EC thinking about monetary cooperation. In April 1964 a committee of EC central bank governors was set up, and the Monetary Committee established in 1958 was given the new tasks of ensuring consultation between member-states on all questions of international monetary relations—with such consultation to take place before the parity of any member state's currency was altered.[3]

Nevertheless, the EC countries continued to play largely individual games within the global cooperative framework of the Bretton Woods system. The German float and revaluation of 1969 (with the French devaluation of the same period) in fact set back prospects for economic union in the EC by at least five years. The German and French exchange rate changes "shot great gaping holes in the CAP [Common Agricultural Policy]" because neither Germany nor France was willing to adjust domestic farm prices to reflect the new exchange rates. "The challenge on monetary union looked to the Six [member-states of the EC] like a call to double or quits."[4]

However, the Werner Plan for Economic and Monetary Union (EMU)—commissioned by the Hague Summit of December 1969 and submitted in October 1970 on the very eve of the collapse of the original Bretton Woods system—originally assumed that the union would be established within the global framework of fixed exchange rates as provided for by the Bretton Woods system. In the first stage of EMU, margins for currency fluctuations were simply to be narrowed so that deviations among EC countries would not exceed EC currencies' deviations vis-à-vis the dollar.[5]

In the monetary area, it took the collapse of the old international system, plus the rather cavalier manner in which the United States euthanized that system, to lead the countries of the EC into a regional, integrationist approach. And they moved in this direction in dispersed order: when in 1979 the European Monetary System (EMS) was finally inaugurated, one key country, the U.K., was still unprepared to participate in its exchange rate mechanism.

The latest push toward European integration was also a product of adversity. After being largely stalled for nearly twenty years, since de Gaulle had put the brake on movement to supranationalism in the European Community,[6] the EC got into gear again in the mid-1980s. In part this was in response to the worsening economic condition of Europe. Eurosclerosis had been diagnosed, and the prescription was a new dose of integration, the fulfillment of the Rome Treaty's provision that the European Community should be a common market for the movement of goods, services, people, and capital.

Bad relations with the United States are another part of the explanation. During the earlier Reagan years, relations between the United States and Europe reached a historic low. Among the incidents of a particularly stormy period were the clash between the United States and Western Europe over the construction of a gas pipeline from Siberia (1982) and the split between the two sides of the Atlantic occasioned by the U.S. attack on Libya (1986). During the latter conflict, Peter Carrington, then NATO's secretary general, said "the situation is as bad between Europe and America as I can remember in the period I have been associated with the Alliance."[7]

These bad relations were only part of the story. They reflected European dissatisfaction with the American policies and actions that rendered Europe less independent—or attempted to do so. But the severity of the resentment, and the impetus it gave to a fresh and stronger European attempt to develop a specific identity separate from the United States and from the alliance which the United States dominated, are explained by the growing perception that the United States' commitment to European security was neither as valuable nor as reliable as before. European worries about this began well back in the 1960s, but two developments of the 1980s—the Strategic Defense Initiative and the INF Treaty—exacerbated them.

Personalities also counted. François Mitterrand, after making a vain attempt to conduct an autonomous socialist policy in France, turned his attention, generally with positive effect, to the broader, less frustrating European stage.[8] Jacques Delors, who combined a certain idealism with ambition and energy, took over the presidency of the European Commission. While other European actors were not so important, Delors did build up a good working relationship with the government of the Federal Republic of Germany; and Margaret Thatcher's personal obsessions, when they were not irrelevant or obstructionist, occasionally had a positive effect, as in her support for the Single Market.[9]

What it all added up to was a resumption of the march toward integration that Western Europe had abandoned nearly twenty years before. This resumption occurred at the same time that the Soviet Union was melting down and the United States was obsessed with geopolitical conflict with the Soviet Union and its allies.

The new integrationist drive had the not-entirely-intended effect of adding to the strains on the alliance caused by the end of the

Cold War. The world no longer was neatly divided in two; *and* the almost inevitable weakening of the links between the elements of what had been the "Western world" was accentuated by the development of greater European inwardness, self-assurance, and autonomy.

Europe, as it stands, is an uncomfortable partner for the United States. The hegemony we enjoyed for a few decades after the Second World War, whatever its psychic costs for Europe, was generally mutually beneficial and acceptable. If Europe were now to develop into a political union, with a common foreign policy, some sort of condominium arrangement might be possible which would create a relationship between Europe and the United States comparable in stability to that of the 1950s.[10] But while the European Union is already more than just a multilateral organization of the normal type, it falls short of being even a loose or heavily devolutionary federal state.

Turning this argument around, while the development of European integration in the late 1980s added to the centrifugal forces within the alliance, it is conceivable that further integration—to the point where the European Union is truly united—might simplify and help resolve the problems in the transatlantic relationship. Having a single partner, with a single governing authority, to deal with, would not just be tidier; it also might make it easier for the United States to accept a relationship of equality rather than to continue its pursuit of dominance through what some Europeans see as divide-and-conquer tactics.

Agreement to the EC Commission's White Paper of 14 June 1985 proposing that the European Community complete the internal market by the end of 1992 led to actions that will strengthen the integration of the European economy. This integration, as it develops, is the best insurance against the European Union's going backward. It does not necessarily ensure going forward to those forms of integration that will turn the EU into a single international actor. But the need to expedite the work of the EC to achieve the target set by the White Paper did contribute to improving the federal quality of the Community. The provisions for qualified majority voting in the Council of Ministers contained in the Single European Act removed the roadblock created by the Luxembourg Compromise—

requiring unanimity in Community decision making—exacted by de Gaulle in 1966.

But if the European Union is to be considered a real union, rather than a collection of states, it must acquire from its members sovereignty in the monetary and political areas. If it does so, it will be subtracting authority from the United States because it will become more nearly an equal with us and less an object of our policy in two spheres of international life—the management of the international monetary system and the management of Western security—which we have dominated for more than forty years.

Prospects are brighter, though hardly unclouded, for Economic and Monetary Union. After Delors's proposal for EMU was presented in 1989, there was a seemingly inexorable movement toward agreement. The Maastricht European Council of December 1991 did leave unfinished business. At that meeting, the U.K. demanded freedom to opt out of the final stage of monetary union. Not long after the meeting it became equally clear that the Bundesbank was unhappy with the package the German government had negotiated, fearing that the lack of movement on political union left too much freedom for member-states to follow fiscal and other economic policies that could undermine monetary union.[11]

Nevertheless, until the financial crisis of September 1992 (which led the U.K. to suspend its membership in the exchange rate membership of the EMS), most observers believed the U.K. would, in the end, join phase three of Economic and Monetary Union, entailing a single European currency and monetary policy, since its not doing so would undermine the role of the City of London in European finance. This logic may yet prove persuasive.

The German attitude toward EMU is interesting—and crucial. The enthusiasm of other countries, notably France and Italy, for full monetary union derives from their belief that they would thereby gain a voice in monetary policy which they have lost within the existing European Monetary System. Until the monetary crisis and breakup of the exchange rate mechanism in August 1993, the Bundesbank set monetary policy for all the members of the EMS and, arguably, still does for many or most of them.[12] If EMU is achieved, a committee composed of the governors of the central banks of the member-states will set the policy. Countries other than Germany would recover at least a share in the monetary sovereignty they have lost. Some nations might seek to push for a somewhat more supple, somewhat less obsessively anti-inflationary policy than the Bundesbank has followed. They might also use their share of control of the European Central Bank to transfer responsibility for funding national budget deficits to the EU level (evidently one of the Bundesbank's fears). Looked at from the Bundesbank's point of view, all of this might be a new way for bad money (the European Currency Unit) to drive out good (the deutsche mark).

The Bundesbank is not isolated in its feverish attention to the threat of inflation: it reflects a large part of German public opinion. If the Bundesbank were to pursue a hidden agenda of persuading the German people that EMU represents one more—and highly significant—case of Germany's sacrificing its own interests for the sake of other Europeans, there could be a negative public reaction to the proposal.

On the other hand, the German government seems to be emphasizing two other, quite different, policy lines. The first, and overt, line is that Germany must prove itself, must legitimize the greater Germany produced by unification, by advocating deeper integration within the European Union. The other line is to assert German leadership within the EU—in a way not seen before. The German government's behavior recalls that of the United States in an earlier period. Just as the U.S. had to make some sacrifice of its narrow economic interests to create and maintain the alliance (e.g., by accepting European discrimination against American exports during the reconstruction era), so must Germany within the context of the EU.

The financial crisis of September 1992 was seen by some as demonstrating an unwillingness on the part of Germany to pay the price of leadership by modifying its own monetary policies. On the other hand, the same episode bolstered the case of those who argue that the EMU proposed by the Maastricht accords is necessary if the countries of the European Union are to have the benefits of fixed exchange rates without submitting to the monetary dictate of Germany—as is now done under the EMS.

The issues raised by EMU and its possible costs to Germany are significant and politically sensitive and constitute a real test of

Germany's willingness to play a leadership role. But if Europe does manage to achieve a single currency and a single monetary policy by the end of this decade, a great transfer of authority to the level of the overall European Union will have taken place.

The creation of a single monetary authority will also have a profound effect on international economic coordination. To some degree, such coordination has existed among the United States, Germany, and Japan. But other nations have participated, especially the other members of the Group of Seven—the U. K., France, Italy, and Canada. And even larger groups, such as the Group of Ten, have had a voice. A Europe that can speak with one voice at least on monetary matters (as it has for some years on trade) changes the structure of the consultations and, given Europe's economic size, could change the ordering of the importance of the participants. This development, which has particular import for the U.S. as the status quo power in the area of monetary policy, is discussed further in chapter 6, below.

Since the beginning of the 1970s the member-states of the European Community have been discussing foreign policy with each other. The process has been classically multilateral; only grudgingly was the EC's central executive organ, the EC Commission, given entrée. European Political Cooperation has created habits and attitudes that cannot be underrated: with the increasing frequency of meetings, European diplomats now see a great deal more of each other—and relatively less of their American colleagues.

The process has had two special values for the Europeans. They can seek to increase their influence, for example in international bodies like the United Nations, by speaking and voting together. Secondly, they now have a place to talk to each other that is not dominated, as is NATO, by the American presence and agenda.

At the same time, the achievements in these two regards should not be exaggerated. Available data indicate that, while there has been some progress in harmonizing positions, recent trends suggest that such progress will not lead to perfect agreement. One statistical measure is the percentage of common EC votes on UN General Assembly resolutions (other than uncontested resolutions). The average in the five-year period of 1975–1979 was 60.3 percent; in the five-year period of 1986–1990, it was only 44.6 percent.[13]

The European Union, furthermore, has not successfully dealt with the question of representation on the UN Security Council; Britain and France tenaciously defend their permanent seats and the present makeup of the council, despite Italy's argument that they should yield their positions, allowing the EU as such to be represented. After years of hinting, Germany informed the UN General Assembly, in a September 1992 speech by Foreign Minister Klaus Kinkel, that it would like a permanent seat on the Security Council. German officials said the step was taken because it appeared that Britain and France would never give up their seats in favor of a single European Community representative. Kinkel repeated his bid in September 1993, less ambiguously, and with French support.[14] By 1994, Germany had European competition: Italy, where a right-wing government had taken office, began to suggest that it, too, should be a permanent member of the Security Council.[15]

And while it is no doubt pleasing to many, though not all, in the EU to be able to talk without Big Brother from across the Atlantic listening in, foreign policy discussions among the member-states tended until recently to avoid security issues, particularly when these verged on strictly military questions. That having been said, however, beginning in 1985 there was significant new movement toward a collective EC foreign policy.

While the Single European Act focused principally on the completion of the economic integration of the European Community, it did give one more formal blessing to foreign policy coordination as well as to the discussion of a certain range of security issues.[16] And by creating a secretariat for political cooperation, the act significantly institutionalized in a collective fashion what until then was a purely multilateral process.

A bilateral agreement—which has potential significance for the effort to integrate the European Community in the security area— gave birth, in January 1988, to the Franco-German Council on Security and Defense. The council—created by a protocol to the Elysée Treaty of 1963 and composed of the heads of state and government, the foreign and defense ministers, and the senior military officer of each country—aimed at the development of a common conceptual approach to defense and security.[17] This bilateral cooperation was seen as a basis for increased multinational defense and security cooperation within Western Europe. Since no one can imagine any sort of European defense entity that does not include both France and Germany, this tighter bilateral cooperation can be seen as the necessary—though not sufficient—condition for progress on a broader front.

These developments predated the crumbling of Soviet dominion in Eastern Europe. That new reality, and the prospect of an end to the Cold War, removed some of the restraint exhibited previously by Western Europeans fearful that defense integration, even security discussions which seemed to separate them from the United States, might lead Washington to rethink its role as protector of Europe.

The Dublin European Summit of April 1990 opened up a process that led finally to the political side of the epochal Maastricht Summit of December 1991, by the participants' agreeing to examine proposals for increased political cooperation among members of the European Community and authorizing foreign ministers to prepare more detailed proposals of political union. The Dublin Summit had been precooked by Mitterrand and Kohl, who on 19 April 1990 issued a statement that the EC should "define and make operational a common foreign and security policy."

From 1990 the Europeans were working to a deadline of 1 January 1993. The aim was, simultaneously with the achievement of a single market, to arrive at a greater degree of political unity, involving some changes in European Community treaties and institutions. The effects would include moving the EC further into the security area.

The process, particularly as it relates to the most difficult area of defense integration, has been bumpy and irregular. It is not clear how far and how fast progress will go, but substantial progress is at best a matter for the latter part of the decade of the 1990s.

The European Community was affected by unforeseen events during the early years of this process. The Iraqi invasion of Kuwait found the EC—while at first prompt and decisive in agreeing to nonmilitary actions—divided and ineffective once the policy agenda shifted in a warlike direction. The Western European Union—made up of nine EC states—performed some useful coordination work, particularly for naval involvement in the Persian Gulf. More significant was the logistical support provided by and through NATO. But the essential reality was that the European states—finally even France—agreed to serve under U.S. command and in response to U.S. decision-making. Paradoxically, despite the revival of interest in European security and defense integration, for the first time the United States received strong support from Western Europe in one of its "out of area" ventures.

But there was another paradox. Some Americans read the Iraq case as proof that the Western Europeans would never get together on foreign affairs and defense. The prevailing view within Europe's foreign-policy community, however, was that the EC's inability to respond cohesively and effectively to the Iraq problem showed the need to move forward to new policies, institutions, and practices that would make the European Community into an international actor in such cases.[18]

Yugoslavia was another test of the EC. The bright side of the picture—at least the brighter side—is that, while there was a range of different attitudes, the EC member-states (with the arguable exception of Greece) did not pursue self-serving independent policy lines. The contrast with the foreign meddling in Yugoslav politics between the two World Wars is encouraging. This ascription of merit needs some qualification, in that Germany's advocacy of recognition of Croatia and Slovenia almost got out of the bounds of collective decision-making. But a sanguine view would be that both Germany's effective advocacy of recognition and Greece's temporary blocking of recognition of Macedonia were games played according to EC rules. As much cannot be said of economic blockade of Macedonia imposed by Greece in February 1994.[19]

The European Community, on the other hand, was ineffective in its efforts to establish and maintain peace within Yugoslavia. To be fair, it took on this responsibility only when the Conference on Security and Cooperation in Europe (CSCE) proved itself impotent.[20] But the experience has shown that the "civilian power" which admirers of EU foreign policy celebrate is ineffective in situations where states do not behave like economically rational decision-makers. And the Yugoslav civil war is a classic instance of behavior dictated by culture, tradition, nationalism—in other words, by the viscera— rather than by rational calculation. Yugoslavia's irrationality rendered the EU's chief policy instrument, its economic power, ineffective.[21]

Germany's combination of a loud declaratory policy with inability to act militarily is the extreme example of the European Union's current inability to get beyond civilian power and into military power. To be both fair and realistic, the unwillingness of many EU states to engage their soldiers in the Yugoslav quagmire is understandable: it's not their problem (Yugoslavia is not a member of the EU, nor did its terrible troubles, in all likelihood, pose a security problem for the EU); and no one can be sure that military intervention on any conceivable scale would succeed in pacifying Yugoslavia. But in some EU meetings, military intervention was discussed, and Germany, though in favor, came up short in terms of participating.

A harsh judgment of the negative impact of the European Union's political cooperation process is that it "guarantees at best ineffective compromises and at worst total self-paralysis. This simple truth has been demonstrated twice in the last four years—the first time as farce, the second as tragedy. The farce was 'Europe's' reaction to Iraq's 1990 invasion of Kuwait. . . . The tragedy is Yugoslavia."[22]

As in the case of Iraq, there are those in the EU who contend that the real lesson is not the EU's impotence but the need to make it more virile. A 1995 report prepared for the EU's external affairs commissioner, Hans van den Broek, characterizes the common foreign and security policy as one of "inertia and impotence" but suggests that the answer is to give a central body, headed by a prominent politician, the right to make policy on behalf of EU.[23]

The effort to invigorate the EU's foreign policy has—to the accompaniment of these loud off-stage noises—gone on throughout the post-Cold War period. Attention has centered on transforming the Western European Union (WEU) into the agent for the European Union in security and defense matters. (The use of this organization, rather than EU institutions themselves, avoids such problems as those created, for example, by Irish neutrality.) In December 1990 the foreign and defense ministers of the Western European Union's nine member-states decided that the WEU has a key role to play both in the construction of Europe and in NATO's modernization. They also agreed that the WEU should make an "appropriate contribution" to the effort to solve European security problems outside Europe.[24]

A doctrinal argument reminiscent of many of the past broke out between those (especially the U.K. and the Netherlands) who insist on the primacy of NATO and those who are more interested in developing an autonomous European defense entity. At one point, in early 1991, the United States joined the argument by sending a message to its European allies warning them of the damage that putative developments in the WEU might do to the alliance.[25]

The rapid developments of the last few years have opened up new possibilities for European defense integration. But the newborn child of a European defense entity finds it hard to compete with the hardened veteran that is NATO. The Franco-German effort to create a multinational European force was quickly trumped by a fundamental reordering of NATO's military structure, producing integration at the corps level (very much as was proposed in the planning for the European Defense Community).[26] The nations of the EU are divided in their tactical positions regarding a European defense entity and its relationship to NATO. In fact, some individual countries seem to be divided within themselves, ambivalent about their own positions on the matter. Yet, though with less certainty than in the monetary area, a process does seem to have been engaged—with at least the consent if not the eager or optimistic support of all EU member-states. And if completed, it is a process that could result in the European Union's having a new personality and a new relationship with the United States.

CHAPTER 4

NATO: TRIUMPH AND TRAGEDY

NATO's nearly fifty-year history is one of repeated "crises" which the Atlantic Alliance survived, only to be faced with the unexpected problem of the demise of its opponent.

From its beginning, NATO had its problems and underwent jolting changes. What began as a rather traditional military alliance was soon transformed by the decision—made in the wake of the 1950 North Korean invasion of South Korea—to create an integrated military command. Next came the problem of how to strengthen NATO by drawing on Germany's resources—something which was seen as necessary by all, but which France, so soon after its humiliating defeat by Germany, found difficult to swallow. Germany was finally brought into NATO, though only after a detour toward the mirage of a European Defense Community.

On the heels of these achievements—which created NATO as we know it today—the question of the nature of the NATO alliance was posed sharply by the controversy over Egyptian President Gamal Abdel Nasser's 1956 seizure of the Suez Canal. At that point Britain and France chose to hope, or believe, that NATO involved global unity; the United States rejected this line, taking a strict constructionist approach to NATO's scope.

Later the United States, increasingly conscious of the drain on its resources of single-handed responsibility for the world, sought periodically to engage NATO in efforts outside the treaty area and, in a neat but discomforting reversal of positions, got negative answers from its European allies.

The United States also sought, as the years went on, to broaden NATO'S focus from the traditional political-military one. As already noted, this effort was not a resounding success.

Underlying these failures to make something more of NATO

was the failure of NATO to engender a sense of community among the nations and peoples of the alliance. The facts of the matter were stated persuasively a quarter-century ago by Harold van Buren Cleveland in *The Atlantic Idea and Its European Rivals*. As Charles M. Spofford writes in his foreword to the book: "In his concluding chapter on the Atlantic idea, Mr. Cleveland finds in it no standard to which Atlantic peoples can be moved to repair or any basis for agreement among their governments, but an existing, cold, inescapable equilibrium of forces. The Atlantic Community (which is a coalition and not a 'community' in the true sense) is cohesive only because of American nuclear power which exercises for all of the states of the Atlantic the basic function of national defense."[1]

Oddly, this less-than-fixed relationship survived quite well the declining credibility of the idea that the United States would expose itself to nuclear catastrophe by defending Europe against the Soviet Union, perhaps because, shakier though the American commitment may have seemed, the Europeans had nothing to substitute for it.

Indeed, it could be argued that the cohesion of the alliance strengthened somewhat as the years went on. The period from the late 1970s through the mid-1980s—from the two-track decision to the Intermediate-range Nuclear Forces Treaty—was one in which the members of NATO made an effort to increase its resources. The greater cooperativeness of the European allies (or rather, their responsiveness to the U.S. lead) may have reflected fear on their part that security was now divisible, that the United States no longer necessarily *had* to provide the public good of deterrence and defense regardless of the European contribution.

NATO was therefore in relatively robust shape at the moment when the East began to disintegrate. Pessimists could, however, view the future for NATO as limited. The cohesion of NATO was at least in part forced on its members by the Cold War's division of Europe and by fear of the Soviet Union. Without these pressures, could (or should) NATO survive? John Lewis Gaddis uses the image of glaciation: "Now that the Cold War is over and geopolitical glaciers are retreating . . . the critical question for the future stability of Europe is the extent to which the Cold War glacier permanently altered the terrain it covered for so long. Integrationist structures like the EC and NATO suggest such alteration; but they could also have been artifacts of the glaciation itself. If so, these organizations will become increasingly vulnerable. . . ."[2]

I would argue that the EU is far less clearly an artifact of the Cold War than NATO, that it has "altered the terrain" of Western Europe and created a sense of community that notoriously did not previously exist. But NATO, which did seem vulnerable, has performed impressively in adapting itself to changed circumstances, especially in defending its corner against competing visions of European security.

Despite the weaknesses of the CSCE, one might have expected it to be given first consideration in an effort to create a pan-European security organization. Notably, it does not have NATO's past as a Western mutual defense entity to live down. But in fact NATO has done well in the competition.

The NATO Summit of July 1990 began the process by stating that the Atlantic Alliance and the Warsaw Pact were no longer adversaries and by inviting the Soviet Union and other Warsaw Pact members to establish diplomatic liaison with NATO. NATO pursued this line with the agreement, at the November 1991 NATO Summit, to move to the creation of the North Atlantic Cooperation Council (NACC), which held its inaugural meeting 20 December 1991. The NACC now includes most of the successor republics of the former Soviet Union as well as the Eastern European members of the dissolved Warsaw Pact.

The NACC did not end the desire of Central European states for something more, nor did it end pressures from within the West to extend NATO guarantees to these countries. Reluctance to extend such guarantees, coupled with a desire to avoid unsettling the Russians, led to another ingenious American idea: the Partnership for Peace (PfP) plan, adopted by the NATO Summit of January 1994. This offered joint planning, training, and exercises to the armies of thirty Central and Eastern European states.[3] Russia's President Boris Yeltsin at one point—in visits to Prague and Warsaw in August 1993—stated his acceptance in principle of NATO membership for Poland (raising the hopes of the other Visegrad states).[4] However, the debt he owed to the Russian military for quelling the October 1993 coup attempt, together with the underlying growth of nationalist sentiment in Russia, led Yeltsin to express his opposition to

NATO expansion in an October 1993 letter to Bill Clinton, François Mitterrand, Helmut Kohl, and John Major,[5] and Russia warned NATO, on 25 November, that admission of the Eastern European countries would force Moscow to take fundamental military countermeasures and would heighten anti-Western sentiment.[6] The strong showing of nationalist and antireform groups in the December 1993 Russian legislative elections only strengthened this attitude.

With this as background, Russia proved hard to get as a participant in the Partnership for Peace. Having for months sought to exact a special sort of partnership for itself, it finally signed up as a member of the PfP on 22 June 1994. Russian Foreign Minister Andrei Kozyrev used the occasion once again to urge that NATO not risk provoking Russian public opinion by rushing to welcome countries like Poland, Hungary, and the Czech Republic into the alliance.[7] When the NATO foreign ministers, at the beginning of December 1994, agreed that by the end of 1995 they would inform prospective members what they must do to be accepted into the organization, Kozyrev refused to sign an agreement regarding Russian cooperation with NATO until Russia had answers to its fears about rapid expansion of NATO.[8] A few days later, Russian President Yeltsin disrupted a summit meeting of the Organization for Security and Cooperation in Europe by saying that NATO's eastward expansion could plunge Europe into a "cold peace."[9]

The Russian-Western honeymoon was over. The next six months was the most difficult period—up to then—in post-Cold War Russian-Western relations.[10] Finally, at a meeting between Presidents Clinton and Yeltsin in Moscow on 10 May 1995, agreement was reached to activate both Russia's program for military cooperation under the Partnership for Peace and a Russian-NATO dialogue, outside the scope of the PfP, on nuclear and nonproliferation issues. Clinton had sweetened the atmosphere by agreeing with Yeltsin that the Conventional Forces in Europe (CFE) treaty should be modified, and the Organization for Security and Cooperation in Europe (OSCE) strengthened. Clearly, however, differences remained regarding the OSCE's role and, even more, regarding NATO enlargement.[11]

Most Eastern European countries would like more from NATO than the NACC, more even than the PfP: a security guarantee, presumably resulting from full membership in the alliance.[12] Part of the explanation for the relative success of NATO's adaptive efforts is the simple fact that these consultative arrangements are the best these countries can get. For the ex-Soviet republics, inclusion in the NACC was evidence of their legitimacy and part of the process of their seeking closer and, it is hoped, more productive ties with the West. Madeleine Albright, the American Ambassador to the UN, said the Partnership for Peace "squared a circle," helping to relieve the Central European states' sense of isolation while reducing Russian fears and providing a new focus for NATO activity.[13] But the fact remains—as some, especially the French government, have perceived—that NATO preempted institutional turf that seemed destined to be the property of the CSCE.[14]

For some years NATO—in fact a coalition of the U.S., the U.K., the Netherlands, and NATO Secretary General Manfred Woerner—also played an excellent defensive game against the creation of a meaningful Western European defense entity. Woerner's attitude was made clear in October 1990 when he said, "The European Community cannot replace NATO. It will take a long time before it can really establish a defense structure. And even then, are you sure that the Europeans could, with their forces alone, balance Soviet power?"[15]

By May of 1991 a rather complete revision of NATO military strategy and organization was ready for consideration by member defense ministers. The revision notably called for the creation of eight corps, seven of them multinational, to take the place of the national army corps that heretofore had constituted NATO's "integrated" forces. This plan, incidentally, mimicked the integrated corps plan suggested thirty years before for the army of the European Defense Community,[16] with the important difference that U.S. divisions would be part of the new NATO corps structure.

On 16 October 1991 came the Franco-German response, proposing that an enhanced version of the already established Franco-German brigade serve as the nucleus for a European force. (In the German, though not necessarily the French, vision of this force, it was to be under the command of the WEU.)[17] This rather tardy gesture provoked negative responses in Washington and London, but the most interesting came from Manfred Woerner. In a speech to the North Atlantic Assembly on 22 October, Woerner said, "It would not make practical sense . . . to create an additional independent European force for the defense of alliance territory." He ruled out the use of NATO units in such a force and said it could not operate on alliance territory.[18]

While the last word on the NATO-WEU rivalry had hardly been spoken, these early skirmishes seemed to leave NATO in command of the field. But the ambiguous results of the NATO Rome Summit of November 1991[19] and the May 1992 unveiling of the details of the Franco-German proposal for a European corps showed that the institutional war was not over.

It took the arrival in office of the new Clinton administration for the fires of the dispute to be banked; the process was aided both by German efforts to relieve American fears and by a moderation of French attitudes toward NATO. Among the steps along the way was the agreement of December 1992 placing the Eurocorps under NATO operational command in defined emergencies. By April 1993 Woerner could say that "a real *modus operandi*" had developed between NATO and the WEU. The next month WEU Secretary Willem van Eekelen noted that WEU's links with NATO had developed much further than those with the EC.[20]

The year 1993 was indeed a turning point in the fight over defense structure between "Europeans" and "Atlanticists." The change in French attitudes was striking—and important. In the early post-Cold War period, French leaders had insisted that European institutions—the EC and the WEU—could set security policy and that Europe need no longer accept American leadership. In 1993 the French ceased to try to marginalize the U.S. They acknowledged that the European institutions would never displace NATO and the U.S. contribution to European security. The change in French views can be attributed in part to the arrival of a conservative government. Only weeks before he became France's foreign minister, Alain Juppé criticized Socialist policy toward NATO, attacking those "neophytes of ultra-Gaullism [who] cling to certainties which today are completely out-dated. . . . Can we maintain, at the heart of NATO, the bad-tempered and conservative attitude that we currently have?"[21] The effect was to diminish the influence of the French Foreign Ministry, the traditional bastion of French particularism. Another factor was the poor EC performance in Bosnia.[22]

Underlying NATO's success in the institutional squabbles with the CSCE and the WEU is the fact that it is a going concern. A newer organization suffers from the comparison. Furthermore, NATO has a staff structure capable of making plans; and it has had the benefit of clear leadership (from the United States with the help of Britain), with the secretary general as faithful executor (particularly during Woerner's tenure), whereas both the CSCE and the WEU are essentially talk shops without institutional direction.

This being said, NATO, while currently in good health and not immediately imperiled, faces problems for the future. It should be noted that these problems do not necessarily threaten the liquidation of NATO, but they may lead to such a radical change in its nature as to transform it in kind.

The first problem is the purpose of NATO. It was created as a mutual defense pact, with the Soviet Union as the obvious threat to be defended against, even if not explicitly named. Even taking the treaty as written, it provides for the defense of its participants in Europe and North America. At the moment, an external attack on the treaty area seems most unlikely.

Particularly during this time of troubles in the ex-Soviet empire, it seems prudent not to abandon a proper deterrent-defensive posture on the part of NATO. But the scale of what is proper is much reduced from the days before 1989.

The Bush administration's plans for 1995 and after would have retained about 150,000 men—a full army corps plus air and logistical support—in Europe. A substantially smaller force—basically limited to providing those support services Europeans need but don't possess, and including few if any ground combat units—would probably suffice, from a strictly military point of view.[23] The Clinton administration came out closer to the second view. During the electoral campaign, Mr. Clinton said he favored reducing the American force strength in Europe to between 75,000 and 100,000 by mid-decade. And at the end of March 1993 NATO defense ministers were informed that U.S. troops in Europe would be cut to 100,000 by 1995–1996.[24]

A second justification for maintaining troops and supplies in Europe is that they can conveniently be used for operations in areas like the Persian Gulf. However, only a very small saving of time is gained from sending forces from Europe, rather than from the United States, to the Persian Gulf. And maintaining these forces in Europe is slightly more expensive than in the United States and considerably less popular with Congressmen conscious of the economic contribution military bases can make to their districts. One can imagine these drawbacks' being compensated for monetarily—just as our troop costs are heavily subsidized by the Japanese government—or politically, by the agreement of Europeans that NATO become an alliance with worldwide scope of action.[25] But neither step has been taken.

Such questions about the defensive imperative have led to emphasis on the contribution NATO can make to stability; this emphasis verges on the idea of transforming what was a pact for mutual defense into a broader collective security arrangement. Such a transformation raises some further questions. Will the American public support indefinitely a large U.S. military presence in Europe if its purpose is essentially political, rather than defensive?

Of course, the preservation of stability may not be achieved merely by the passive presence of U.S. troops in Europe. A broader collective security arrangement might, unless we are very lucky, occasionally require the use of military force. Answering such a need would put us far beyond our past military commitment to Western Europe—a commitment to the defense of an area of vital political and economic interest to us. In the future we could be committed to peacemaking and peacekeeping in a much broader area, where conflict would be more likely and our interests would not necessarily be directly engaged.

Furthermore, the transformation of NATO to something broader in geographic scope and more political in purpose would raise the question of the defense of Western Europe. If NATO were pan-European (and North American), it could hardly serve the same functions it now does. Yet Western Europe has for more than forty years entrusted the core of its defense to NATO (and, through NATO, to the United States).

The something new that would substitute for the old NATO should not be a revival of individual national defensive systems in Western Europe: the step would clearly reverse the integrative progress of the post-World War II period. And there is little sign of desire for this kind of change; even France may realize the futility of it. But if NATO turns into something broader and fuzzier than a defense pact, the logic of a Western European defense entity grows stronger.

Such a development would not necessarily mean the severance of a defense link between the United States and Western Europe. But that link might take the form of a traditional military alliance, without the presence of U.S. troops in Europe, much less their integration into a collective force.

This series of reflections aims at suggesting that updating NATO's character does not solve the question of the U.S.-European relationship in defense. Rather, it could render more acute the questions that already exist about the continuance of something like the status quo ante.

The Bush administration seemed to find the idea of a substantially transformed U.S. military role in Europe very hard to accept. Its resistance to proposals for a more European defense of Europe, as in its attempt to sabotage the proposal for a European force founded upon a Franco-German corps, showed a great deal of tactical skill but ignored the need to economize and to do so by transferring the defense burden, at least in large part, to the Europeans. It may be that this particular European initiative will not succeed, but this is not a motive for wishing it ill.[26] The Clinton administration, to its credit, abandoned the effort to block the creation of a European defense identity.[27] It is understandable that the U.S. wants to have a voice in European affairs, but preservation of the historic U.S. military commitment is not a necessary condition for that privilege.

While for years one thread of U.S. policy, expressed through NATO, was to preempt the CSCE's becoming the dominant security organization in Europe, it may not be necessary to choose one of these organizations to the detriment of the other. They could be complementary. We could aim at an updated NATO whose functions remain essentially military and are in the service of a delimited group of countries, while leaving to the OSCE the difficult problems of collective security in a "Europe" that runs from the Atlantic to the Pacific.

CHAPTER 5

CAN EUROPEAN SECURITY BE
BASED ON THE OSCE?

"Collective security does not work: if everybody is allied to everybody else, nobody is allied to anybody."[1] This dictum expresses the problem many see in making the Organization for Security and Cooperation in Europe (OSCE) *the* security system for all of Europe.

The OSCE is an ongoing multilateral forum involving all the countries of Europe plus the United States and Canada. It took shape in the early 1970s, during the period of East-West détente, as the Conference on Security and Cooperation in Europe (CSCE)[2] and produced in 1975 the Helsinki Final Act. The act's provisions are divided into three "baskets": general principles and security issues; economics, science and technology, the environment; and humanitarian issues.

The CSCE was born of the Soviet desire for legitimacy and, as such, was not regarded with great warmth by the United States. It came to symbolize the process of détente for many West Europeans and, in that guise, again aroused negative feeling in Washington. Eventually, the U.S. government found a certain purpose in the CSCE process—it provided a forum, and a semi-juridical basis, for attacking Soviet human rights policies.[3]

But right up to the end of the Cold War, the United States had great reservations about the CSCE, especially as an agency that might be involved in security matters. As such, on one level it was viewed as a threat to NATO. The State Department finally prevailed over the National Security Council (NSC), and in a speech in Berlin in April 1990, Secretary of State James Baker enunciated the idea that CSCE and NATO were complementary. But for months thereafter, the United States, whose policy was much influenced by the NSC staff, opposed institutionalizing the CSCE to deal with emergencies, on the basis that NATO was the right organization to manage crises in Europe.[4]

On another level the CSCE was seen as inappropriate, as not reflecting the geopolitical reality of the division of Europe and the world. The United States was much more comfortable with bloc-to-bloc relations and negotiations, a preference that continued to be significant as late as the opening of the negotiations on Conventional Forces in Europe (CFE), in March 1989. In that case, the U.S. insisted on negotiations being conducted between the NATO states and the Warsaw Pact states, rather than in the CSCE context, as advocated by France: thus, the neutrals were excluded.

The collapse of the Warsaw Pact changed the argument. It left the Central and Eastern European states at loose ends from a security point of view. Their initial reaction was to use the CSCE as the basis for new security structures. However, it took little more than a year for them to rethink. In February 1991 Czech President Vaclav Havel, once one of the most outspoken proponents of the CSCE, said that NATO is Europe's "only functioning democratic security framework." By that point, most if not all of the ex-Soviet satellites seemed to want to take shelter, in some shape or fashion, under NATO's wing.[5]

This shift in East European thinking reflected the CSCE's weaknesses as a security organization. These deficiencies were fully demonstrated a little later in 1991 when Yugoslavia began to come apart.

CSCE foreign ministers, meeting in Berlin, agreed on 20 June 1991 to a new emergency mechanism for dealing with crises in Europe. Any member state which considers that an emergency has arisen as the result of "major disruptions endangering peace, security or stability," or a violation of the principles of the Helsinki agreement, can ask clarification from the state or states concerned. If the situation remains unresolved, an emergency meeting can be requested by any state, provided its demand is supported by twelve or more other member-states. The agreement was reached over initial Soviet objections that the procedure could undermine the Helsinki Final Act's principle of nonintervention in the internal affairs of a state.

The mechanism did lack teeth—no decision could be imposed; recommendations remained subject to the unanimity rule that still governed CSCE meetings. But it represented a breach in the barrier previously created by the consensus rule. And, taken together with the CSCE foreign ministers' statement of 19 June supporting the "democratic development, unity and territorial integrity of Yugoslavia," it seemed to presage a new collective security role for the CSCE. As German Foreign Minister Hans Dietrich Genscher said, it had been generally recognized that the internal situation in one state can often affect a wider region.[6]

The new procedures soon got a test. Ignoring the CSCE's appeal, Croatia and Slovenia declared independence on 25 June. On 27 June the Yugoslav Federal Army went into action against Slovenia. On 2 July the CSCE's Vienna-based Conflict Prevention Center at its first meeting urged an immediate cease-fire in Yugoslavia and the return of army units to their barracks.

On 3 July the CSCE met in Prague at senior official level under the new special emergency procedure. A declaration was quickly adopted calling for an immediate end to hostilities, the return to barracks of both the Yugoslav and the Slovenian forces, and the resumption of political control over all armed forces in Yugoslavia. But the "delegates to the conference . . . made no attempt to hide their scepticism about the practical contributions they could make. 'It's always too late. Such a conference cannot send troops to Yugoslavia,' said Mr. Jiri Dienstbier, the Czechoslovak Foreign Minister." Czech President Havel tried to go beyond words by proposing that an observer group be sent to Slovenia and Croatia; its report would be the basis for the CSCE to decide whatever further action it deemed necessary. But Yugoslavia and the Soviet Union objected to motions that endorsed an EC observer mission and a CSCE "good offices" mission—the Soviet delegate making clear that Moscow considered it inappropriate to intervene in the internal affairs of a member country.[7]

The *Economist* wrote that, "if you wanted to design a perfect test for Europe's new collective security arrangements, you would invent Yugoslavia. Collective security looks like flunking it. The crisis-prevention procedures being set up by the Conference on Security and Co-operation in Europe (CSCE) are too slow and weak to prevent conflict. The CSCE lacks both clout and a mandate to intervene in Yugoslavia's 'internal affairs.'"[8]

But this was not the end of the story. Early in August, Austria requested another meeting of the CSCE to discuss the crises in Yugoslavia; the senior officials met on 8 August. At that meeting, Western diplomats hinted that they would not rule out an international peace conference if Yugoslav's leaders were unable to establish a lasting cease-fire and negotiate the future of the country's internal borders. Yugoslav diplomats firmly rejected the idea of an international peace conference and said they would call their own peace talks.[9] While it continued to hold meetings on Yugoslavia and to send observers there, the CSCE by default passed the ball—or hot potato—to the EC and the UN after the summer of 1991.

Yugoslavia was a tough case; maybe it made "bad law" in the sense that it seemed to presage a complete inability of the CSCE to serve a purpose in the real and potential armed conflicts likely to develop in the eastern half of Europe. Nils Eliasson, the director of the CSCE Secretariat, was undoubtedly right when he said, "The crisis came a little early—the new structure has not matured."[10] But, beyond this, it is fair to say that the new structure, like the old nonstructure, was and is peculiarly ill-adapted to deal with actual military conflict. The CSCE may be able to help avoid conflict—it may come to play a very useful role in this regard—but it has two great drawbacks in dealing with conflicts when they break out: the unanimity principle and the lack of military forces.

When the CSCE convened again at ministerial level in Moscow in September 1991 for a meeting supposedly devoted to the "human dimension," German Foreign Minister Genscher proposed that the CSCE countries consider developing a sort of antitotalitarian task force. He recalled the attempted coup just the month before in the Soviet Union and said it had taught other states that they must immediately isolate would-be putschists. The CSCE, he said, had a responsibility to underpin its human rights ideals by deploying observers in countries which had fallen victim to a coup or which suppressed human rights—even where permission to do so was refused by the country's government. British Foreign Secretary Douglas Hurd said Britain backed these "far-reaching" proposals: "We are certainly in favour of moving beyond the present situation where everything [in the CSCE] happens by consensus." The example of Yugoslavia had "shown the limited value" of CSCE mechanisms, where central authority had failed.[11]

Indeed, the effort to make something more effective out of the CSCE seemed to revive in early 1992. The foreign ministers of the CSCE met in Prague in January. The headline-catching business was the admission of ten new members from the Commonwealth of Independent States.[12] However, there was also a clash of points of view regarding the future of the organization, and there was one important institutional decision.

The correspondent of the *New York Times* wrote, "The Americans have long sought to keep the conference limited, so that it would not challenge the Washington-dominated NATO alliance as the preeminent European security organization."[13] While there had, prior to the meeting, been growing media comment on a shift in interest by Poland, Hungary, and Czechoslovakia from the CSCE, with its disappointing record, to NACC (as a surrogate for the unattainable NATO),[14] Czech President Vaclav Havel in fact challenged the U.S. attitude.

Havel called for structural changes in the CSCE mandate: "Europe is now faced, for the third time in this century, with the task of building for itself an arrangement that would not only rule out the danger of another world war—hot or cold—originating in its territory, but making sure that no fighting takes place here anymore. . . . The C.S.C.E. is a political environment that might play a critical role in this respect." Havel proposed that states joining the organization eventually be asked to subscribe to its human rights standards in the form of international treaties subject to verification and sanctions. He suggested that the CSCE give its secretariat broader powers so that it was no longer simply a "debating club" but a force that could assume certain peacekeeping functions; an unarmed force of five thousand would be used to help enforce conference decisions in conflicts such as Yugoslavia. And he called for clear "functional links" between the CSCE and other major pan-European organizations, saying he could "even imagine that NATO, especially if it opens itself to new members, might one day become one of the instruments of collective defense of all the [CSCE] countries . . . and an organizer of local interventions the CSCE would deem necessary."[15]

American officials, clearly unenthusiastic about Havel's propos-als, said they would "study" them.[16] In other words, the proposals did not gain instant acceptance. They did get support from Genscher (the most consistent advocate of the CSCE among the leaders of major countries), who said it was time for the CSCE to expand its security role: "The CSCE should provide for the possibility of creat-ing CSCE 'blue helmets' and CSCE 'green helmet' missions to safe-guard peace and the environment."[17]

The meeting made one important (if limited) decision, consis-tent with Genscher's call for a change in the rules of consensus: to modify the unanimity rule in "very serious" cases. Decisions could now be made without the agreement of the state concerned if it were in "flagrant, serious, and persistent" violation of its CSCE commit-ments. The impact of such decisions would be limited: action would be confined to political declarations or other "measures of a politi-cal nature." Stiffer measures, such as embargoes and the dispatch of missions of inquiry, could be taken only on the basis of CSCE una-nimity.[18] Nevertheless, this decision was a second, more important modification of the debilitating consensus principle.

The conflict in Nagorno-Karabakh gave the vision of a different role for the CSCE a new test early in 1992. In late February the CSCE sent a mission to Armenia and Azerbaijan. On 28 February the senior officials meeting in Prague put forward a plan for a cease-fire, renewal of the Russo-Kazakh mediation effort, and the deploy-ment of cease-fire observers drawn from CSCE countries, if the warring communities agreed to accept such observers.

This sort of effort requires a military element, if only acting as observers, and the CSCE was bereft of such a resource. But NATO Secretary General Woerner had suggested, a little earlier, that NATO could make its military expertise, and even troops, available for missions ordered by the CSCE, and there were supportive murmurs from within the organization, including the United States.[19] A cou-pling of the two organizations began to seem possible.[20]

In the weeks preceding the July 1992 CSCE Summit, movement toward making NATO resources available to the CSCE took place. At the NATO Council in Oslo in early June, ministers stated they were "prepared to support, on a case-by-case basis in accordance with our own procedures, peacekeeping activities under the responsibility of the CSCE, including by making available alliance resources and expertise."[21]

The situation quickly became more a competition between NATO and the WEU than an effort to make the CSCE effective. The WEU, meeting at Petersburg, near Bonn, later in June, made a similar offer to aid the CSCE.[22]

This competition dominated the CSCE Summit. The WEU states held a foreign ministers' meeting to decide on and announce the sending of a naval surveillance squadron to the Adriatic; getting wind of this, NATO foreign ministers met later the same day and agreed to do likewise.[23] Neither decision was taken in the CSCE framework.[24]

The CSCE did agree to declare itself a regional organization under chapter eight of the United Nations Charter and therefore capable of authorizing peacekeeping without recourse to the UN itself. It also agreed that it might call on NATO, the WEU, or individual member countries to provide peacekeeping forces.[25]

However, it was clear that until the CSCE found a way of breaking away from its consensus approach, perhaps by creating something like the Security Council, it was unlikely to become an effective peacemaking body.[26] As a member of France's President Mitterrand's delegation to the CSCE Summit put it, "It's the League of Nations, only worse."[27]

While NATO displayed a willingness to help fill the gaps in the CSCE's ability to deal with conflicts, it also, as noted, poached on the CSCE by the creation of the North Atlantic Cooperation Council (NACC). This body is similar in composition to the CSCE (the NACC does not, however, include the neutral nations of Europe), and it gets into some of the area traditionally cultivated by the CSCE. As a consolation for nonmembership in NATO, membership in the NACC has the effect of building a country's confidence and sense of security, a traditional concern of the CSCE. The NACC seems to have an appropriate role in discussing the implementation by the successor republics of the Soviet Union of the arms control agreements signed by Moscow. But even some of this work could hypothetically be a CSCE function, since while the Conventional Forces in Europe agreement was negotiated between the nations of NATO and those of the Warsaw Pact, it was under the CSCE umbrella.

While it has its justification, the development of NACC has been all the easier because the United States—though it has accommodated itself to the idea of a somewhat more tangible and active CSCE—continues to put NATO first in its affections and policies. The more recent Partnership for Peace plan is another example of the same approach. Regrettably for the CSCE, this helps to dampen its attractiveness to those countries which were initially most committed, the countries of the eastern part of Europe, including the ex-Soviet Union.

France's attitude toward the CSCE turned cool because of the U.S. presence within that organization—regardless of the less-than-forceful U.S. support for it. Conveniently for France, there is another, long-existing organization that matches up with its Atlantic-to-the-Urals concept of "Europe"—the Council of Europe. If, as a result of French efforts, the council becomes somewhat more effective, it will eat away at other areas of the CSCE, human rights in particular.

France took another step that at least initially undercut the CSCE when it came up with the "Balladur Plan"—proposed by its Prime Minister Edouard Balladur—at the June 1993 European Summit in Copenhagen. Under it, East European states were to reach "good neighbor" agreements on respecting borders and protecting the rights of minorities if these states were to be eligible for EU membership. This sounded to many like a replay of Mitterrand's 1991 plan for a pan-European confederation (though without its anti-American overtones); in any event it clearly invaded the CSCE's area of competence and interest.[28]

At the CSCE's biennial summit in Budapest in December 1994, it was agreed to change its name to the Organization for Security and Cooperation in Europe. Aside from that, however, the only significant positive action was agreement in principle to send a peacekeeping force to Nagorno-Karabakh to monitor the cease-fire agreed to there in July 1994. The rest of the meeting, aside from being dominated by Yeltsin's attack on NATO enlargement, did not resolve the clash between two basic models for the organization's future. The Russians want the OSCE to be the supreme security organization in Europe, with both NATO and the Russian-dominated Commonwealth of Independent States subordinate to it. The OSCE would be endowed with a UN-style Security Council. The United States, supported by the West, sees a role for the OSCE in preventing conflict and maintaining human rights, but it does not agree to putting NATO under an OSCE with a Russian veto. Though Boris Yeltsin and Bill Clinton agreed at their May 1995 meeting that the OSCE should be strengthened, it is apparent that they did not agree on how to do so.[29]

Thus, the OSCE presents the paradoxical picture of an organization which is much more active and much more visible than it was during the Cold War but which now seems unable to extend its influence and power, and even to defend its own turf from other organizations. The OSCE needs to change if it is to become important to the security of Europe.

There are two quite divergent paths that it might take. The first, somewhat similar to the one indicated by the Russians, is to evolve in the direction of being a European Security Organization, as Richard Ullman suggests.[30] This would create a true collective security organization, subject to several conditions being achieved, including a substantial reduction in the level of armaments, to the point that offensive war would be very difficult.

Substantial barriers stand in the path of this evolution. Existing organizations would lose their roles. Nations would abandon sovereignty more radically than other European organizations have yet demanded; in this case, the form of supranationality might come before the foundation of feelings and loyalties was created. But the biggest problem is that of transition—the transition from a divided Europe, still divided after the end of the Cold War and of communism. It is important to try to include Russia in a system of European security, but very difficult to let down the military guard against a state with such power, a troubling past, and an unpredictable future. Whatever the ultimate merits of the idea of a European security organization, it is difficult to envisage its rapid implementation.

The second path, which does not exclude an ultimate movement to a "European Security Organization," is to accept the pluralist organizational reality of today but to try to make it work in a more synergistic way. One idea is, for example, to make the OSCE a more effective forum for the discussion of and possible decision-making regarding European security problems. This aim in itself would entail significant change in the organization: the abandonment of consensus and the creation of a council of states whose power would be greater than that of the others, for example. A UN-type security council may be too far to go, but a council that acts as a steering committee could be envisaged, and it might have the advantage of being accepted by the Russians as a step in their direction.[31] The Bosnia contact group—created at the end of April 1994, at French and Russian instance, and made up of the U.S., Russia, France, Germany, and the U.K.—is suggestive of the possibilities.[32]

Moving in this direction would require the United States to give up its efforts to duplicate the OSCE in NATO. As Henry Kissinger has suggested, the task of relating Russia to the Atlantic nations should be entrusted to the OSCE (which he suggests renaming the Partnership for Peace).[33] Vaclav Havel has made a similar point, seeing the OSCE as a uniquely suited institutional environment in which the West can communicate with and draw closer to Russia, which "has a very specific position in Europe. It is an enormous Euro-Asian power. . . ." Havel's suggestion that the West might want to engage in "institutionalized cooperation" with the Commonwealth of Independent States—accepting it as a "developing regional structure"—may hold out another way of responding to the Russian agenda for the OSCE without accepting its dangerous features.[34]

NATO would be left with the substantial role of building confidence and stability when Europe is in search of such comfort in a period of unprecedented change. Giving this role to NATO is not the same as making NATO coterminous with Europe—something that would simply turn it into the OSCE. It should continue to be a mutual defense pact among a group of like-minded countries. Without being comprised of all the nations of Europe, it could serve a deterrent and enforcement function throughout the Continent, with the sanction of an OSCE freed from the unanimity rule. The OSCE might call upon NATO to provide the military expertise and, if necessary, force to implement its decisions.[35] It has to be added that the WEU (or a European defense force under another name) might also serve this function of being the "secular arm" of the OSCE; the essential difference is that NATO exists and functions, and the WEU is an infant, in terms of operational ability.[36] NATO also has the merit, for most OSCE members, of including and involving the United States.

CHAPTER 6

THE EUROPEAN UNION AS AN EMERGING ECONOMIC SUPERPOWER

The European Union (for most of its history, called the European Community) has been an important fact of international economic life for nearly forty years.

Once the Treaty of Rome began to be put into effect in the late 1950s, there was a clear potential for the European Community to become a key player in international trade. The United States recognized this and initiated two major multilateral trade negotiations—the Dillon Round of 1960–1961 and the Kennedy Round of 1963–1968—intended to reduce in advance the potential for discrimination inherent in the setting up of a large European customs union.[1]

From the very beginning, U.S. attitudes and policies were tinged by ambivalence. We favored a united Europe, but increasingly, as the years went on, we feared its impact on us.

Similarly, we favored European unity, but we yielded to the temptation to exploit national differences in order to prevent or frustrate common European policies regarded as threatening to our interests.

American fear and resentment of the European Community has had two principal themes. We worried about the development of the EC into a protectionist bloc. This was a horizon that constantly receded. While the internal procedures of the EC were frustrating, its market remained quite open, indeed became more so. But fears of its becoming protectionist did not ease. To the contrary, these fears developed new strength when the EC adopted its program to achieve a single market by the end of 1992. When, belatedly, Washington and the American business community realized what was happening, the virtual knee-jerk reaction was to talk of "Fortress Europe." More understanding—and modifications in the

Community's proposals—abated this fear. By late 1994 concern about economic competition from the European Union had diminished among both the public and leaders in America. It ranked last among nine possible threats to the U.S. over the next ten years; only twenty-seven percent of the public and eleven percent of leaders viewed the EU as a critical economic threat.[2] Yet there remains today a latent fear of a closed-up Europe.[3]

A more specific source of U.S.-EU differences has been the EU's Common Agricultural Policy (CAP). From an economic point of view, this policy is probably most costly to the EU itself and, secondly, to certain other countries, both developed and not, which are highly dependent on agricultural exports, and only thirdly, to the United States. But politically speaking, the CAP is highly important. This exception to the rule of EU trade openness has been the focus of U.S. criticism of the European Union. There is domestic politics on both sides of the question.

Agriculture is one issue that never was successfully dealt with in the multilateral trade negotiations prior to the Uruguay Round (1986–1994). Typically, the United States stated at the outset that liberalization of agricultural trade was the sine qua non of the negotiation, only to accept a result that largely omitted agriculture.

That this was not the case in the Uruguay Round was due not just to the position of the United States (which might once again have yielded to European intransigence) but also to the linkage established in these negotiations between European agricultural concessions and trade-liberalizing actions of some less developed countries.

It took the European Community a generation to move much beyond trade in its international economic impact. When in the 1970s it made some tentative efforts to expand its scope, friction developed.

One of these set-tos developed over the proposal made by Commissioner Hendrik Vredeling to require worker participation in the management or, more precisely, in the supervision of larger firms established within the EC. The proposal can be seen as an effort to impose a "German" style of company organization on the entire European Community, though in fact many other Western European countries have similar systems. While the proposal was conceived as an element of "social policy" attractive to workers and unions, its reception differed according to the labor relations history of the EC countries—provoking at best a mixed reaction, for example, from the British unions.

The United States, while having little legal standing in the matter, was pushed by American firms with European subsidiaries into joining forces with Europeans negative to the Vredeling proposal. This is best seen as simple response to constituent pressures. But it also reflected two other, broader attitudes.

Vredeling, by imposing these conditions on firms wishing to operate in Europe, would have erected a new barrier to entry, or at least would have reduced the almost miraculous freedom of American firms to operate in Europe without assuming onerous responsibilities and unfamiliar practices.[4] Significant enough in itself, Vredeling could also be seen as the opening wedge for making Europe less unconditionally open to foreign direct investment.

Vredeling never made it from proposal to enactment (though the worker participation issue is not dormant).[5] But the other innovatory European economic policy of the 1970s—the European Monetary System—was agreed to. Again, the United States had little legal basis, after the demise of the original Bretton Woods arrangements, on which to object to whatever Europeans decided with regard to their monetary regimes. But this fact did not prevent many knowledgeable Americans, including officials, from reacting negatively.

The criticism of some American academics was unexceptionable both in form and substance. In arguing that economic coordination or convergence should come before the attempt to stabilize exchange rates,[6] they were taking up a theme already familiar in European discussion of the subject—and one which has continued to be current in regard to the movement to European Monetary Union.

Other American reactions were less constructive in their motivation. The very idea of European independent thinking and action in a matter affecting the international monetary system aroused the bureaucratic defensiveness of U.S. Treasury officials. They tended to argue that the European Monetary System wouldn't work but that, if it did, it would be a bad thing.

In judging that the EMS would be bad for the U.S. and the world, the Treasury was expressing not just the reaction of its officials but the assessment of the Carter administration of the impact of EMS on U.S. policy. This was the period when the United States was trying to stimulate the world economy by proxy—specifically, by prodding Germany into the role of "locomotive." The Carter administration feared that the result of the EMS—if it worked and didn't fall apart immediately—would be to spread to the rest of Europe the deflationary bias of the Germans. In the old Keynesian eyes of the American administration, the result would be to depress economic growth in Europe and therefore in the rest of the world, including the United States.

Both the Treasury bureaucrats and the higher levels of the Carter administration had other, less explicitly stated, reasons for viewing the EMS with concern. They viewed it as a threat to American dominance of the international monetary system and as a threat to the dominant role of the dollar as an international transactions and reserve currency—both of which were viewed as significant for American politico-economic well-being. The partial supplanting of the dollar had the potential, it was felt, to make the financing of the U.S. deficit more difficult.[7] European independence of the United States in this sensitive sector was seen as a threat to America's world dominance.

The EC's 1992 program had the potential to elicit even greater opposition from the United States, and it did; the full liberalization of the movement of goods, services, capital, and labor within the EC, in certain respects, has created specific difficulties for the United States. Criticism was tempered by the EC's willingness to modify its proposals to meet U.S. objections (as in the case of the revision of the Second Banking Directive). Concerned elements in the U.S. business community and the government also came to realize that whatever elements harmful to our interests might still lurk in the massive 1992 program, they were outweighed by the opportunities it would give to U.S. enterprises doing business in Europe and by the stimulus it would give to European economic growth—with a favorable secondary effect on the United States.

The degree of economic integration created by the Single Market program is not fully understood in the United States. In many regards it will produce a more nearly unified market than exists in

54

the United States after more than two hundred years of federal life. American banking and insurance still are largely state-regulated, with barriers to entry across state lines and considerably different regulatory policies among the individual states. State environmental and other regulations constitute barriers to the free movement of goods comparable to those the apostles of the Single Market attacked. The list could go on; the costs of "non-market" in the United States must be at least comparable to those identified in the EU.

The elimination of these barriers within the EU will give the West Europeans a competitive advantage over the United States, for there is no general movement in the United States to follow the European lead. The closest comparable effort—the Bush Treasury's attempt to reform American banking legislation inter alia to make multistate banking easier—ran into the political sands. Resurrected, legislation permitting true interstate banking by 1997 was finally enacted in 1994.[8]

Both the static efficiency gains from these actions and the dynamic impetus they will give to the European economy will contribute to increasing the prosperity of the West European economy relative to that of the United States, though, to be sure, this contribution will to some extent be offset by Europe's continuing structural rigidities, particularly in the labor market.

This sweeping economic integration should also contribute to the unity of the European Union, both in the psychological sense and in terms of domestic and international politics.

It will increase the sense of unity of West Europeans because in many practical aspects of day-to-day existence barriers have ceased to exist. Europeans are largely free to live and work where they want; they are able to invest their money in whatever part of Europe they want; their goods *and* their services are increasingly provided from a wide variety of national sources. The establishment of a dense intra-European network of personal and business connections—or, rather, the rendering yet more dense an already significant network—is creating vested interests in the preservation, and perhaps the further development, of an economically integrated Europe.

Politically, a great swatch of decision-making terrain has been transferred from the member-states to the EU level, with a consequent transfer of the interests of citizens, pressure groups, and politicians. And the integration of the European Union in areas outside trade will make it a more generally competent, as well as more formidable, actor in international relations.

The geographic scope of the Single Market, and of the contribution to a sense of common Europeanness which it makes, has expanded since it was first proposed. This was the result, first, of the agreement between the EC and the European Free Trade Area (EFTA) to create the European Economic Area (EEA). While the EC-EFTA agreement did not extend all features of the Community to an eighteen-member grouping, it did so in key areas.[9] The accession of three former EFTA nations to the European Union in January 1995 was a second important expansion of the Single Market.

But this is not the end of the story. The years from 1985 through 1991 witnessed an institutional renaissance in the EC; that substantial achievement, the Single Market, may be only the first of a series of unifying actions. The most important of these prospective steps is Economic and Monetary Union (EMU).

EMU was not part of the Single Market program but is both facilitated and made more appropriate by it. The probable increase in the proportion (already high) of all transactions accounted for by other countries of the European Union, and in the mobility of factors of production within the EU, makes the creation of a single currency—the end objective of EMU—both possible and desirable.

The apparent success of the European Monetary System—success defined as the reduction of exchange rate changes, and subsidiarily as the reduction of economic divergences that necessitate parity changes—was another springboard for the call for full monetary union. The EMS's success was not instantaneous; indeed, in the first years after its inauguration in 1979, it seemed vulnerable to collapse. But a transition took place from 1982 to 1984 as West European governments adopted theories and practices of economic management that were compatible with maintaining fixed exchange rates.

The most significant change of policy direction, both symbolically and substantively, was that made by France in March 1983. The attempt by Mitterrand and the Socialists to manage the French economy as if it were independent, in the hope of achieving a higher growth rate, was abandoned for the realities of interdependence. France, and other European countries, accepted the inevitability of managing their own economies sufficiently similarly to the Federal Republic of Germany to permit the maintenance of a fixed exchange rate with the deutsche mark.[10] This meant, most notably, reducing the difference between their inflation rates and that of Germany. Thus, the economic convergence which Germany had long argued must come before monetary union was the sequel to the establishment of the EMS, but was the necessary condition for its success.

Once a degree of convergence was achieved, however, further progress was not made. The remaining possibility for adjustments; the lack of ultimate credibility in an admittedly transitional regime; even the sense that, assuming ultimate movement to absolutely fixed rates or a single currency, countries should first use their freedom to achieve a competitive permanent rate—all were, and still are, disturbing factors. From within the EMS, therefore, there emerged an internal logic to moving to full monetary unification. The freeing of capital flows within the European Community and the integration of the financial sector as part of the EC's 1992 Single Market program have added to these pressures. With free capital flows, moderate divergences in inflation rates result in substantial interest rate differentials and consequent pressures on exchange rates. Since parity adjustments and capital controls run against the logic of both the EMS and the Single Market, the answer must be *greater* policy coordination: independent national monetary policies are not compatible with fixed exchange rates and free capital movements.[11]

The Delors committee's *Report on Economic and Monetary Union in the European Community* (April 1989) made, in the light of this situation, proposals which were approved at the Maastricht Summit of December 1991, and which seemed—at least until the financial crisis of September 1992—to enjoy very widespread support. The countries of the European Community should aim at permanently fixed exchange rates and, since in such a situation twelve (or more) currencies would serve little purpose, a single currency. This currency, and the monetary policy underlying it, should be managed by an independent body, a European central bank, plus a "system" of central banks equating with a committee of the national central bank governors, all of whom are to be (unlike past and present situations in many countries) independent of government dictation. The central bank would have a constitutional mandate to aim at price stability.

Karl Otto Pohl, for many years head of the Bundesbank, said in 1990, "If we are to have a European monetary regime, then it has to be as good as, for example, the Bundesbank's. And a European central bank can only achieve price stability if it is independent in its monetary policies of the EC institutions and governments."[12]

The aim of the Delors Report, and of those who subsequently tinkered with it, was to meet Pohl's test. There is, in Germany, considerable doubt as to whether EMU will in fact be an equal trade for the existing German monetary system, whether a mediocre ECU may not replace a good deutsche mark. The day after the Maastricht Summit agreed to EMU, the banner headline of Germany's leading circulation newspaper, *Bild Zeitung*, read "The End of the D-Mark." The front-page story began: "In the Dutch town of Maastricht yesterday could be heard the sound, quite softly, of a funeral bell. It tolled for the symbol of German prosperity, of the German economic miracle."[13] The tests of fiscal probity that Maastricht adopted for eligibility for membership in the last stage of EMU—the public policy equivalent to the Calvinists' proving by their behavior on earth that they are among God's elect—sought to respond, at least in part, to these concerns.

There can, in fact, be some doubt as to whether a new European central bank will act as if it were the Bundesbank. Aside from questions of pride or European supranationalism, there would seem no reason for a European central bank to substitute for the Bundesbank if the latter were entirely acceptable as the monetary governor of Europe. Two knowledgeable Europeans have asserted that "the EMU is not only an economic project, but also a means to overcome what some perceive as the monetary hegemony of the German Bundesbank."[14] Therefore, Germany's willingness to accept EMU is evidence of its continuing willingness to sacrifice its own national interests (up to a certain point) for those of Europe. (It has to be added that this sacrifice will be made only on the basis of conditions the Germans did much to specify. Furthermore, it is a sacrifice that serves the purpose of making Germany, and German policies, more generally acceptable within Europe.)

The measure of monetary sovereignty the other members of the EU will have to yield in moving to a single currency is less than it was before the EMS. Even after the collapse of the formal EMS exchange rate mechanism in August 1993,[15] many EMS states continued to follow a monetary policy aimed at maintaining parity with the deutsche mark, with varying success.[16] But the commitment involved in the final stage of EMU will be far less reversible than was involved in the EMS.[17]

EMU is an interesting constitutional development. Until now, European Union policies have been devoted mainly to creating circumstances in which market forces can operate more freely. EMU will involve control over member-state policies in an area generally considered part of the core of state sovereignty.[18] While the practice of EMU may not match intentions, it will be governed by a body which is supposed to be much more supranational, much less intergovernmental, than the EU's current policy-making organ, the Council of Ministers. (The EU Commission is supranational but has the power only to propose, not to make, policy.) The formal mandate to maintain price stability given the European central bank is also interesting in that it means setting a policy objective, on the order of a constitutional prescription, which is independent of either popular or intergovernmental political argument.[19]

Sweeping though this surrender of power in the monetary area is, the effect goes further. While member governments' nominal fiscal independence will largely remain, they will be subject to surveillance and to conditions intended to keep them from adopting fiscal policies that disturb the monetary union.

The United States has for years had to take the European Union seriously as a negotiating partner in trade. But the EU Commission's powers in the trade area, while real, do not compare with those to be assigned to the European central bank. If EMU comes to pass, the U.S. Treasury will have to make a double jump—difficult for a not-very-agile institution—from dealing with a few financially important European countries, each with its own interests and policies, to dealing with one monetary (and fiscal) authority; and from dealing with its own counterparts in finance ministries to dealing with a group of central bankers.[20] Not only will the familiarity and ease of relationship that now exists be, at least temporarily, lost, but also the relative strength of the U.S. bargaining position will likely decline. A single European monetary authority might even steal from the U.S. its lead in monetary initiatives. The EU Commission has taken a similar view of these prospects: "EMU will . . . mean that the Community will be better placed, through its unity, to secure its interests in international coordination processes and negotiate for a balanced multipolar system."[21]

It could be expected, further, that a single European currency would to some degree replace the dollar as a transactions and reserve currency. There could be some costs to the United States as a result of portfolio substitution away from the dollar. (There also might be costs to Europe, in the form of appreciation of the European currency vis-à-vis the dollar.)[22]

It remains to be seen whether by January of 1999 EMU will have gone into its final stage. The Maastricht Treaty is categorical on this point: ARTICLE 109j(4) states that "the third stage [which begins with the irrevocable locking of exchange rates between participating countries] shall start on 1 January 1999." It probably will, given not just the letter of the treaty but the political determination of France and Germany, the motivating forces of the European Union.[23] But the number of EU states that will be ready to proceed at that time is less predictable. And while, in the intervening years, there will be a rehearsal of Europe's monetary future (the European Monetary Institute came into being in January 1994 as the designated precursor of the European central bank), only practice will demonstrate how well EMU will work.

In 1994–1995, work did begin on the mechanics of EMU's inauguration. On 31 May 1995 the EU Commission released its ideas; they represent what is probably a majority, but not a unanimous, view of the start-up stage. There would be three phases: the decision to go ahead, and the designation of the participant countries; the irrevocable fixing, within twelve months, of the parities of those countries' currencies; and within three years after that, the transition to a single currency, with its coins and notes introduced over a few weeks at most.

Virtually no one believes that the Maastricht Treaty's requirement to begin EMU on 1 January 1997 will be met—that a majority (eight out of fifteen) of the member-states of the EU would have met the treaty's convergence criteria. Assuming, therefore, that the decision to proceed and the designation of participants will take place on 1 January 1999, currencies should be irrevocably linked by the beginning of the year 2000, and a single currency introduced no later than 1 January 2003.[24]

The financial crisis of September 1992, which led to the exit of the U.K. and Italy from the EMS's exchange rate mechanism, strengthened the view that EMU will, indeed, begin with a narrower group of countries. On present reading, that group consists of Germany, Benelux, France, Ireland, and Austria; it will also include the U.K. and Denmark, assuming they can get over their political hang-ups. The process of convergence toward the German norm of inflation, and especially to the Maastricht criteria for government deficits and public debt, will be too difficult, or at least will take too long, for the other EU countries to qualify for EMU.

On the other hand, the nature of the 1992 crisis and that of August 1993, caused by the inability of other EMS participants to influence the Bundesbank's monetary policy, suggests the desirability of an early date for the start-up of EMU.[25] In EMU, other countries would, at least in principle, have an equal voice in setting interest rates. Furthermore, these crises are evidence that the transitional nature of the EMS renders it perennially subject to speculation; best, therefore, to move quickly to the final stage of EMU.

The battering the EMS took in 1992–1993, coupled with the other troubles of the post-Maastricht European Union, raises the question of the political will to move to EMU. There seems little doubt about the continuing commitment of political and business elites in much of Europe to go ahead. Popular sentiment is less clearly positive; pro-EMU feeling clearly fell in Germany after 1990, for example. Yet there is evidence of popular support for monetary union, especially for its anti-inflationary effect. A sufficient level of consent probably exists to permit a core group of countries to proceed with EMU.[26]

Germany is insistent that the necessary concomitant of EMU—and its price for playing this game—is progress toward political union: the broadening of the political base of EU institutions and an increase in their power. This is contested by some, especially those in the U.K. who favor EMU but do not wish to counter the widespread

British reluctance to make the EU more like a political union. Aside from the intrinsic logic of the German position (surely such powers over the lives of European citizens as the EMU will have require some sort of political consent and support), there is the brute fact that EMU will be created with Germany as a willing participant or it will not be created.[27]

If EMU does come to pass, it will be a new *political* fact of great importance for U.S. relations with Europe and, indeed, for the U.S. role in the world.

CHAPTER 7

THE "EUROPEAN UNION": POLITICAL UNION OR OVERREACH?

A NEW TACTIC

The European Community was the creation of a group of leaders whose ultimate goal was some form of political union.[1] However, after a flurry of activity in the early post-World War II period openly aimed at this target, the tactic of proceeding toward political unity by way of and by means of cooperation in functional areas—the tactic associated with Jean Monnet—was adopted. As French Foreign Minister Robert Schuman put it in 1950, "Europe will not be built all at once, or as a single whole: it will be built by concrete achievements which first create de facto solidarity."[2]

"Functionalism" prevailed over efforts such as those of General Charles de Gaulle to reverse course and stress cooperation in foreign and security policy at the cost of the EC's developing supranationalism in functional areas. The process and its result are well described by Walter Russell Mead:

> The European Union is at once the greatest and the dullest achievement of 20th-century statesmanship. On the one hand, the collection of ancient enemies and historical rivals that created the EU dramatically overcame centuries of hatred and suspicion to fashion the largest political entity in Europe since the death of Charlemagne. . . .
>
> But if the European project is inspiring, the European Union can also be prosaic. The labyrinthine bureaucracies of Brussels and the mare's nest of consultative and decision-making bodies that make up the day-to-day realities of the European Union remain one of the world's most daunting and incomprehensible structures.[3]

The habit of political cooperation did develop, representing, if one wishes, a spillover from functional integration. This habit became more entrenched and more significant in the 1980s, and especially after adoption of the Single European Act.

But the events of 1989–1990 produced a change in kind, as well as degree, in European Community thinking about politics and security. Rather abruptly, the vocabulary shifted, reflecting an apparent shift in tactics from the classical, Monnet, approach. The movement to monetary union, with its significant effect on political integration, was already in the cards; suddenly a new track, aiming not just at more cooperation but at political union, was added.

In retrospect the institutional effort that went into the political decisions at Maastricht seems to have suffered from excessive concentration on what might well be the last, not the first, step in political union: defense.[4] This is understandable in the context of the liberating effect the end of the Cold War had on European thinking about defense. It may, nevertheless, have been a case of overreach.

Europe, it would now seem, has first to deal with two more fundamental problems. First, the same thaw that elevated the issue of European defense to the level of discussion, if not action, created new demands for accession to the EU, raising political and institutional questions as well as posing economic problems. Second, the psychological and institutional bases for a common foreign policy, much less a common defense, have not properly been laid. The familiar criticism of the "democratic deficit" in European Union institutions was accentuated, not calmed, by the Maastricht Treaty. There is a sense that today the European Union is an enterprise severed from the will of the people. This may be true in some ways; but, equally important, the reluctance to cede sovereignty to Brussels and to act collectively has rendered the EU impotent before problems like Yugoslavia.[5]

DEVELOPMENTS OF 1990–1992

The change in the European Community approach to politics and security can conveniently be dated from 19 April 1990. François Mitterrand and Helmut Kohl, meeting in one of the periodic Franco-German summits, stated that the EC should "define and implement a common foreign and security policy."[6] The statement seemed significant to Washington, even if it could be seen as the product of diverse motivations: yet another French effort to rope in a uniting Germany, yet another German concession to keep the French sweet. But significant of what?

It left almost everything to be clarified at some future dates. "Security" is a capacious category. Presumably, Kohl and Mitterrand proposed going beyond the discussion of the political and economic aspects of security authorized by the Single European Act. But was the statement the overture to another effort at a European Defense Community? Did it presage the creation of an integrated European military command structure? If so, what would happen to NATO's existing structure?

Washington was puzzled about how far Kohl and Mitterrand intended to go. But then, deciphering what Europeans mean is a perennial problem for our government. David Bruce, seeking in 1951 to explain to Dean Acheson just what was going on in the negotiations for the European Defense Community, said, "the Europeans like to do things in a way which seems to us like beating up a souffle of generalizations." Our government, then and now, finds it hard to follow the advice Bruce then gave: "It would come out all right, if we would leave it alone and worry about something else."[7]

Almost immediately after the Kohl-Mitterrand declaration, the European Council, on 28 April 1990, set the target of 1 January 1993 for arriving at a greater degree of political unity simultaneous with the completion of a single market, and agreement to economic and monetary union. Read together with the Kohl-Mitterrand statement, this plan made it seem plausible to foresee the EC moving deeper into the security area within a relatively brief period of time.

Rhetorically, all of this was a great leap forward. Traditionally, the EC countries had been nervous about broaching the subject of security because they thought talk of their own independence would weaken the U.S. commitment to Europe's defense. Reopening the subject was, quite evidently, motivated by the perceptions that the Soviet threat had declined, that the U.S. commitment would in any case be reduced, and that it was important to integrate Europe in this as in other ways to limit German independence.

In practice, progress has been slow. The reservations that Ireland, Denmark, and Greece displayed in the early 1980s regarding extending European Political Cooperation (EPC) to defense issues had led France and Belgium to suggest, toward the end of 1984, the revival of the Western European Union (WEU), which had been moribund since 1974.[8] Several shots of adrenaline, usually administered by the French, had modest effect. Perhaps the United States took the WEU more seriously than the Europeans did. Richard Burt, then assistant secretary of state for European Affairs, at least aroused attention when he wrote WEU governments in the spring of 1985 to ask them not to adopt agreed positions on arms control in meetings not including the U.S. Later, the Jacques Chirac government's "Charter of European Security," floated in the WEU, suffered from widespread European suspicion of French motives and intentions.

Nevertheless, as noted in chapter 3, in December 1990 the foreign and defense ministers of the WEU agreed that it had a key role to play both in the construction of Europe and in NATO's modernization, and also that the WEU should make an "appropriate contribution" to European security problems outside Europe.[9] The WEU seemed once again to be chosen by those European Community countries interested in some form of defense cooperation because it excluded the countries that are negative about the EC's having a defense role.

Doctrinal argument soon broke out between those who insisted on the primacy of NATO (especially the U.K. and the Netherlands) and those more interested in developing an autonomous European defense entity. As already noted, in early 1991 the United States joined the argument by sending a message to its European allies warning them of the damage putative developments in WEU might do to the Atlantic Alliance.

There was also some agreement among the EC countries. Most, including the U.K., were quite prepared to discuss security, and even defense, matters together. The WEU was generally accepted as an interim solution to the problem of a locus for this work. The divergence came over the relationship to NATO, with the British, and some others, fearful of anything that would weaken the alliance. The French, while paying lip service to the alliance, seemed unconcerned about this effect and determined to create a competing defense arrangement. The Germans agreed with both sides.

As noted, so far the Franco-German efforts to move ahead on an independent European line have been outdone by NATO's efforts to revise its structure. And NATO continued, well into 1992, to seek to repel its perceived rival: we will recall the unseemly competition between NATO and the WEU to send naval squadrons to the Adriatic in the summer of 1992 (squadrons whose function was, in each case, extremely unclear—almost a case of the unspeakable in pursuit of the uneatable).[10]

At Maastricht, in the treaty establishing a European Union, the EC agreed to an intergovernmental common foreign and security policy (CFSP) "including the eventual framing of a common defense policy, which might in time lead to a common defense." Responsibility for the European Union's decisions and actions having defense implications was delegated to the Western European Union, "which is an integral part of the development of the European Union" and "the means to strengthen the European pillar of the Atlantic Alliance." The policy of the European Union "shall respect the obligations of certain member states under the North Atlantic Treaty and be compatible with the common security and defense policy established within that framework."[11]

In this statement, there was something for both nervous Atlanticists (the references to NATO and its policies) and the Europeanists (the reference to common defense policy and a possible common defense). But it is the latter set of references that was innovative for the EC. Another sign that Maastricht was a cog in forward movement on a European defense policy was its agreement to the French proposal that defense arrangements be reviewed in 1996.[12]

The treaty provides that when the Council of Ministers decides, by unanimous vote, that an area or matter "covered by foreign and security policy. . . should be the subject of joint action" and such joint action is decided, the joint action "shall commit the Member States in the positions they adopt and in the conduct of their activity." In a separate declaration, member-states affirm that the following topics may be the subject of a joint action: industrial and technological cooperation in the field of armaments; the transfer of military technology to third world countries and the control of arms exports; nonproliferation issues; arms control issues, including negotiations on arms reduction and confidence-building measures, particularly in the context of the Conference on Security and Cooperation in

Europe (CSCE); involvement in peacekeeping operations in the United Nations context; involvement in humanitarian intervention measures; questions relating to the CSCE; relations with the Soviet Union; and transatlantic relations.[13]

This ambitious list certainly covers many security issues, but it stops short of a common defense policy. Movement *toward* one may be made through the WEU, but basic decisions are left for negotiation at the 1996 conference.

At the same time the French and German governments were leading the European Community down the path to political union, they were taking bilateral steps, ostensibly in the cause of ultimate action by the EC as a whole, notably the proposal of October 1991 to increase the size of the existing Franco-German brigade as the basis for a multinational European force.

The chiefs of defense staff of the WEU nations were invited to a meeting in Bonn in February 1992 to flesh out the Franco-German plans and explore reconciling them with an alternative Anglo-Italian plan for a European rapid-reaction force to operate outside the NATO area.[14] Only those "seriously interested" in setting up an integrated European defense corps need attend. The initial London comment that some skeptical countries might send "quite low level people to take notes" indicated that variable geometry might be emerging in European defense.[15] German diplomats tried to smooth things over by giving the impression that the European force they were planning would operate independently only outside NATO territory, but British officials said the Franco-German plan still looked like an attempt to set up a rival military structure, circumventing the Maastricht compromises in a way that was dangerous when leading American politicians were questioning the U.S. commitment to NATO.[16]

The subsequent Kohl-Mitterrand proposal of May 1992 to create by 1995 an army corps based on French and German contributions, but open to participation by other Europeans, aroused suspicion and dissent rather than contributing to European unity. Several European governments—not just Atlanticist U.K. and the Netherlands, but also Europeanist Italy—reacted negatively to the Paris-Bonn Eurocorps. Other Europeans were in some cases restive about Franco-German dominance. They also feared the U.S. reaction—

which was not long in coming, in the form of a barrage of monitory messages from Washington. The most important was, it is said, a message from Robert Zoellick (under secretary of state and intimate of Secretary James Baker) to the German foreign ministry's political director, stating that this development would have a negative effect on the continued willingness of the American public to support the U.S. military commitment to Europe.[17]

The Germans, as always, tried to calm their American partners; but their assurances about the Eurocorps—for example, that it would be available to NATO in case of need—were not fully accepted in Washington since the Germans might not be speaking for the French. However, at the end of September 1992 French Defense Minister Pierre Joxe stressed that the corps's first duty was to defend the alliance and that its troops would come under NATO command in case of emergency. Joxe also expressed an interest in France's taking "part more fully than previously in political-military discussions" in NATO.[18] This chapter of dissent was finally closed in January 1993 when the French and German chiefs of staff signed an agreement with NATO's Supreme Commander, General John Shalikashvili, whereby the Eurocorps would be placed under NATO command in case of crisis.[19]

WHY THIS ATTENTION TO "EUROPEAN" DEFENSE?

Despite all the attention to the questions of a defense policy and an ultimate common defense, it seems clear that these are developments which should, perhaps must, follow from a truly common foreign policy. As already noted in chapter 3 above, while there is a growing density of consultation and coordination among European Union countries, the end results, in terms of common policies, have not been startlingly successful. And the Maastricht Treaty does not change the basic coordination process: unanimity is still the general rule after Maastricht, despite some hortatory language about minorities yielding their position.

There are some within the European Union, though their voices tend to be drowned out, who would argue that for the EU to stress the creation of a common defense is to ignore the new realities of the world and who contend that the EU could, as a "civilian power," using its immense economic and considerable political influence, play a significant world role. Hans-Dietrich Genscher, German foreign minister from 1974 to 1992, went along with the French-inspired emphasis on a defense aspect to the EC, but seemed to hold and practice views similar to those of the civil power school.

The preponderant view, however, is that the European Union is almost forced to seek to develop some sort of defense policy, if not a common army. One argument is that the EU will not play the role in the world that befits it—that Europe's voice will not be heard—if it lacks what is still one of the principal attributes of power, military force. EC Commission President Jacques Delors, in a March 1991 speech, argued that "the Gulf War has provided an object-lesson . . . on the limitations of the European Community. The only option compatible with the complete vision of European union is to insert a common security policy into this framework. . . ."[20] And the Maastricht Treaty, in ARTICLE B, states an objective of the European Union is "to assert its identity on the international scene, in particular through the implementation of a common foreign and security policy including the eventual framing of a common defense policy. . . ."[21]

Another, more practical argument is that U.S. withdrawal from Europe is virtually certain and that a European collective defense would be preferable (at least, as second best to the unsustainable status quo of NATO) to a renationalization of defense, which would be inconsistent with the progressive integration of the EU in other areas—and dangerous, to boot.[22] However, so long as U.S. troops remain in Europe in substantial numbers—even the 100,000 left in Europe in the mid-1990s are a substantial force—and so long as NATO is nimble about reordering its reduced ranks, the EU is un-likely to make much progress toward a European defense force.

To listen to Europe's leaders is to hear a chorus of voices saying in unison that they don't want us to go. In most cases, this state-ment is sincere. Few Europeans may think there is a current or fore-seeable need for American forces to deter or defend against an attack from the East: the chaos in the former Soviet Union is as good a deterrent as NATO ever was. But many can imagine useful roles for our troops and the political commitment that goes with them, as a contribution to stability or, more crudely, to counterbalance the Germans and keep them from dominating Europe.

At the same time, there seems to be an underlying doubt that our forces will stay in Europe. This concern didn't, and doesn't, equate with a judgment that they will all leave at once. But, in the medium term, by the mid-1990s two-thirds of our troops had left. And the fear is that all will leave by the end of this decade.

Early in the post-Cold War period there were two principal sources of this feeling. The first is still alive. Europeans believed that the U.S. would read the reduction in the threat from the East more or less as they themselves had and that below some minimum threshold-level of threat, it would be politically impossible for the U.S. to pay the political and monetary price of maintaining a troop presence in Europe. While the process of withdrawal has been drawn out, this argument still seems valid and is nourished by voices Europeans hear in the United States.

Second, they had doubts about the long-term willingness of Germany to play host to large U.S. army and air forces. So far, Germany has *not* shown signs of preparing eviction notices, even though many thought it would come to feel that the continued presence of foreign troops—at least troops from another continent—was an anomalous relic of the forty-five-year occupation and of German singularity. (There is no indication whatever that France, however vocal it has been about wanting American military forces to remain in Europe, would be willing to play host to units displaced from Germany.)

What remains valid in this second point is that if the United States did totally withdraw, substitution of a European force for the Americans in Germany might have some political attraction. A European force might not be as strong militarily. However, it would remove the image of occupation yet avoid creating fear in other Europeans about a rebirth of German nationalism.

Another motivation for emphasis on security is purely political. Halting though progress toward making Europe into a political unity has been, European ideological statements have repeatedly stressed this as a goal. Cart-before-the-horse though the approach may seem, giving the EU a greater security role is seen as part of the process of making the EU more of a political institution (desirable in and of itself but also as a way of limiting German independence). This political motivation leads to proposals for defense integration that seem to ignore technical realities and to run ahead of policy coordination.

Finally, the habits built up over twenty years of European political cooperation make further foreign policy and security cooperation seem inevitable.

This last point may seem weak, but it is not. Well before the end of the Cold War it was noted that the evolving European Political Cooperation process had progressively shifted emphasis and importance away from political consultations in NATO and toward the European Community. Some years ago, a pro-NATO European wrote that while the EPC processes are hardly "efficient," they had developed a certain esprit de corps among participants, such as ministers, directors general, and departmental directors. They know each other personally, are in daily communication, and feel as if they are participating in a laudable enterprise. On the other hand, the NATO consultative mechanism, formal and highly structured, is not conducive to close personal relations between participants, particularly policymakers like foreign ministers and directors general of political affairs.

Still, the renewed interest in a European Union security role would not have developed except under the influence of the perceptions that the military threat to Western Europe is reduced and that the United States is on the verge of a massive cutback in its European military presence, regardless of what the Europeans do. Europeans have traditionally been wary about proposing too much by way of the European defense entity, for fear this would precipitate a departure of the United States from Europe. A U.S. military pullout is now less worrying, although it is still not desired. In any case, it seems to be a possibility independent of European actions.

A judgment dating from before the events of 1989–1990 seems prophetic: "If the U.S. commitment to Europe were to disappear, the EC, as the dominant European cooperative arrangement, could be considered as the basis for a new alliance; indeed, it would be unlikely that the economic and social dimensions of the Community could survive the breakup of NATO unless an alternative vehicle for Western European defense solidarity was produced."[23] Or, as former French Prime Minister Edith Cresson put it in July 1991, "It is evident that the United States is disengaging from Europe.... It cannot leave and ask us not to have a defense of our own."[24]

WHAT SORT OF EU SECURITY ROLE?

What might be the form and substance of an EU role in security? Even now, after years of rather intensive discussion, the answers are speculative. I suspect that even those European politicians who have given a lead to consideration of this subject within the EU are not sure what exactly they mean.

This is not an unusual way for the European Union to proceed. The European technique has been to state very fuzzy goals, amounting to no more than a sense of direction, and then begin working toward them, with definitions and specificity following, not preceding, the process: first the deed, and then the thought. The questions posed by Mrs. Thatcher's government during the latter part of her term as prime minister were in many cases well-taken—showing, as they did, a measure of skepticism about just what might be involved in a greater degree of political unification. But the dominant European sentiment was: "This is the right direction to go; we will work out the details as we travel."

I believe there are three principal aspects to a security role for the EU: (a) discussion of security issues, aiming at common policies; (b) coordination of defense production and procurement; (c) actual military integration.

Discussing security issues such as the CSCE and arms control is something the European Union has done for some time; the list of areas for joint action in the declaration appended to the Maastricht Treaty is indicative of where the EU may go in the future.

Discussion within the EU does not, in European eyes, preclude discussion of the same subject in NATO. But EU countries could increasingly arrive at NATO with an agreed position, changing what has been a discussion among sixteen nations to a dialogue between the U.S. and the EU.[25] Until very recently, operational military questions have been regarded by the EU as in NATO's domain. While the EU countries continue to participate fully in NATO discussions ranging from the truly operational to NATO's "new strategy," they may also discuss similar matters in the WEU.

"Out-of-area" actions—that is, outside the area of the North Atlantic Treaty—were long a bone of contention between the United States and its European allies, with the U.S. striving for years without success to lure them into agreeing to collective military ventures beyond the NATO pale. (The crisis in the former Yugoslavia changed attitudes.)[26] While the Europeans were not unwilling to *discuss* out-of-area problems in NATO, the EC was able to go further with these discussions than NATO. It was able to adopt common diplomatic positions of some significance: the high point—or the low, in the view of the U.S.—was the position on the Middle East adopted by the Venice EC Summit of June 1980, which, inter alia, backed Palestinian self-determination and participation in negotiations, called for the end of Israel's occupation of the West Bank and Gaza, and condemned Israeli settlements in the occupied territories.

But the EC's ability to coordinate actions, as opposed to verbiage, was limited. In much of the world, where the European Union countries' interests are limited and where the range of possible EU action is equally limited, the EU can achieve an impressive unity—impressive, but not very consequential. But on the Middle East, the extra-European region of greatest moment to the EU in those cases where it could have an effect on the situation, the strength of national positions and national interests has made a common policy difficult to achieve. The EC was, for example, able to adopt sanctions against Libya in 1986, but at the same time, it divided sharply over the U.S. attacks on Tripoli and Benghazi, with Thatcher's Britain lending us assistance and other EC countries criticizing or condemning our actions.

A real test of the effective unification of the foreign policies of the EU countries will be whether they can act collectively with regard to the Middle East, despite the sacrifices of national interests and perceptions that will be involved. The crisis provoked by Iraq's invasion of Kuwait in 1990 gave some evidence of progress. The EC was able to maintain a unified attitude throughout, though partial credit for this unity must be given to the special circumstances and to the support given to the EC by the UN's ability to achieve agreement.[27]

So far, the EU has not met the Middle East test. To be fair, it was forced by the United States into a marginal role in the Middle East peace process that began after the Gulf War. But it seemed all too willing to cede the Eastern Mediterranean and the Persian Gulf to the U.S.[28] The EU has come up with new Mediterranean programs, but they are of a piece with its old attempt to make economic power work without political and military complements. Indeed, the most innovatory step taken was by NATO, which early in February 1995 agreed to open a dialogue with Egypt, Israel, Morocco, Tunisia, and Mauritania because of concerns about Islamic fundamentalism and missile proliferation.[29]

Integrated defense production and procurement is an approach to the security issue that should come naturally to the EU, given its history of following functional pathways to unity and its record of accomplishment in economic integration. There have been a variety of developments in this regard—the Intra-European Program Group (IEPG) and, more effective, ad hoc "variable geometry" arrangements to produce specific weapons systems. But to date, cooperation has frequently been ineffective, even where attempted; and the efforts have generally been disconnected from the European Union institutions.[30] If one considers potential roles for the EU in security, this one logically comes before development of integrated military forces, if after development of common policies. In all aspects of security, the efficiencies of integration conflict with the divergent interests of each nation. However, in the production and procurement area, the military industrialists of each country—a particularly powerful group of vested interests—dig in their heels.

Yet the fault does not lie simply with the business interests. The problems faced by European defense firms are serious. The defense budgets of NATO's European members dropped from $93 billion in 1989 to $83 billion in 1994 (in 1985 dollars) and are still declining. Procurement spending is falling much faster. The market is divided among many products and firms: Britain, France, and Germany each produce a main battle tank; the United States, only one. Three advanced fighters are under development by different firms or alliances in Europe, only one in the United States. The U.S. defense industry has gone through a wave of mergers. The largest, the 1994 combination of Lockheed and Martin Marietta, produced a behemoth with military sales three times those of British Aerospace, Europe's largest defense firm; its sales in fact now exceed those of the entire French defense industry.[31] The world export market for major conventional weapons fell by nearly half between 1989 and 1993. The U.S. more or less maintained its level of sales, accounting for about half of the total in 1993; Europe lost market share to the technologically superior and lower-cost American suppliers.

Faced with this bleak situation, some industrialists have begun to think of transnational mergers, despite lack of encouragement by their governments.[32] In June 1994 a group of companies representing seventy percent of the European land-warfare defense industry issued a statement calling for the creation of a European defense industry community, with preference for European products, an industrial policy, and an open intra-European market, as well as mergers and alliances between firms.[33]

While industrial and technological cooperation in the field of armaments is on the list of areas adopted at Maastricht for joint action within the political cooperation context, this area is one where a role for the EU Commission seems possible—and could develop. The Commission's efforts to subject defense imports to the common commercial policy, plus some of its research and development programs, constitute the embryo of an agenda for the Commission. The classic EU combination of import protection and internal subsidies could have significant impact on Europe's defense industries. An expanded effort to render competition more open between European defense industries, through regulation by the Commission, would be another potential tool. Finally, an EU Commission staff responsible for the defense industry could constitute the nucleus for a European Ministry of Defense, should the EU proceed to military force integration, the third and most difficult aspect of security cooperation.

The EU could get around to part of this program at the 1996 Intergovernmental Conference, amending ARTICLE 223 of the Treaty of Rome, the "national security" exemption from the normal rules on openness and competition.[34] The commission study, *European Security Policy in the Run-up to 2000,* issued at the end of January 1995, had a different focus, however: more on "high policy." It recommended qualified majority voting (except for military interventions); appointment of a politician responsible for intergovernmental Common Foreign and Security Policy (CFSP), with powers similar to those of the Commission president; creation of an EU intervention force; movement toward a collective defense capability with strong links with NATO and the WEU; and establishment of a CFSP budget.[35]

More prosaic, and probably more effective, would be the creation of an EU-wide procurement agency; a number of proposals are in the field.[36] This agency would manage common procurement programs—e.g., for a new large transport plane—and seek to impose commercial discipline on them. It could also promote common rules on export regimes, bidding, and technical standards, and try to prevent the duplication of research and development.[37]

Distant possibility though *military integration* probably is, there has been considerable, if intermittent, discussion of it in the last few years. Perhaps too much attention has been devoted to the various French permutations on the theme of Franco-German military integration. While it is difficult (but not impossible) to conceive of a "European" force that does not have French and German units at its core, it may be more productive to ask what a European force means rather than to assume that it is something whose genetic code can be found in the Franco-German brigade.

First, what is the right level at which to integrate?[38] Second, how would an integrated European army (and air force) relate to the NATO integrated commands, assuming they survive—and to the American units, assuming they remain? Third, how would the French and British nuclear deterrents fit into this integration of military forces?

Answers to these and other such questions must be extremely speculative, particularly since there is no authoritative European proposal on the table. One can, at least, clear away some underbrush. An integrated military force—even one more truly integrated than NATO's has been—does not necessarily, or probably, involve the disappearance of national ministries of defense or national armies and air forces. One can well conceive of a situation in which these national entities continue to exist—and spend—to support the forces which, by collective agreement, they contribute to the integrated force. One can use an EU analogy: membership in the European Monetary System involves the acceptance of obligations, but these are met by nationally determined and executed policies. (But just as the EMS seems to be headed in the direction of full EMU with a common currency, there may be a logic of development that would carry military integration further.)

The French have at times seemed tantalizingly close to "Europeanizing" their nuclear deterrent.[39] In January 1992, speaking to a

National Conference on Europe in Paris, President Mitterrand noted that only two of the EC states possessed nuclear forces: "They have a clear doctrine for their national defense. Is it possible to imagine a European doctrine? That question will very quickly become one of the major issues in the construction of a European defense." (This came as a surprise: Mitterrand had, in March 1991, after the Gulf War, answered no to the question of whether France should change its defense strategy, adding that France's "nuclear-deterrent force is and remains the pivot" of that strategy.) However, Mitterrand did not want to go as far as Jacques Delors who, speaking to the same January 1992 Conference on Europe, said, "One can't help thinking that if, one day, the European Community has a very strong political union, then why not transfer the nuclear force to this political authority?"[40]

Mitterrand may have been thinking of something like the British position connecting its nuclear deterrent to NATO: "France would continue to be able to make independent decisions about the use of its nuclear force, while putting it at the wider disposal of a future European government."[41] Jacques Amalric argued, similarly, that Mitterrand had to recognize that the development of a common European defense is not compatible with the maintenance of a completely independent French deterrent force—something pointed out by several European leaders, "beginning with Mr. Genscher, the German Foreign Minister."[42]

France, of course, is not the only European power with nuclear forces. The British reaction to Mitterrand's initiative combined skepticism about just how far France really would go and a distinct unwillingness to go any further toward multilateralizing Britain's own nuclear forces. Such interest as the British have displayed in European nuclear cooperation is, in fact, limited to bilateral cooperation with France.

After months in which Mitterrand's characteristically Delphic statement seemed to be getting neither foreign response nor French follow-up, the issue was raised again, in the autumn of 1992, by Prime Minister Pierre Bérégovoy and Defense Minister Pierre Joxe. What they said lacked detail, but they suggested an expansion of the nuclear deterrence guarantees of Europe's two nuclear powers to cover all of Europe—or at least the European Community.

This time, the British response, by Defense Minister Malcolm Rifkind, was somewhat more positive. He welcomed the idea of discussions on a European nuclear doctrine. But he reminded the French that it was unrealistic not to link a European deterrent to the American one.[43] Rifkind's response led to the formation of a Franco-British Joint Commission on Nuclear Policy and Doctrine. At the Franco-British Summit in July 1993, British Prime Minister John Major and France's President Mitterrand made the Joint Commission permanent. British officials have kept the commission's work secret, but expressed great satisfaction with it.[44]

When the right-wing parties took over the French government in early 1993, they had already talked of reassessing French defense policy. Among the ideas suggested was a French nuclear guarantee to Germany as part of a Europeanization of the French deterrent force.[45] The issue was raised again by Alain Lamassoure, the French minister for European Affairs, in December 1994. Speaking to a Franco-German conference, he said—stressing that it was only his "personal wish"—that France, along with Britain, consider extending the umbrella of their nuclear deterrents to defend the European Union.[46]

The French Defense White Paper of February 1994 declares that "with nuclear capabilities, Europe's defense autonomy is possible. Without them, it is out of the question."[47] But for the moment, the nuclear issue does not seem of burning urgency. Germany, the non-nuclear odd-man-out among Europe's greater powers, does not exhibit any great interest in the subject as a whole, much less in acquiring its own nuclear capability. The dominant German view seems to be that nuclear weapons have become an irrelevancy. There is certainly little German inclination to give Britain and France leadership credit balances on the basis of their nuclear capabilities.[48] But in the longer run, if European defense integration does get anywhere, this issue will have to be confronted.

The Backlash

The most difficult question about a European defense identity has to do with its relationship to NATO. Some Europeans were reluctant to go along with the Franco-German mainstream. The Danes reacted negatively to the Maastricht provisions making the WEU responsible for executing military decisions reached under the common EC foreign policy. Antipathy to defense cooperation, and fear that it would weaken NATO's role, was at least one of the factors leading to rejection of the Maastricht treaties in the initial Danish referendum of 2 June 1992.[49]

The split within Europe had been displayed at the Munich "Wehrkunde" meeting of February 1992. Martin O'Neill of the British Labour party made an outspoken attack on the French-German plan for a European defense corps, warning it could drive the U.S. out of NATO. He saw the plan as the greatest threat to the Atlantic Alliance, accused France of "at best, a semi-detached relationship" to NATO, and called for clarification of how the Franco-German command structure would relate to the NATO command, who would have responsibility for French nuclear weapons, and whether the force was intended to have any role outside Europe.[50]

It was clear that while the *idea* of European military integration had emerged, the *reality* would be hard to achieve. Yielding military sovereignty is hard for most of Europe's countries, except possibly the very smallest (and even this exception is doubtful—see, for example, the very different but real reservations of Denmark and Ireland). There are, furthermore, two specific and fundamental problems to be resolved before the process can get much further:

1. The British, while quite willing to discuss security matters with their European partners, whether in EPC or in WEU, have strong reservations about European military integration— not just for reasons of sovereignty (though this is not a negligible consideration) but also for fear of the withdrawal of American military forces from Europe. Moving in this direction would, they argue, precipitate such a withdrawal, and that is something nobody professes to want. Underlying this objection—which has some resonance elsewhere in Western Europe, e.g., in the Netherlands and Portugal—is a more fundamental and more distinctly British unwillingness to opt decisively for the European as opposed to the Atlantic connection.

2. The bona fides of the French in proposing European military integration was widely suspect. The French have talked a good integration game but have been unwilling, in the final analysis, to sacrifice their own independence in defense, and not just as regards the use of their nuclear deterrent.[51] Mitterrand's new willingness at least to discuss this issue, and the general acceptance within France of his initiative, save for Jean-Marie Le Pen and the National Front,[52] may

have been the beginning of the process of building confidence in French intentions. The process continued under the government of Prime Minister Edouard Balladur (1993–1995), which quietly reentered NATO councils (though not the integrated military structure) and made clear its desire for a strong continuing U.S. commitment to European defense. But suspicions linger.

A Continued Role for NATO

Until these doubts and reservations are put to rest—and even thereafter—the European Union countries will want to preserve NATO. The strength of this desire has, if anything, grown over the years since the end of the Cold War. Events such as the hostilities in the former Yugoslavia have made Europeans aware not only of their lack of a powerful military instrument but also of the unlikelihood of their creating one in the near future.[53] For this and other reasons France has substantially modified its previous skeptical and negative attitude toward a U.S.-led NATO (though it would prefer some Europeanization of the organization).

NATO itself—under that American leadership—has contributed to its European popularity. Partnership for Peace, whatever its intrinsic merits and regardless of its usurpation of the CSCE's role, has responded to the feeling of some Europeans, especially the Germans, that reaching out to the East is an imperative for the West. Even Mitterrand took a favorable view of PfP.

At the same January 1994 NATO Summit that launched the PfP the decision was taken to create "Combined Joint Task Forces" (CJTF). Under this concept, NATO can lend its assets to WEU for the latter's operations. The CJTF concept may be, as one commentator puts it, "NATO's most radical piece of new thinking in its 45-year history."[54] More certainly, it represents a definitive shift in the American response to European defense cooperation from resistance to encouragement.[55]

As of mid-1995, the only clear pressures for an end to the American military involvement in Europe are coming from the United States, not Europe. Europe wants NATO to continue as it is and has been.

This desire would probably exist even if U.S. forces were totally withdrawn from Europe. In that case, NATO would become an alliance without much subordinate structure, certainly without the integrated military command. This change in structure would not conflict with the Treaty of Washington that created NATO. European interest in preserving NATO in some form would be strong, especially if it were felt the existence of NATO would improve the chances that the U.S. would continue to extend its strategic deterrence to Western Europe—even if there were doubts that the U.S. would actually use its forces to protect Europe.

ENLARGEMENT COMPLICATES THINGS

But there is another complication. What "Europe" would the U.S. commit itself to? An issue which hardly existed before late 1989—and which seemed, as late as 1990, likely to be postponed— now seems unavoidable: how soon the European Union, including its nascent defense and security aspects, will be enlarged to comprehend at least part of Eastern Europe.

Until the implications of the revolution in the East sank in, the stress within the European Community was on "deepening" the existing EC of twelve members. The absorption of East Germany as part of the existing German member state was a significant, but not Rubicon-crossing event. Indeed, the primary motivation for emphasizing the deepening of the European Community became the need felt to engage Germany in an integrative process that would preclude its taking an independent course. Thus, far from being a step toward incorporating the rest of Eastern Europe into the EC, German unification became a reason for not going any further.

Some of the pressures for enlargement do predate the revolution of 1989–1990. The desire of some of the countries of European Free Trade Area (EFTA) to join the EC was a product, not of that revolution but of the fears and hopes created by the EC's movement toward a unified single market. The EFTA countries went along with Delors, when he, to avoid enlargement, concocted the idea of a European Economic Area (EEA) to satisfy some of EFTA's desires. But several of the EFTA countries regarded the EEA as an inadequate solution.

The end of the Cold War and the demise of the Soviet Union made it easier for these EFTA countries to come to the decision to apply for EU membership. Finland might never have done so, but for the revolution in the East. And the way was also smoothed for Austria and Sweden. Austria no longer needed to fear a Soviet veto.

Sweden, like the other neutrals of Europe, found neutrality a viti-ated concept in a world no longer divided between two adversaries.

While any enlargement adds to the already-substantial prob-lems of policy determination and management of the European Union, the EFTA countries are relatively small, easy morsels to swal-low, and are at a high level of economic development: they seem more likely to be fit for membership in the EMU at the end of this decade than many of the current member-states of the EU. The na-tions of EFTA are culturally and economically part of Western Eu-rope. Politically, they remained on the Western side of the great European divide after the Second World War; their political disabili-ties or disqualifications for European Union membership were elimi-nated by the end of the Cold War, even in the extreme case of Finland (for which the disintegration of the USSR was especially liberating).

Accession negotiations began with Austria, Sweden, and Fin-land in February 1993 and were concluded in March 1994, in time for entry into the EU on 1 January 1995.[56] The three EFTA coun-tries were willing to sign on to all of the EU's aspects, including the Common Foreign and Security Policy—though it is unlikely that these formerly neutral applicants will soon apply for NATO mem-bership.[57] The process was faster than normal because the EEA ne-gotiations constituted a sort of pre-accession negotiation and because the European Union wanted to get this phase of enlargement over before its 1996 institutional review.[58]

Eastern Europe is a different story entirely. Its countries are the product of a very different history, in the postwar era and before. They have varying degrees of cultural linkage with the West; they share an enormous economic retardation compared to Western Eu-rope, as was demonstrated by the adjustment problems of the most advanced East European economy, that of East Germany. While the chaos within the former Soviet Union liberated them to choose other alliances, they remain geographically vulnerable to their great neigh-bor to the east, Russia.

Unlike the EFTA countries, none of the countries of Eastern Europe was instantly ready, either economically or institutionally, to enter the European Community. The EC looked to its precedents in cases of less-developed applicant countries and offered associa-tion agreements to most of the countries of East Central Europe.[59]

83

These agreements, sometimes referred to as "Europe Agreements," provide for generally free entry of these countries' products into the European Union—and for economic assistance.[60]

At the Copenhagen European Council of June 1993, the EC committed itself, for the first time, to the understanding that the purpose of the association agreements is to prepare the associates for full membership, when they are ready for it.[61] These agreements do not for the moment pose the question of security guarantees that accession will.[62] The European Union has created an even more delicate potential question of security guarantees by signing, in mid-1995, association agreements with the Baltic states of Estonia, Lithuania, and Latvia—the only former Soviet republics that have secured such agreements.[63]

The EU can and should enrich its association agreements by increased political consultation and better economic treatment. But some, at least, of the associated states are insistent on early membership, not just for the economic benefits but for the stabilizing impact and the security, in a broad sense, that participation in the EU will give them. Since few of them will qualify economically in the near future, the EU must consider whether to admit some countries quite soon for political reasons, on the understanding that they will need long-term economic assistance after accession.[64]

Alternatively, the European Union's tendency toward an à la carte approach might be exploited with regard to the states to the East, letting them participate in certain EU programs and policies without full membership. But this approach would run into opposition both from within the EU and from the prospective beneficiaries—from the latter because they would achieve neither the security nor the legitimation conferred by full membership in the EU.

The EU's Essen Summit of December 1994 took up the question of enlargement to the east, but mainly it issued a directive to the EU Commission to prepare an inventory of what policies and rules new states must accept and adapt to in order to become members of the EU. This inventory was produced in May 1995. Neither the Essen Summit nor the inventory clarified the timing of the enlargement or the countries that would enter first. Rather, the summit agreed that substantive talks on eastward enlargement would have to wait until after the 1996 intergovernmental conference to review the EU's institutions. Nevertheless, the Hungarian and Czech prime ministers both said they were planning on the year 2000 for their entry into the EU.[65] And Jacques Santer, on the threshold of becoming president of the EU Commission, said in an interview that he hoped to see the six Eastern European associates join the EU around the turn of the century.[66] The Eastern European states, in any case, are not first in line. The European summit of June 1994 decided to put Cyprus and Malta on its list for enlargement; negotiations with these countries are to begin immediately after the 1996 intergovernmental conference.[67]

How much will "Europe"—i.e., the European Union—grow by the year 2000? The best bet is that most if not all of the Visegrad states (Czech Republic, Hungary, Poland, and Slovakia) will be members of the EU, or on their way to becoming members, aided by the strong German pressure to expand the EU to cover Central Europe. So will Malta and Cyprus. The EU will have risen from its 1995 level of fifteen members to twenty or so.

"Europe," in other words, will still be a subset of Europe. Though its frontier will have inched eastward, it will still not include any part of the former Soviet Union (though the Baltic states will be closely associated with the EU). Nor is it likely to include any state in Southeastern Europe. Slovenia (which considers itself Central European) has a chance for relatively early accession. But Romania, Bulgaria, Albania, the other republics emerging from the old Yugoslavia, and Turkey seem likely to be left outside the EU pale for as far ahead as one can foresee.[68]

The answer for them could be the development of a subregional alliance in Southeastern Europe. There are embryonic elements of such an alliance among the Balkan countries. The troubles in the former Yugoslavia may make such an arrangement seem implausible. However, the very fractionation of what was Yugoslavia adds to the need for some sort of regional confederation, which could presumably be associated with and receive economic and political help from the EU.[69]

A best estimate of the changed political structure of Europe as of the year 2000 therefore sees the EU enlarged, in Western Europe, Eastern Europe, and the Mediterranean, but not including all of the countries to the west of the former Soviet Union. And while broader groupings—the Organization for Security and Cooperation in Europe, the North Atlantic Cooperation Council, and the Council of Europe—will include the former Soviet republics, it seems entirely unlikely that the EU will. Except for the Baltic states, these republics are even more distant from Western Europe, culturally and economically, than are the countries of Southeastern Europe. And Russia is just too big to swallow, even if it did not share the other disabilities.[70] Even within Western Europe, a few thoroughly Western countries, like Switzerland and Norway, may stay outside the EU as a result of inward-looking, anti-integrationist nationalism.

Whether or not a European defense community is fully developed, EU membership could be a way of associating a broader range of countries with the U.S. in NATO, via the eligibility of EU members for membership in the WEU. This may not matter a great deal in the case of some recent and prospective additions to the EU. However, such an effective if indirect association with NATO via the EU could cause concerns, in the case of the East European countries.

One should not exaggerate. The loudly negative Russian response to enlargement of NATO has been recounted in chapter 4, above. The Russians have not opposed enlargement of the EU as such and have been only mildly critical of the "associate partnership" status in WEU offered by the EU to countries—the East European and Baltic states—with which it has association agreements.[71] So some expansion of the EU seems possible without incurring Russian wrath and without causing security concerns for the moment, since the chances of Russian aggression—taking into account both capability and intentions—are currently small.[72]

The Clinton administration finessed the NATO enlargement issue in 1993–1994 by refusing early membership in NATO to all—but stating that it was a long-term possibility for any democratic state in Europe and offering, in the meantime, the Partnership for Peace.[73] An ongoing polemic on the subject developed and continues.[74]

Without going deeply into the substance at this point, I would suggest, first, that the stability the East Europeans of the Visegrad group (the group that is most desirous of admission to NATO) is more likely to be provided by the economic and political benefits of EU membership than by anything NATO can offer. Second, the risk involved in a back door security guarantee by virtue of their EU membership is small and would become significant only if Russia became actively aggressive toward them—at which point we might in any event want to consider their applications for NATO membership. It is true that there should be consultation between NATO and the EU regarding their respective enlargements. The December 1994 NATO Summit said: "The enlargement of NATO will complement the enlargement of the European Union, a parallel process which also, for its part, contributes significantly to extending security and stability to the new democracies in the East."[75] For the moment, that consultation might take the form of encouragement to the EU to move rapidly on enlargement to the Visegrad states.

A Bridge Too Far?

The process that led up to the Maastricht Treaty provisions on foreign and security policy has run into many obstacles. This is reflected by popular attitudes in Europe. According to a March 1993 poll, while a large majority of Europeans felt NATO should be reorganized to give the EC countries more influence, they had serious worries about security in the next few years, and mixed views about European defense cooperation.[76]

It has become evident that although the Maastricht Treaty was approved with little difficulty by nine of the twelve member-states, the treaty's political chapters went both too far and not far enough— too far for what was practical in terms of defense at this stage of the European Union's development without resolving fundamental differences between the approaches of the member-states. Agreement was reached by masking these differences. Britain and France, while differing constantly about what sort of line to take on European defense, were agreed in demanding intergovernmental, rather than supranational, control of foreign and security policy. Germany's stress on a more integrated European Union did not really win the day.[77]

And the reception of the treaty was cold, and deservedly so, because of the completely undemocratic way in which it was developed, the technocratic detail of the document itself, and the failure of governments to educate their citizenry, even after the fact, about what had been agreed to. The EC's handling of the treaty differed little from how it had usually operated, but clearly, in this case, the stakes were higher. The result, as one experienced EC-watcher says, was that the "democratic deficit finally reached out of the various national political swamps to catch the Brussels mechanism firmly by the ankle. The fun that ministers, national civil servants, and Eurocrats were having free of the democratic restraints that inhibited them at home finally came to an end."[78]

Europe may have entered a new sclerotic period. One EC Commission official said early in 1993 that it's "common for people to say the Community advances in good times and falls back in bad, but no one's too sure when the sky is going to clear this time." Delors himself told the European Parliament that "the very idea of a united Europe is in peril."[79] (By 1995, however, two European insiders detected a "shift toward optimism and self-confidence.")[80]

But a more measured view is that a lesson has been learned. The overreaching toward a common defense has been replaced by a more practical approach. Time may give the European Union the opportunity both to develop a closer consensus and the material wherewithal to be a political-strategic, as well as an economic, actor on the world scene. The intergovernmental conference of 1996 will be a good test of how well the EU is succeeding. Time—or the actions of others, including possibilities such as the further diminution of American interest and commitment in Europe—may demonstrate that while the pace and the methods were wrong in 1990–1992, the goal of a politically integrated Western Europe is not only desirable but necessary.

CONCLUSIONS

Let me try to distill some conclusions from this chapter:

—If the Cold War had not come to an end—with the quenching of the threat from the East leading almost inevitably to both a reassessment of Europe's need for American protection and a reduction in America's military presence in Europe—the movement toward political and security union in Western Europe might have continued to be very slow and would probably have continued to follow, not accompany, new steps to economic integration.

—The end of the Cold War accelerated the process, but this speed-up does not mean that political union, including the development of a common defense, will be consummated at any early date. (Even moderate progress will have to await the results of the intergovernmental conference of 1996.) The more likely and more definite movement toward monetary union will add another functional basis for political union. But there are also countervailing forces.

—The least of these is the historically neutral position of some Western European countries. The end of the Cold War has measurably reduced the force of neutralism. Incorporation of East Central European countries poses much greater problems.

—The prospective incorporation of additional European countries into the European Union will put a burden on the EU's institutions. It will be difficult enough to manage the economic life of a community of twenty-plus instead of fifteen countries; getting twenty-odd to agree to subject their security to a common policy will be even more difficult.

—But even the fifteen would find this difficult. A litmus test of readiness to abandon national decision-making in security matters may lie in the nuclear area. Despite forthcoming murmurs, France's willingness to abandon nuclear singularity is open to doubt, and there is no indication of a greater willingness on the part of Great Britain.

—Nevertheless, there are strong pressures, particularly from within the political elites of the Continental core countries of the European Union, to move in the direction of defense integration. They feel not just that a common defense is a natural aspect of political union but that a common defense will contribute to political union.

—Shaky though this prospect seems to be, it is, from an American point of view, preferable to the only likely alternative: a renationalization of European defense. And since, for many years to come, Europe is unlikely to be able to produce a self-sufficient collective defense of its own, this trend will give the United States a role to play in defense cooperation during that period. The form could remain: the NATO treaty may continue to serve. But the substance would change to a real division of labor, with the United States providing the specialized technical, air, and naval capabilities Europe will still lack, and with Europe shouldering the main burden of providing land forces.

CHAPTER 8

U.S. INTERESTS

There is a striking continuity in the definition of U.S. interests over the last forty-five years—at least, if one excludes the extremes in American foreign policy thinking. From George Kennan in 1947–1948 to the "finite containers" of the present,[1] the principal aims of American strategy have been seen as preventing an attack on the continental United States and, connected thereto, preventing any one power from achieving hegemony in the key areas of the Eurasian land mass. Knowledgeable and realistic politicians have held similar views.[2]

Key areas were and are defined as those countries (or possibly close coalitions of countries) having a major industrial-military capability. Kennan thought of five such—the United States, the U.K., the countries of the Rhine valley (France and Germany and their hinterlands), Russia, and Japan.[3] Today we might be tempted to substitute Western Europe or the European Union for the two centers of strength Kennan identified in the western half of Europe, but to keep the number the same by adding China to the list. We might also add one: the crucial importance of oil to the economies of the United States and those major countries that have been allied to us, along with our collective dependence on imports for that oil, makes the Persian Gulf a special area of interest.[4]

While few would question the importance of keeping Eurasia from falling under one dominant power, which would leave the United States both isolated and overmatched in the world,[5] plenty of room remains for argument as to how such a fate is to be avoided. In March 1992 a paper prepared within the Department of Defense was leaked to the *New York Times*. It proposed that the United States act to prevent the development of truly competitive great powers in Eurasia by preempting Germany and

Japan from acquiring the nuclear capability that would give them that status.[6] The Pentagon paper can be dismissed as essentially a rationale for maintaining a large military establishment: to be able to play the role of the world's policeman. Yet while it advocated an extreme position,[7] the paper did represent one way of solving the conundrum of how the United States can avoid an unfavorable balance of power deriving from the acquisition of dominance by one Eurasian power or a group thereof.

For fifty years the United States has acted like a European power. This represents a reversal of the traditional foreign policy of the United States, which was to avoid foreign alliances and entanglements, especially in Europe. The end of the Cold War gives us the opportunity—in fact, the need—to examine whether such involvement in Europe continues to be either necessary or desirable.

The peculiar form our involvement in Europe took was not foreseen, even in the years when American forces were fighting in Europe. The grand scheme that animated U.S. foreign policy was, in the early 1940s, a universalist one, aiming at a world order within which there would be peace, free trade, and the other usual goals of liberal thinking.

Only the perception of a challenge from the Soviet Union, followed by the division of Europe, led to a new emphasis, not on the world as a whole but on the world as divided. In this divided world, Western Europe, though at the moment in economic crisis, would, because of its potential economic and technical power, play a key role as ally to the "leader of the West."

Even with this change of policy direction, U.S. involvement in Western Europe did not instantly take the shape that is now so familiar to us. We started out in a more traditional alliance mode—and the mode of an alliance that would be other than permanent. Few in the late 1940s would have conceived of American troops remaining in Europe in the last decade of the century. And when the Marshall Plan was proposed, the offer of aid was tied to intra-European cooperation. We wanted a stronger Europe as an ally—but at that point we still were thinking of Europe as a partner rather than as something we were part of.

One cannot date the shift even from the North Atlantic treaty of April 1949. Rather, it came with the fears aroused by the Korean

War regarding the sufficiency of the West's defenses in Europe. The Council of the North Atlantic Treaty Organization (NAC), in a communiqué issued 27 September, 1950, stated its agreement to "the establishment at the earliest possible date of an integrated force under centralized command . . . to deter aggression and to ensure the defense of Western Europe."[8] On 19 December 1950, the NAC announced the naming of an American, General Dwight D. Eisenhower, as supreme commander of NATO.[9]

The form of our involvement in Europe could be changed by a sort of fast rewind to the status quo prior to the creation of an integrated force in 1950. But, for the moment, the question is what our interests are; form can come later.

The reason our involvement in Europe initially took the form it did was fear of the Soviet Union and doubt that Western Europe—even a Western Europe on the road to economic recovery—could or would stand up to the Soviets without American involvement and leadership. As matters now stand, this reasoning is no longer valid.

The Soviet Union has come apart, and even though Russia continues to possess a world-class nuclear armory, it seems to have neither the intention nor, perhaps, the capability to threaten the rest of Europe. One can imagine a chain of developments that would re-create the Russian threat, and actions which could prevent this certainly should be considered and, if possible, undertaken. But neither the presence of U.S. troops in Europe nor the extension of our nuclear deterrent to Europe is crucial to determining the future of Russia, and neither is needed at the moment unless we view them as being justified by factors other than the Russian threat.[10]

A second argument is that the U.S. has an interest in the preservation of peace and stability within Europe. As this argument is usually put, we do not want to repeat the history of the first half of the twentieth century, when Europe twice tore itself apart and the United States was twice compelled to intervene to restore order.

There is an American interest in European stability, which starts but does not end with the security and profitability of our economic interests in Europe. That stability could be disturbed in a number of ways, of which the following seem possible, though not equally likely:

1. The former Soviet Union could fall into greater turmoil—not just the economic turmoil of today, not just the wars within

the successor republics, but war between the republics.

2. Similarly—but with a different scale and effect—turmoil, ethnic or otherwise, could develop in Central and Eastern Europe: Yugoslavia writ large.

3. Western Europe, in which a sense of community has grown over the last forty years, could experience a reversal, possibly due to the resentment and resistance of others to German efforts to exercise dominance.

U.S. INTERESTS IN THE FORMER SOVIET UNION

There is little by way of positive U.S. interest in the countries of the former Soviet Union.[11] Ironically, unless and until they are fully integrated into the capitalist world economy, their economic disaster is of little economic or direct political moment to the United States. (This is not to deny the attraction of certain potentials within the ex-USSR: a highly productive oil industry would not only be of interest to Western investors but also would diversify the sources of a strategic import.)

While countries to the west of these states may well fear a migratory horde propelled by chaos and starvation in the East, such an invasion is not a threat to the United States. Should this kind of migration become a destabilizing force in Central and Western Europe, it might marginally impinge on our interests in these areas and should be judged in that light.

A widely read article held, in mid-1991, that the "violent disintegration of the Soviet Union would pose first-order threats to vital American interests. The U.S. stake in the Soviet Union's future merits a strategy of engagement as robust and refined as America's Cold War strategy."[12] Shortly thereafter, the USSR disintegrated. While it is true that Russia, by itself, has formidable nuclear warfare capacity,[13] the prospect for its being a direct military threat to the United States is small. Russia's nuclear war capacity is a good argument for our seeking further nuclear weapons reductions and for an American contribution to the cost of dismantling the weapons Russia has already agreed to eliminate. Technical and educational assistance to Russia surely is also desirable. But Russia's military strength, such as it is, is not a good basis for massive economic assistance. Such an effort would in any case have an improbable objective—to rescue Russia from its troubles. Russia can and must rescue itself.[14]

What if the turmoil in the ex-Soviet lands led to war between the successor republics—more seriously, what if Russia sought by military force to reestablish dominion over some of its formerly subordinate republics?

A more assertive Russia has emerged from two traumatic developments of late 1993. In October of that year, Yeltsin was forced to seek the help of the military to shore up his authority and put down the revolt of the parliamentary leadership. Then, in December, nationalists and communists won nearly half the seats in the newly elected parliament. Perhaps because of his debt to the army—more certainly, out of a desire to stem the flow of support to the more authoritarian wings of Russian politics—Yeltsin has become more forceful in international politics, and particularly with regard to the "near abroad," the other republics of the former Soviet Union.

Some, notably Zbigniew Brzezinski, and with particular reference to the largest of these republics, Ukraine, have argued that the United States should abandon its allegedly pro-Russian policy and work to avoid the re-creation of a Russian empire.[15] There may, arguably, be good reasons to prefer the division of the former Soviet Union. But an effort to reestablish Russian dominance within that territory would be neither a clear threat, in and of itself, to the United States—which, after all, tolerated well the existence of the old Soviet Union—nor a justification for prior commitments or after-the-fact response.[16]

Calculations of interest frequently clash with moral and political sentiment. Russia's clumsy, indeed brutal, attempt beginning in December 1994 to suppress the movement for independence in Chechnya enraged many Americans. It is well to remember the principle stated by John Quincy Adams, and recommended by George Kennan: "America goes not abroad in search of monsters to destroy. She is the well-wisher to the freedom and independence of all. She is the champion and vindicator only of her own."[17] We can, directly and through institutions like the Organization for Security and Cooperation in Europe (OSCE), encourage better Russian behavior in Chechnya, but what Russia does there does not threaten our national interests.[18]

In April 1995 Russian Foreign Minister Andrei Kozyrev said Russia was prepared to use "direct military force" to protect the interests of the twenty-five million ethnic Russians who live in other parts of the ex-Soviet Union.[19] Russian military action against an independent formerly Soviet republic would surely be cause for sharper international criticism than in the case of Chechnya, which is legally part of Russia.

Yet can or should our reaction take a military form? Even in the case of the Ukraine, clearly the most important of the non-Russian ex-Soviet republics, it is hard to perceive either a direct American interest strong enough to warrant taking the risk of a nuclear war with the Soviet Union, or American popular support for military intervention.[20] Russia probably does not desire to reincorporate most of the other ex-Soviet republics. It would be satisfied by their treating their Russian minorities well and giving Russia due deference as dominant state in the Commonwealth of Independent States. (Of the two cases where this may not be true, Ukraine and Belarus, Belarus seems more eager to return to Moscow's fold than Moscow is to receive it.)[21] In these circumstances our role should be to encourage peaceful coexistence between Russia and the other republics, rather than to create false, and potentially dangerous, expectations about American intervention.[22]

Some of the bellicosity in Russian rhetoric in the period after the autumn of 1993 has no doubt been pitched to a domestic audience. However, the touchiness within Russia about its decline from greatness is so widespread that the U.S. might do well to make gestures toward enhancing Russian self-esteem, where these gestures are reasonable in and of themselves. We should emulate the Congress of Vienna, where France was welcomed back into the club of great powers.[23]

The western powers have taken some steps in this direction, such as inviting Russia to take part in the political portions of the annual G-7 summits.[24] More such efforts, obviously, are needed, but not gestures like the letter reportedly sent to Yeltsin by Clinton early in May 1995 stating that the U.S. has no objection in principle to the "new Russia" becoming a member of NATO.[25] The offer was both unwise and unnecessary—unwise because to admit Russia to NATO would be to rob it of its nature as a mutual defense alliance,[26] and unnecessary because there was no indication that Russia wants to be part of NATO. In an interview a few days after Clinton's proposal, Secretary of Defense William Perry stated that he could not foresee Russian membership in NATO. A "new Russia," said Perry—attributing the term to Secretary of State Warren Christopher—might want to join NATO, but the *current* (my emphasis) Russian government wanted a security relationship with NATO.[27]

These steps, among others, might contribute to a stable security relationship with Russia:

1. NATO could enter into a treaty of global security cooperation with Russia.[28] This treaty—while proposed by Brzezinski in the context of NATO's admission of the Czech Republic, Hungary, Poland, and Slovakia to membership by the end of the 1990s—makes sense in and of itself. It received a degree of endorsement by Assistant Secretary of State Richard Holbrooke, who noted that it responded to proposals made by Yeltsin in 1993 and that there had already been preliminary discussion of the possibility between Christopher and Kozyrev.[29]

2. We could accept another of Brzezinski's suggestions and upgrade the OSCE as a venue for security consultations.[30] In chapter 5, above, I suggest a steering committee of larger countries, on the pattern of the Bosnia Contact Group, as one way to do so.

3. We could follow up on Clinton's May 1995 statement to Yeltsin that the Conventional Forces in Europe (CFE) treaty should be modified. Russia has a case for pressing for this; the treaty was concluded with the defunct Soviet Union and applied to a very different security situation to the south of Russia.[31]

4. We could, finally, gradually "legitimize" the Commonwealth of Independent States (CIS), which the Russians clearly want. One suggestion is to begin this process by discussion of CIS peacekeeping in the North Atlantic Cooperation Council (NACC). Such discussion could be a way of acknowledging the CIS as a valid security instrument, while at the same time exposing it to scrutiny and the influence of outsiders.[32] Conceivably, though with less ability to control the process, we could do the same through the OSCE.

This is, I think, a fair reading of what our national interests dictate with regard to the countries that formerly composed the Soviet Union. It does not assume that Russia is just another normal democratic country that can be fitted into the existing transatlantic and Western European institutions. It does recognize that Russia—

not the Ukraine or any other of the ex-Soviet republics—is the key to European security.[33]

Trouble in Central and Eastern Europe

The United States has had opportunities in Central and Eastern Europe to exert influence and acquire allies which it has not fully exploited. This failure, however, is probably not of enormous significance so long as the result is not to unbalance Europe as a whole—e.g., by creating a void in which German power grows so much as to lead either to German aggressiveness or to a defensive reaction to the growth of German power by other countries. In fact, over-involvement by the U.S. would pose comparable dangers, because the U.S. interest in these countries, while real, is limited. That interest also is uneven, depending on historical, cultural, and ethnic links, and on the degree to which the countries make themselves attractive and important by democratizing and becoming significant producers and consumers. Poland, Hungary, and the Czech Republic—and after them, Slovakia and the western republics of the former Yugoslavia, Slovenia, and Croatia—are likely, on these grounds, to have first claim to our attention.

That the Central and Eastern European nations feel a void in terms of security relationships and have turned to the United States, through NATO, to fill that void is understandable from their point of view. But it does not by itself mean that the United States has sufficient interest in these nations to commit itself to their defense— even if it may want to give them encouragement and other forms of assistance. Two types of danger to the Central and Eastern European states are posed by the security void in which they now exist. The first is that their newly acquired independence might be threatened by a resurgent, and aggressive, Russia. The second is that their stability might be disturbed by problems from within their own countries or between the countries of Central and Eastern Europe.

It is useful for my argument to start with a discussion of the second possibility—which is somewhat more probable than the first. If instability within or between countries of Central and Eastern Europe seemed likely to destabilize Western Europe, or some part thereof, the situation would have to be taken seriously. The threats posed by such instability seem to fall in two areas: economic losses and migration.

If there is a strong growth in Central and Eastern Europe's production and trade, it is likely that the countries of Western Europe, their natural trading partners, will develop strong economic interests in their eastern neighbors, with possible spillover into other relationships with them, such as to render developments in Eastern Europe of moment to them. Even before a strong recovery in Eastern Europe has taken place, Germany has already developed such an interest. On the other hand, development of Eastern European economies and of their links with the West would almost certainly make serious instability less likely. As matters now stand—with a gap in Central and Eastern Europe between economic aspirations and expectations on the one hand and realities and foreseeable prospects on the other—instability with at least one root in economic discontent seems quite plausible, but of little direct economic consequence to the countries of Western Europe. Eastern Europe as yet has but marginal significance for their economies.

Migration is perhaps a clearer present threat to Western Europe; there have been enough prodromal trickles and flows to demonstrate this. Three things have to be said, however. The first is that the Western European states have the capacity—if they have the will—to wall themselves off from these flows. Italy's surprisingly ruthless treatment of Albanian boat people in the summer of 1991 showed that even one of the weakest and most humanitarian governments in Western Europe was capable of forestalling mass immigration. The second is that immigration from Eastern Europe clearly ranks second to the flows from the southern rim of the Mediterranean as a Western European bugaboo; Western Europeans find the Easterners much less threatening, for reasons of color and culture. Up to a point, migratory flows from Eastern Europe may, despite the problems they cause, be tolerated in the West. Third, even if Eastern European migration should be a major problem, it is almost impossible to conceive of its threatening the stability of Western Europe.

The U.S. could help avert the problems Western Europe, and its interests in Western Europe, might face from these two sources, mainly by contributing to the economic reconstruction of Central and Eastern Europe. Western Europe's military security is most unlikely to be threatened by instability in Eastern Europe, and therefore—aside from the question of direct U.S. interest—there is no role in this regard for U.S. military deterrence or defense. The answers to the area's problems, and to the problems the area can pose for its neighbors (and the United States) are, in the short term, an open European Union market for their exports, and assistance and guidance; in the medium term, admitting at least the more advanced countries of Central and Eastern Europe to the EU. NATO is not the answer, either for these countries' economic problems or for fostering political stability; and to suggest that it was the answer forty years ago in Western Europe is to forget the importance of the Marshall Plan, and also the differences between the two situations.[34]

What if Russia were to try to reestablish hegemony in its formerly vassal states in Eastern Europe? Such an attempt seems highly unlikely in any foreseeable future. If it were to be made, however, it would pose a dilemma for the United States. These states do not and will not add much to the economic, technological, and military strength of the Atlantic countries. Committing ourselves to their defense would seem to be an unnecessary risk incommensurate with our interests and without compensating benefits.[35]

Yugoslavia has been a test case. It could, regrettably, set the pattern for some other countries in Central and Eastern Europe, but this is far from certain: Yugoslavia's process of disintegration predated the end of the Cold War and is the product of historic conflicts within an artificial multinational state; unhappy though some of the other states of the area may be, none of them is as predictably explosive as Yugoslavia.[36] Most significantly, after the peaceful division of the old Czechoslovakia into the Czech Republic and Slovakia at the beginning of 1993, the other Central and Eastern European countries do not suffer from the same ethnic turmoil and strife as the former Yugoslavia. While, as Jacques Delors said, after several years' bitter experience, Yugoslavia's problems were beyond the reach of the EU's essentially economic power,[37] those of most of the other Central and Eastern European countries are not.

Yugoslavia's neighbors and near-neighbors in Western Europe have, while expressing great concern about the situation, evidently not found it a clear enough threat to their collective interests to intervene with military force.[38] If this is the response to Yugoslavia—with which the West and particularly the countries of the European Community have had rather close ties for a number of years—one can imagine the response to similar developments elsewhere in the Balkans.[39] The attitude is reminiscent of Disraeli's: he hoped that the Balkan troubles would "burn themselves out beyond the pale of civilization."[40] There might of course be more Western European concern and possibly more EU response to gross instability in Poland, Hungary, and the former Czechoslovakia, but such instability seems less likely there.

If Western Europe, rationally assessing its interests, does not find instability in Central and Eastern Europe a threat to its own stability, there seems little ground for the United States—whose interest is largely a secondary one based on its interest in Western Europe—to take it as a threat.

This judgment, realistic in terms of international politics, may underestimate the force of idealism or moralism in American domestic politics. American reactions to the Yugoslav tragedy demonstrate there is a sense that Eastern Europe belongs to our moral community in a way that many other parts of the world do not. Even if the United States manages to resist armed involvement in Yugoslavia, this reaction is a warning sign.[41] The United States might have to take more to heart a repetition of this tragedy in other Eastern European countries with a still greater hold on American sentiments—such as Poland, Hungary, the Czech Republic, and Slovakia.[42]

It is that feeling for these four countries that led Congress, even before the 1994 elections, to require favorable treatment for them in logistics and weapons acquisition, and for the Senate to favor their inclusion in NATO. One of the bills included in the Contract for America package pushed by House Republicans in 1995 contained a requirement that the same four countries be invited to join NATO by January 1999. However, before the bill went to the House floor, it was amended simply to single out these countries as deserving early consideration for NATO membership, provided they met political, military, and economic criteria.[43]

Acting on these sentiments is something that should be given very careful consideration, and not just out of a desire to placate Russia, whose opposition to NATO enlargement has become very clear since 1993.[44] The core of NATO, and of the desire of many Central and Eastern European countries to join NATO, is the commitment in ARTICLE 5 of the North Atlantic Treaty: that members will consider an attack on one or more of them an attack against all, and that they will assist the party or parties so attacked. Does the sum of American national interests and sentiment equal a willingness to commit ourselves to the defense even of the four Visegrad states?[45] To put the issue most sharply, would we risk a nuclear war in their defense? ARTICLE 5 leaves to the member-states the decision as to how to respond. Even short of that hard question of risking nuclear war, a failure to respond to a lesser conflict in a part of Central and Eastern Europe that was within NATO's accepted security zone would extinguish the credibility of NATO.[46]

Just as incorporation of these states into the EU is the best solution for their problems of stability, so may it be a way out of this problem. If the European Union decides to extend its boundaries to include these states, they would form part of the "Europe" to which we have committed ourselves. It would then be easier for us (and incidentally for Russia) to accept them into NATO membership. This would be all the more true if NATO were to evolve into a U.S.-EU pact.

WESTERN EUROPE: INTERESTS AT RISK?

Western Europe is not perceived as our great economic rival; Japan is, though its economy is considerably smaller than that of Western Europe.[47] Nor is it a military threat to us in the way Russia, potentially, is: it does not have an equivalent capability; and, while we may not have achieved "community" with Western Europe in the broad sense, Western Europe and the U.S. constitute a security community in the sense that war between us is virtually inconceivable.

We have two strong, positive interests in Western Europe. The combination of transatlantic trade and the two-way exchange of investment with Western Europe is unmatched in relations with other regions of the world. These are the outward and visible signs of the interpenetration of the two economies which has created extremely strong links between the private business sectors in Western Europe and the United States.

While the conflict with the Soviet Union is over—the USSR no longer exists—the world has not been returned to an Edenic state. Beneath the ashes left by the Second World War, George Marshall and George Kennan —and the other architects of our postwar foreign policy—saw an economic strength in Western Europe which would, if coupled with that of the United States, permit us to balance and contain the Soviet Union and its satellites. Some might say that having Western Europe as an ally permitted us to dominate the non-Communist part of the world. The world has changed, but Western Europe is still one of the other great power centers. We certainly would not want it aligned against us; and inchoate though the threats of the post-Soviet world may be, to have Western Europe on our side would be comforting, at least—and possibly vital.

These interests could be jeopardized in three ways. If the United States were to adopt a harshly protectionist and otherwise narrowly nationalist posture, the relationship we have built up with Western Europe would, at the least, become less fruitful and reliable, and could potentially come to an end. This would be a political and economic calamity. For in a postmodern, advanced technology world, it is difficult to imagine even the United States prospering through autarky; and the available substitutes for Western Europe as partners either are insufficient in economic size and political power (e.g., Latin America) or are unlikely to be equally compatible allies (e.g., Japan and East Asia). The costs of such a course seem clearly so high, however, that its choice seems unlikely.

There is also a mirror-image possibility: that Western Europe finds us dispensable. Americans have fantasized over such a possibility for years: the depiction of the EC-1992 process as the creation of Fortress Europe was a case in point. There are two developments that lend a bit of plausibility to this scenario. The ending of the Soviet threat means that Western Europe needs our protection less than it once did. The processes of economic and then political integration within Western Europe have reduced the relative importance of linkages with the rest of the world—even the most important part of the rest of the world, the United States.

While Western Europe may need us less than before, it finds value in a reasonably close relationship with us. Since 1989 there have not been stentorian calls for "Americans out"; rather, there have been repeated statements of an interest in preserving the American military commitment to Europe. Economically, the relationship, if dwindling relative to intra-European economic activity, is still valued and profitable. Western Europe still finds us somewhat useful as insurance against the uncharted perils of the political future and clearly valuable as a market, source of technology and goods—and a co-victim, in the eyes of some, of Japanese economic aggression.

The third threat to American interests in Europe is the least likely to develop but the one that could have the worst consequences— i.e., repercussions beyond the economic realm which would perhaps include costly warfare. It is the threat of serious instability within Western Europe. Such instability could have external or internal sources. I have already discussed the potential for invasion from the east (Russia is the only potential aggressor) and of disturbances spilling over from Central and Eastern Europe—though this latter is an unlikely source of grave Western European instability. Russian aggression seems quite unlikely too, but Russia's military potential is great enough to make the risk one that has to be taken seriously. Western Europe should be capable by itself of deterring or, if necessary, defending against such an attack—but, after all, it should have had such a capability during the many years in which it remained highly dependent upon the United States for its protection against the Soviet Union.

Since the early 1960s the United States has been trying to strike a new balance between its interests in Europe and the potential costs of defending those interests by extended deterrence. Europeans worried whether it was really credible that the United States would sacrifice itself for the sake of Europe. The risk of America's being "called" is now smaller—it probably never was very great. But at the same time, with the reductions in the Russian nuclear and conventional armory—both those that were planned and those that occurred through disorganization—it is more than ever arguable whether Europe should need American help to deter potential aggression from the east.

The United States may wish to provide help for a quite different reason, as dues for continued membership in at least the outer circle of the European club—or, to put it another way, to create a sense of obligation on the part of the Europeans that will diminish whatever tendency they have toward an economically and politically introverted regionalism. For the moment, Europeans are inviting us to continue our military involvement on their continent. But we should judge whether the military costs and risks are commensurate with the benefits we derive in other spheres. And if we are at some point invited out, we shall indeed have to find ways to preserve our European interests without the payment of military tribute.

There is another external threat to Europe's well-being and, perhaps, its stability: its dependence on oil from the Middle East makes it vulnerable to developments in that area. With the end of the Cold War, and therefore the end of the inhibition on use of force by the West in the Middle East, Western Europe should in principle be able to protect its own interests in the Gulf. The recent action against Iraq showed, on the other hand, how incapable Europe is at the moment of independent action on the requisite scale. Europe may have a need for U.S. help in this regard; the U.S. shares an interest in Gulf oil, and has a quite different but intertwined interest in Israeli security. These interests lead the U.S. to adopt an active role in the area in any event.

The U.S. interests are in fact so strong, and the lack of substitute or surrogate defenders of these interests so evident, that it is easier to construct a rationale for continued presence of the Sixth Fleet in the Mediterranean than it is for maintaining American land forces in the middle of Europe. The same need to protect a corridor to the Middle East-Gulf area creates a special interest in good relations with the Mediterranean nations of Southern Europe, especially those which provide (but could deny) base rights and overflight permission.

U.S.-European cooperation in the Middle East was difficult from the 1950s through the 1980s. More recently—and particularly beginning with the action against Iraq—U.S. and European policies and decisions have seemed more harmonious. In this new context, U.S. action to preserve its own Middle East interests may be valuable in terms of U.S.-Western European relations by creating a sense of community or even obligation on the part of Europe.

The other threat from the south perceived by Europeans, from the countries of North Africa, is hardly a conventional security threat; it is the threat of continued migration at a rate which Western European cultures cannot accommodate. The United States, whose interests in the area are much smaller, and which is physically distant from the problem, cannot do a great deal directly to help. However, the example of America's more effective response to its comparable problem of actual and potential immigration from its immediate southern neighbors, especially Mexico, may be instructive. Finally, the insecurity felt by the countries of Southern Europe increases the value they find in alliance with the United States, even if the Sixth Fleet is not the policy tool most adapted to this problem.[48]

A discussion of U.S. interests is abstract and not very useful unless it attaches some sort of price or cost to them. The interest in avoiding an attack on the United States is obviously of so primal a nature that multiple zeros can be attached to any assessment of its value. However, at the moment, plausible attacks on the United States are hard to identify. Russia is capable of one but is almost as unlikely, at the moment, to do so, as are Britain and France (which also have this capability).

Isolation of the United States by a coalition of Eurasian powers is also so significant in terms of the potential which such a coalition would have, even short of war, for depriving the United States of well-being, that there is a prima facie case for doing a good deal to avoid it. Yet even in this instance, there is reason to examine how best to achieve the objective of avoiding isolation. It is not transparently clear that an emphasis on Western Europe that entails large military expenditure is the most profitable one.

Where there is a hard choice is between Western Europe and Japan (and Japan's economic satellites sprinkled down the eastern shores of Asia). Here, ironically, the prospective stability and friendliness of Western Europe is an argument against maintaining the Atlantic connection in ways that are costly. Western Europe will probably remain stable, without outside help, and is also likely to remain friendly to the United States. This is less true of East Asia. Left to its own devices, that area could turn sour, could become hostile, could be the zone for renewed Japanese imperialism, or, more likely, nuclear muscle-flexing by China. No natural, mutually satisfactory order seems as likely to follow an American military withdrawal as is the case in Western Europe. The right, if demanding, prescription seems to be for the United States to attempt to play a balancing role in East Asia akin to the one played by Great Britain in Europe during the nineteenth century.[49]

On the other hand, there is in East Asia a dependence on the United States, at least as a market, that is greater than the European dependence on the United States after the evaporation of the Soviet Union. This means that the United States is likely to be able to exact a higher price, however measured, for a presence in East Asia than for one in Europe. In terms of cost and benefit, therefore, it would seem desirable to expend costly U.S. military resources in East Asia in preference to Europe. But this is a very provisional judgment, one contingent especially on the belief that American interests in Europe, which are greater than our interests in East Asia, can be preserved with policies involving relatively low costs.

CHAPTER 9

WHAT ARE OUR OPTIONS?

It is not true that the United States has permanent interests. While ensuring national survival is a constant, our interests, considered at a more detailed level, change with external circumstances and with developments within our country. The factors shaping our national interests have changed substantially from those of the period immediately after World War II when our national policies largely took form.

Significant changes from the initial matrix emerged as long ago as the second half of the 1960s—especially in the economic sphere, where the recovery and vitality of Europe and Japan began to deprive us of the economic dominance we had acquired largely by the destruction of these areas in World War II. It is arguable, in fact, that our relative economic standing is not much different now from what it was twenty years ago. In the less favorable economic period that was ushered in by the oil crisis of 1973, U.S. performance, while not scintillating, has more or less matched that of the rest of the world.

But the loss of dominance has now become more important. With the changes in the politics of the world, with the collapse of the Soviet Union and the end of the threat to which only we had the answer, we can no longer readily borrow influence from the political-security side of the ledger to compensate for lost economic dominance. That is the major change in the equation, producing a major, and negative, change in U.S. power.

It is common to talk of France's failed bet on gaining power through nuclear capability. In post-Cold War Europe, France's economic weakness relative to Germany counts for a great deal more than the *force de frappe*; in fact, the *force de frappe* may not count for very much at all. While America's scale and circumstances are different, our situation has a certain resemblance to that of France.

There are, furthermore, prospective developments that are largely independent of the end of the Cold War and that may add to the strains on our existing foreign policies. Chief among these, at least for the purposes of this book, is the growing integration of Western Europe, which may, during the remainder of this decade, develop into the integration of a broader area including Central Europe. It may also, in the same time frame, go far beyond the traditional European Union agenda of trade, to monetary integration, and perhaps a significant degree of political integration.

A second such development is the increased strain evident in the international economic system which developed after the Second World War. This system has already gone through several transformations and is, in fact, functioning quite well. But there is a generalized sense that it is increasingly inconsistent with the radically transformed basic political-economic structure of the world because it does not properly reflect changes such as the decline of American economic dominance and the supposed growth of regionalism.

Third, the prestige of the United States, and more particularly of its political leadership, has declined in Europe over the last generation. Certain presidents were viewed particularly negatively. Jimmy Carter was disliked and distrusted. He did not seem to fit the role. He made U-turns on policy, both macro (regarding the Soviet Union) and micro (the neutron bomb), and his personal relationships with European leaders, especially Helmut Schmidt, were poor. The fear with which some Europeans greeted Ronald Reagan, and the irritation, or worse reactions, caused by some of his early actions and statements, later abated. Yet Reagan's dealings with the Soviets, especially when at Reykjavik he was ready to plump for the zero option on nuclear weapons, confirmed his unreliability in the eyes of some Europeans.[1]

While George Bush enjoyed a good deal of respect, Bill Clinton created puzzlement and displeasure by his combination of expansive humanitarian rhetoric with behavior that was vacillating, frequently indecisive, and on most issues determined in fact by a narrow view of U.S. interests. The impression he gave initially of an indifferent if not slightly hostile attitude toward Western Europe (later modified) did not help his standing there.

The point of view I've just expressed may seem surprising. It conflicts with the image of America as the only superpower and the rest of the world as disoriented and meandering. Events have, over the last half-decade, made the United States seem more dominant than ever—or at least as having the opportunity to be more dominant.

But the political climate in the United States and the attitude toward the United States in sophisticated foreign circles are evidence for my view: the election campaign of 1992 (as well as an enormous and growing literature) emphasized the need for the United States to focus on salvaging its domestic economy before decline goes too far. While the remedies proposed by the Republicans who won the congressional elections of 1994 were different from those Clinton had advocated in 1992, their concentration on domestic problems was equal to his. And friendly foreigners tend to agree that America's first priority should be to tend to its own affairs. Even those, perhaps particularly those, who want the U.S. to continue to exercise leadership in the long term think that in the short term it must strengthen the economic foundations of leadership.[2]

Finally, the concern both of the American public and political leadership for the world in general, and Europe in particular, has declined relative to what may have been an exceptional period of outward-looking, Eurocentric attitudes in the half-century beginning around 1940.

This psychological and intellectual change should not be overstated. While there is no doubt that domestic concerns have come to dominate the attention of Americans, they continue to think the U.S. should play an active role in the world. Europe continues to be regarded as more important to the United States than Asia. After a dramatic decline in the latter 1980s, leadership support for maintaining the current level of U.S. commitment to NATO snapped back in the first half of the 1990s. As of 1995, public support for NATO remains unchanged, and is solidly positive. Western Europe is one of the few areas of the world to whose defense a majority of Americans would be willing to see U.S. troops committed.[3]

These attitudes are reflected by politicians. The Republicans who came to power in Congress in the November 1994 elections were divided between those who wanted to spend more on defense and those who thought cutting the federal budget was a more vital concern. (House Speaker Newt Gingrich, in an effort to bridge the gap, described himself as a "cheap hawk.") They were uninterested in the less-developed world and eager to cut foreign aid; and they were hostile to a United Nations that could lure the United States into peacekeeping or peacemaking efforts in situations in which the U.S. has no stake. On the other hand, they seemed supportive of NATO and not negative about Western Europe.[4]

Still, a change in attitudes has to be taken into account, along with our material national interests, in formulating realistic policy options.[5] With that as a brief premise, what are the options for our relationship with Europe?[6]

A. Maintain — or Try to Maintain — the Status Quo ante 1989

This was, in fact, the policy that was pursued by the Bush administration. It was not pursued rigidly, but with verbal nuances and even some course adjustments. It was possibly conceived to be in the spirit of Lampedusa's *The Leopard*: in order for everything to remain the same, everything must change.

Some of the adjustments that were made were major—but not really voluntary. For a substantial period of time, our government seemed to be consumed by nostalgia for the old bipolar world. Yes, there had to be changes: the USSR of Gorbachev no longer fitted neatly into the role of adversary. Well, if not adversary, then partner. And for a substantial period of time, a considerable effort was made to turn the old enemy into a fellow traveler of the United States.

Some of this effort was required by the tactical situation inherited from the old order. The Soviet Union, with its permanent seat on the Security Council, could block U.S. actions there. This was an important fact of the game during the Iraq-Kuwait crisis of 1990–1991. The USSR still had some assets in the Middle East, which added to the need to get at least its passive support for U.S. initiatives.

But the U.S. effort to preserve a senior role for the USSR went far beyond this. We treated it as a major player in the Middle East by making it a co-host for the Middle East Peace Conference we organized. (The contrast is sharp between the role we accorded the USSR and the marginal one we gave to the European Community, which arguably had and certainly will have more interests and influence in the Middle East than the USSR did.) We were more careful not to challenge a continuing role for the USSR in Eastern Europe than the USSR was to maintain one. For as long as it was possible—and for a bit longer—we sought, insofar as we could, to tip the balance in favor of the preservation of the Soviet Union and against its disintegration.

Again, some of these positions are understandable, especially as expressions of healthy respect for a state still retaining enormous nuclear capability. But some seemed to proceed from a fear that removal of the Soviet Union from the world power equation would change the equation in ways which were unpredictable and potentially negative and from a false belief that as a way to avoid radical changes in the world, the Soviet Union could be preserved somewhat as it had been.

After a few years—during which the Soviet Union collapsed and Russia itself changed enormously but was far from establishing itself either as a truly great power or an eternal friend of the West—public judgments varied. But Russia and the Commonwealth of Independent States (CIS), which feebly took the place of the old Soviet Union, were no longer viewed in the same self-deluding way. For some, partnership now will have to follow, rather than precede, "integrative processes within Russia and the CIS." Another view is that the Bush and Clinton administrations' hopes for a "strategic partnership" with Russia are fading; it will be difficult enough, in the years to come, to preserve such understanding between Moscow and Washington as has been achieved. Finally, some argue for supporting other power centers within the former Soviet Union. Trying to make Russia into a partner is bad for it as well as for us, they contend.[7]

The adjustment in the U.S. stance with regard to the integration of Western Europe involved more than a touch-up job on previous positions but fell far short of a thoroughgoing revision of policy. President Bush and Secretary of State James Baker gave important speeches in which they revived an American policy of support for European integration that had not been voiced in such positive terms since the 1960s. In some cases, most notably with regard to aid to Eastern Europe and peacemaking in Yugoslavia, the U.S. yielded the lead to the European Community—explicitly, in the case of aid to Eastern Europe. In doing so, the U.S. recognized the limited nature both of its interests and capabilities.

On the other hand, where issues seemed more central to America's great power role in Europe and to its continued dominance of its alliance with the countries of Western Europe, U.S. behavior was different. When Washington caught wind of discussion about creating a European defense entity, it dispatched a monitory warning. Long after most European nations thought economic aid to the new Russia was in order, after ex-President Nixon weighed in to the same effect, the Bush administration belatedly decided something should be done. It then threw together a package of assistance. The haste with which this proposal was developed, coupled with its airy assumption that other countries would ante up the sums expected (most of this aid was to come from non-American sources), gave the proposal the appearance—rightly or wrongly—of a Potemkin village. But the most interesting and disturbing element was the clear expectation that when the United States spoke, others would act. (Only Germany—in recent years, frequently singled out for special attention by the United States—seems to have been fully consulted.)

This expectation lived on in a Washington that seemed little affected by the manifest changes both in relative U.S. power and in the need that Western Europe has for us. An excellent example of this failure to acknowledge new realities was the threat allegedly made by Vice President Dan Quayle at the Wehrkunde conference in Munich in early 1992: if the European Community were not more forthcoming in the Uruguay Round of trade negotiations, support for a continued U.S. military commitment to Europe would be rendered difficult.[8]

President Bush shortly thereafter denied that there was any such linkage. The fact is that the EC performance in the Uruguay Round *was* frustrating and potentially dangerous to the international trading system—and therefore, ironically, to the European Union, which is more dependent on foreign trade than the United States. The linkage was made, not so much by the Vice President as by other Americans, some of them in Congress. In doing so, they were repeating an argument which originally came from Congress in the form of a demand for burden sharing (the Mansfield Amendment) as far back as the 1960s, and which was turned by John Connally, President Nixon's secretary of the Treasury, into a very similar trade-defense linkage. Nixon and Connally tapped into the feeling, in the words of William Diebold, "that the United States is carrying an unfairly large share of the burdens of maintaining security in the world and is somehow made a victim of the actions of others in international trade."[9]

But the basic change in the transatlantic relationship seems to have been lost on the Americans who reiterate this old demand. Western Europe no longer *needs* American protection in the same way it did when the Soviets were united and menacing. It finds our military commitment convenient and comforting, possibly useful to preempt undesired developments; but there is no longer an ultimate threat to which it responds.

Indeed, some West Europeans may see our desire to remain militarily involved in Europe as founded on our desire to use Europe as a base—a mammoth collection of hangars and garages—for military intervention outside Europe, especially in the Middle East. Some may see it as founded on a desire by the United States to dominate European politics.

When the American military commitment was more valuable to Western Europe, it had a calming effect on transatlantic trade relations. Europe did not want to push its security provider too far; most European countries did not adopt General de Gaulle's cold-blooded position that the U.S. would defend Western Europe no matter how independent, indeed ornery, France was.[10] (America also tended to avoid straining the bonds of the alliance by pushing trade arguments too far.)

But even in the palmy days when the extended deterrent met a felt European need, it was impossible for the United States to extract specific trade concessions, or a totally compliant trade policy position, from the West Europeans. How can we hope to do so now, when the need is much reduced, and of a different kind, and when Europeans may suspect our military commitment as having foundations that are unconnected to the defense of Europe?

Again, President Bush rejected a crude trade-NATO linkage. The mainstream of administration (if not congressional) thinking seemed to be to preserve NATO as at once the means for the exercise of U.S. influence in European security politics and a way of coopting the West Europeans for U.S. military ventures outside Europe.

NATO did play a useful role in the military effort against Iraq in 1990–1991. But this role was largely passive and instrumental: forces committed to NATO were utilized in the Gulf, and the NATO infrastructure helped support the intervention. NATO did not act as an integrated body, either politically or militarily. Decisions were taken elsewhere, and military coordination was handled, ad hoc, by the American command.

And while what NATO did was important and useful, its activities did not set a precedent for NATO's becoming an alliance with worldwide scope. Even the contribution that NATO was allowed to make might not be available in the future: the Gulf intervention was the product of a degree of consensus between the United States and its European allies regarding an out-of-area incident that has rarely been seen. One can easily conceive of future cases where the European members of NATO will want to take their distance from U.S. actions and will preclude such use of NATO facilities; after all, this has happened before, notably with regard to U.S. actions against Libya.

For the moment, there is no strong challenge to the continuance of NATO, and indeed, as I have noted above, NATO has displayed a certain survival quotient by responding with relative agility to the new political-military situation. Doubts nevertheless exist that NATO can and will be changed enough to fulfill in the future the same purposes it has in the past.

At some point, when the U.S. military commitment becomes exiguous, Europeans will begin to wonder whether the old tradeoff, in which they accepted our presence and leadership in return for protection, continues to be valid—and sufficiently desirable to offset the barrier this may pose to the development of their own political and defense identity. Something akin to this sort of reflection emerged in 1992. Some Europeans—convinced that only NATO could act effectively in former Yugoslavia, and regarding NATO as blocked from acting by U.S. unwillingness to have its forces engaged—warned that U.S. persistence in this line would lead to the demise of the Atlantic Alliance.[11]

Americans will, more or less simultaneously, begin to wonder whether the cost of defending a Europe that no longer seems to need to be defended—both because the traditional threat is gone and because the Western European nations are completely capable of collective self-defense, if they will it—is tolerable for a United States that is encumbered with many costly domestic problems. The savings to the United States from a final retreat from Europe—which would certainly radically change NATO—would be modest in financial terms. But the cost of our continued involvement, in terms of diversion of attention from more urgent national needs, may be seen as overly high.

Furthermore, the United States may increasingly view the world through economic rather than security lenses. Indeed, President Clinton does so. He made a classic statement of his point of view in a speech he gave immediately before leaving for Europe and the Naples Summit of July 1994. Clinton argued that foreign policy must focus on the economy. The ability of the United States to promote economic expansion is the key to peace and stability throughout the world.[12]

It was difficult for leaders who for decades had stressed security concerns to look at the world this way, but popular sentiment and the arrival of a new generation of politicians may be forcing the issue. An enfeebled NATO is unlikely to do much if anything for U.S. economic interests. Trade disputes, unmediated by fears about the security relationship, may become more acute; U.S. monetary leadership may be challenged; and NATO will be neither a brake on these developments nor a forum in which resulting differences can be worked out. Stressing NATO may not serve our primary foreign policy needs as we move toward and into the new century.

While the mainstream of the Bush administration's approach to Europe was a dogged insistence on preserving NATO—changing it but enhancing it—that administration did make some gestures toward a more pluralist relationship with Europe. It took a less negative tone about the Conference on Security and Cooperation in Europe (CSCE); it even allowed that the CSCE has a potential usefulness. But it jealously protected NATO from any conceivable encroachment by the CSCE, so much so that it impeded the CSCE's effectiveness even where no challenge to NATO was really evident and, in fact, encroached on the CSCE; an example was the development of the NACC.

In the case of the European Community, the Bush administration not only said more positive things; it recognized the potential development of the EC by efforts to develop a closer relationship. One such effort involved picking up some German hints and pushing for a treaty; then, when that could not be achieved, signing a joint declaration with the EC. However, these efforts did not have a profound effect. The EC, while offering more consultations with the U.S., was neither eager nor prepared to do anything very imaginative. Its mental energies, aside from the politics of the issue, were absorbed by the EC's internal processes at a time when momentous changes were taking place.

But the U.S. was not itself able or willing to put much into this effort. It was hard to attract high-level attention to the problem. It was even difficult to insert much content into the expanded schedule of consultations. And the United States did not come up with a coherent proposal for a truly new and closer relationship with the EC. The essential crystallization of policy did not take place.[13]

For all of the good words and goodwill, the U.S. was left at arm's length from the European Community. If the Bush administration's line were continued by its successors, the U.S. would remain there, in an era when this may be costly.

B. PARTIAL WITHDRAWAL

The attempt to keep things as they were, or at least to pretend that they are, entails stretching depleted resources to maintain America's status and influence in the world. Another possible response—of which one sees some anticipatory signs—is to save on foreign policy resources, perhaps transferring them to domestic concerns, by a partial withdrawal from global responsibilities, including responsibilities in Europe. This measure could be seen as restoring the solvency of our policy.

Many Europeans (and Americans) saw in Bill Clinton the personification of this alternative response. During his campaign and in his early months as president, he was perceived as domestically oriented—an image he encouraged by proclaiming his intention to focus on the domestic economy with laser-like intensity. Some Europeans thought this was best for the world; others believed it would result in the end of the alliance. None thought Europe meant as much to Clinton as it had to Bush.

In all likelihood, a partial withdrawal from global and European responsibilities would have as its positive counterpart a greater emphasis on the Western Hemisphere. Those who might find a withdrawal attractive often differentiate between the American role in this hemisphere, seeing it as a traditional and natural one, and a broader American world role, seen as a temporary phenomenon produced by World War II. Another motivation is the perception that there is a worldwide trend toward the formation of economic blocs which we must either fight, or cope with, by forming our own bloc.[14] The European Union, particularly with the completion of the single market in 1992, is seen as one such bloc; more hypothetical is an East Asian bloc centered on Japan.

The United States does not face any threat from within the Western Hemisphere. Nor, at the moment, is its security threatened by any of the powers on the Eurasian land mass. Pursuit of this line of policy, pushed to an extreme, would free the United States of a large part of its defense burden. The U.S. would wish to maintain nuclear superiority over any country other than Russia, but this is a relatively cheap form of defense.

In other than an extreme form of this policy, however, the United States would wish, by a combination of diplomacy and military capability, to achieve two objectives: to avoid the development of a hegemonic and potentially dangerous state or coalition in Eurasia, and to preserve a free flow of oil from the Middle East.

U.S. strategic nuclear forces would contribute to the first objective. The U.S. would probably also want to use the tools of diplomacy in this task. Some sort of treaty arrangement with Western Europe might be appropriate. What Senator Henry Cabot Lodge and the moderate opponents of the Versailles Treaty were willing to contemplate in 1919—a guarantee treaty for Britain and France— suggests what would be consistent with this approach. Even the NATO treaty, stripped of an active American military presence in Europe, might be consistent with it. More probably, however, we would want something more flexible and less binding; the aim would be to leave our hand free to try to play the balancer in Eurasia, without making lasting commitments to any one country. We would not maintain regular military forces that would be instantly capable of the sort of ground war on the Central Front that once provided the plot for the books of military futurists.

We might, in addition, seek when necessary to enter into short-term alliances with other consumer countries to keep oil flowing from the Middle East. (This is, after all, what we did in response to the Iraqi invasion of Kuwait.) In support of this effort we might wish to retain a moderate-sized army, navy, and air capability to conduct an expeditionary war in the Middle East. However, consistent with our desire to avoid undue involvement as well as undue expense, we would hope that such efforts would be rare—that normal economic forces would, for the most part, ensure that the oil flowed. (We might, just conceivably, turn to energy conservation as a way of promoting our security.)

Such a scenario does not require abandonment of the United Nations. The UN puts few demands on the United States—except when those demands are instigated by the U.S. itself. Without incurring heavy costs, America could well play a cooperative role in a UN that would be at least as activist as it has usually been.

What are the flaws in this strategy? First, we too readily assume that Latin America would welcome a strong U.S. focus in the hemisphere. The Latin American attitude is apt, rather, to be ambivalent. The history of U.S. relations with Latin America is not an entirely happy one—especially as seen from the south. America is still regarded by many as a bad hegemon. A renewed U.S. interest could evoke the sentiments a family has when an abusive father decides to return home after a separation. Many Latin Americans have resented American political interference and, as they see it, economic exploitation. Even those who are less extreme in their judgments of past American behavior, or who think the future might be better than the past, have absorbed traditions of national identification by means of differentiation from or opposition to the United States. Finally, even on the economic side, while Mexico (in many ways a very special case) is eager for a high degree of economic integration with the United States, many other Latin American countries are at a level of economic development or have other disabilities such as to make an opening to the U.S. more a frightening than an encouraging prospect.

Economically, a reorientation of U.S. interests to the hemisphere has limited attraction. We have a very large volume of interaction with Canada and Mexico, but free trade with these countries has already been agreed. The rest of the hemisphere is a relatively low-income area; if its markets were opened to us, our exports would benefit but the level of demand is not high. Perhaps more important in a dynamic perspective is that these countries offer little by way of technology; they even offer little by way of competition. Economic integration works most productively when economies are competitive, not complementary—where trade diversion is not the name of the game.

At the same time, the United States would be turning its attention away from the developed areas of the world where, increasingly, it buys and sells goods, technology, and services, where its direct investments have been growing, and with which there is a dense network of commercial and human interchanges. It would be falsely apocalyptic to predict that such a redirection of American policy attention would instantly and generally put at risk its economic stake in the developed world, especially Europe but also East Asia. But insofar as this policy shift were to have any effect on established business relations, it would be negative. A change adopted in part in reaction to a perceived trend toward the division of the world into economic blocs would accentuate that trend. And the bloc we would be left with would be a "low rent" or "down market" one.

One can argue that while the international economic system we now have is nominally a multilateral one, it has become, de facto, a several-tier system, with the United States and the industrial countries of Europe and Asia in the first tier. This is not, in the geographic sense, a bloc, but it is a coherent grouping of countries and economies. Trading it—if it can be preserved—for hemispheric hegemony would not be an attractive deal.

Finally, and most important, could we successfully achieve what has to be a fundamental American objective, to avoid the emergence of a hegemonic force on the Eurasian land mass, while following an essentially hemispheric policy? The United States is not incapable of a balance of power approach to international relations. Our policy in the Middle East and Persian Gulf over the last few decades was just that, and for years it worked. At a cost mostly of economic assistance, coupled occasionally with modest military interventions (such as Eisenhower's in Lebanon), we generally succeeded in avoiding the development of a coherent force that could imperil our two essential interests, the flow of oil and the survival of Israel. This policy suffered a temporary failure in 1973–1974, and a more notable one in 1990, when we were forced to respond massively to Saddam Hussein's bid for regional hegemony.

Attempting to do the same in the great Eurasian game, while at the same time seeking to limit the assets we put at risk, may be difficult. Advocates of an approach of this kind often refer to the example of Great Britain in the nineteenth century. The example is not entirely encouraging. Particularly after the rise of German industrial-military power, British influence on European developments became quite limited. Its military strength—a large navy but a tiny army, basically devoted to non-European tasks—did not give it much weight on the Continent. While Britain was still first among the powers at the beginning of this century, in the series of events prior to World War I it seemed more the victim in the drama than the stage manager. Can we play a similar hand more skillfully and effectively than Britain did?

The Clinton administration's foreign policy sometimes, in some ways, has resembled this approach.[15] This reality has been masked by periodic statements of broad intent: enlarging the area of democracy in the world is one of these. In practice, however, the Clinton administration has been averse to risky action and happy to leave problems to others. Its one notable military intervention was in Haiti—part of our hemisphere. It stressed economic motivations and interests. But what it did not display was the stuff of Castlereagh or Palmerston. It is difficult for a democracy to conduct their kind of foreign policy;[16] even more difficult when a domestically oriented politician with an aversion to force is the director of foreign policy.[17]

C. SEEK A NEW RELATIONSHIP WITH EUROPE

If we feel on the one hand that our interests in Europe will not be well served by a massive reduction of our commitment to, and withdrawal of our assets from, the old world, and on the other that these interests cannot be preserved by seeking to maintain the old order, because it is unsustainable, then we have to search for a third way—which may, of course, not exist. My view is that it *could* exist.

Such a policy would have to take into account certain realities:

—The world is no longer divided between the United States and the Soviet Union, with other countries adopting positions in relation to these poles. A monocular alliance aimed at the Soviet Union no longer serves. The alliance can be preserved only by massive change.

—The United States is no longer economically dominant and cannot expect to continue to dominate international institutions (a fact which does not deny it the possibility of leadership).

And a changed relationship with Europe will have to meet certain conditions. To reiterate:

1. It will have to be founded on a basis other than the continued presence of substantial U.S. military contingents in Europe, which, absent the Soviet threat, the American public will not support.

2. It will have to take account of the changing nature of Europe and, in particular, the increasing integration of the countries of the European Union. We are used to dealing with the EU on trade. But its foreseeable development in this decade will make it our necessary interlocutor on monetary issues—and probably on politics and security.

3. The relationship will have to be a much more equal one than we enjoyed as NATO leader; we are now weaker than we once were, and the European nations have become not only stronger but, despite the post-Maastricht syndrome, increasingly united.[18]

Different though such a relationship with Europe would be, it still could be highly productive for the United States and could be the cornerstone for a reordering of the entire international system. Suggesting a permanent alliance with Europe—to be precise, with the European Union, which is unlikely to be coterminous with Europe—involves a rejection of a pure balancing approach which could, conceivably, involve switching support and relationships to another of the great Eurasian powers. The Bush administration displayed a faint glimmer of interest in such a balancing approach when it was pursuing the will-o'-the-wisp of peaceful condominium with the Soviet Union during the latter's last days. (The assumption seemed to be that Western Europe would accept this, just as it had accepted the old confrontational bipolar world.) In 1992 disgruntlement with Western European behavior contributed to a revival of interest in an alternative alliance with Russia.[19] But there are solid grounds for seeking a special relationship with Western Europe.

First, while I have argued that there is a difference between the transatlantic and the European relationships—the European Union is a community, the alliance is not—the ties between the United States and Europe are close, long-standing, and mutually productive. If we are to choose any other nation or group of nations with which to ally ourselves in the new era of world politics, Western Europe seems by far the most obvious, and easiest, choice.

Second, Western Europe constitutes by far the most valuable ally we could have, greater than all the others in both economic power and military potential.

Third, because of this, an alliance with Western Europe—an alliance that corresponds to new realities of the world by being at least as much about the international economy as about international security—could dominate international relations and provide a stabilizing substitute for the old, lost, hegemonies. Such an alliance—which need not preclude good relations with some or all of the powers not participating in it—would seem to have considerable value and attraction.

For two reasons, however, it is difficult to imagine such an alliance taking shape.

Western Europe is now coming together and losing its need for an umbilical cord to the United States. New nations (as was the case with our own) are notoriously wary of alliances, particularly with their old masters; and, stretching things a bit, the European Union of 1999 may be something like a new nation.

The United States is so habituated to the imperial position it has held for many years that accepting another sort of relationship—one that implies equality rather than superiority—comes hard, psychologically and politically.[20] Unless an enormous effort is made, the United States is likely, in the years to come, first, to attempt to preserve its old place in the world order and then, when this becomes patently impossible or at least too costly for our current means, to seek to "play the field," retiring from old exposed positions but seeking a balancing role in the world.

A candid assessment is that following the third option of seeking a new relationship with Europe would not be easy. Even making the decision to attempt to follow it would not be easy. But the value it would have for the United States and for the world is great enough to merit an effort to spell out just what sort of relationship would be desirable and possible and how we might proceed to achieve it.

CHAPTER 10

BUT WHAT IF EUROPE BREAKS APART?

September 1992 was the cruelest month for Europe. A financial crisis severely strained the European Monetary System and led to the departure of the U.K. from the EMS's exchange rate mechanism. Before this storm had time to abate, the French referendum on the Maastricht Treaty added to the sense of crisis by producing a barely visible favorable majority. Not surprisingly, these unfavorable developments were accompanied by a round of intra-European acrimony, with Anglo-German mudslinging particularly heavy and particularly atavistic.

Maastricht was eventually ratified, and with its entry into force on 1 November 1993, the European Community officially became the European Union. But September 1992 was only the worst stretch in a generally unsettling aftermath to what had been hailed at Maastricht, in December 1991, as a momentous, perhaps definitive, step toward European union—*union* in a sense that transcends nomenclature. However, despite the stormy passage the European Union has had since the Maastricht Summit, the likeliest hypothesis is that the process agreed there will continue, though perhaps at a slower pace, and with some countries lagging behind in certain aspects of unification. The strongest argument for this belief is that some part of the EU is likely to continue on this path, whether or not all the member-states do; and those nations that do not stay with the convoy would be left in a weakened and vulnerable condition.

Nevertheless, one cannot exclude the possibility that some countries will decide they cannot continue. The strains of 1992–1993 suggest that the potential nonparticipants fall into two groups. First, there are countries which are averse to the transfer of sovereignty, political and monetary, involved in the Maastricht Treaty. The two clearest cases are Denmark and the U.K. Then, there are the countries which find the economic standards of a developing union too high to meet, at least for now. Despite the financial crisis the U.K. got into in 1992, it probably should not be put in this group, but several Southern European countries, most notably Greece, but also Italy, and probably Spain and Portugal, are unlikely to be prepared for full monetary union by the end of this century.

The major difference between the two groups is that the first countries, while probably capable of keeping up economically with the pacesetters of Northern Europe, have continuing difficulty in giving up independence in favor of community life. The Southern European countries, on the other hand, would if they could; they do not have the self-confidence, the sense there is an alternative to going further along the path toward integration.

This difference in desire and intention suggests a difference in attitude toward the two outlying groups on the part of the core group of the European Union that would proceed toward monetary and political union. The Southern Europeans would be tolerated as a group of countries that, given further progress, could be expected to sign on for the full obligations of EU membership. (Spain, especially, has made a great deal of progress and may in a few years be close to the level of economic convergence required to make the European first division.)

A failure by Great Britain to climb back onto the European Union omnibus would arouse very different feelings. The history of post-Second World War Western Europe is largely the tale of its division by British pride and obstinacy.[1] If, after having seemingly changed policies over the twenty years since its accession to the European Community, the U.K. were to revert to its old standoffish policy and opt out of the European Union's further development, the reaction of "the Continentals" might be severe. Unlike the Southern Europeans, the U.K., because of its past record and present attitudes, has no credit bank of good will to draw on.

The negative reaction would be all the stronger because the U.K., despite its secular decline, still counts for something. It is still a relatively important player in terms of military power and international finance, to name two key examples. Denmark, the other stubborn nationalist among the European Union countries, has the advantage of being a charming featherweight; its unwillingness to cooperate in "building Europe" matters less and could be better tolerated than British recalcitrance.

A European Union without Britain—a high-speed union clustered around the Rhine—could still go ahead. It probably would go ahead, if only because France, especially, and, in a different sense, Germany itself see the dangers of opening the way to full German independence. Such a European Union would still be a major industrial and trading entity. But it would have significant weaknesses as a result of the absence of Britain. The U.K. is one of the two nuclear powers in Europe, and its military traditions and capacity make it an important potential contributor to any credible European defense entity. London continues to be one of the three financial capitals of the world.

Looking at the problem more politically, a European Union without the U.K. would be even more unbalanced: German power would loom very large indeed. Finally, while a union that includes all of the more important powers of Western Europe has the potential to speak very loudly in international politics (even if that potential has yet to be realized), a European Union which does not include the U.K. cannot be seen as speaking for "Europe."

Such a development would present the United States with a mixture of superficial advantages and profound dangers. A divided Western Europe would not give us the problems of adjustment, political and monetary, that a uniting EU would. Split into several parts, Western Europe could not hope to supplant NATO; the bureaucratic warriors along the Potomac could rely on the United States' being surrounded by a group of smaller and diverging entities rather than potentially confronted with a single European defense entity. Somewhat similarly, a European monetary union of six or seven countries would change the international monetary landscape, but not in the same way an Economic and Monetary Union (EMU) including all of the countries of Western Europe would. The dollar might continue to be number one; in any case, the economic, political, and psychological losses involved for the United States in the case of an EMU of fifteen (or twenty) countries would not be incurred.

This last is the most positive point that can be made. And remember that the costs for the U.S. as a result of EMU would be mainly psychological.

On the other hand, with the indefinite postponement of the prospect of Western European unification, we stand to lose, or at least risk, a great deal. The greatest risk is that Western Europe would begin to develop again its traditional tendency to competitive, and even aggressive, nationalism. The danger of this attitude's leading to armed hostilities is small, but the potential cost is so high that the low probability cannot be the end of the calculation.

The splitting of Western Europe is the more likely and dangerous because the division of the world of the Cold War days is over and because the United States no longer has the will or the capacity to impose discipline on its half of the world. (Nor would that half necessarily accept a discipline which, absent the Soviet threat, no longer seems necessary or even tolerable.) While NATO might gain some more years of vigorous middle age as a result of Western European dissension, it will never again play the role it did before 1989.

Indeed, the United States—whatever the schadenfreude along the Potomac about the indefinite postponement of European unity—should reflect on whether it wants, or is likely, to maintain a significant military presence in Western Europe for many more years. If, as I think, the answer is no, the best possible military future for Western Europe takes the form of a unified defense. The alternatives are likely to be dangerous: disunity would create collective weakness; renationalized military forces might revert to fighting each other.

More broadly, a united Western Europe has the potential to be a strong ally for the United States; the two sides of the Atlantic could gain from sharing leadership and responsibility. A divided Western Europe, particularly one divided acrimoniously, leaves us with the present unsatisfactory situation, only worse. There will be no one person or group who will be able to speak for Europe. The United States will either have to seek to play a balancing role (and we seem to be losing our enthusiasm and energy in this regard), or withdraw possibly to await one more round of intra-European fighting. The choice we would have is similar to the one we faced at the end of the First World War. The situation is not as dangerous as it was then, but our relative power may not be as great, either.

The United States, as well as Europe, could lose from a division of the European Union. Fortunately, it may not happen, at least in a harsh and damaging form. The key is the U.K. Its presence or absence, as noted, means a good deal to the substance and credibility of the EU.

Britain's leaders and people should reflect on the effects of dropping out. This would wound the European Union, but it would not kill it. The prospects for the U.K. are far worse. When Great Britain stood outside the European Community of its own will in the 1950s, and even when it was excluded by General de Gaulle in the 1960s, it could be seen as the major power in Western Europe, and it had a cluster of like-minded states to keep it company on the periphery of the EC. Now, however, the U.K. is far weaker than Germany, and even weaker than France economically. While once it had its followers in the European Free Trade Area, some of those erstwhile members of the British claque are now members of the European Union—and en route to membership in the prospective Economic and Monetary Union.

A Britain that does not go on with the European Union will be isolated. Its international financial role will be sapped by exclusion from EMU, even if that is a smaller Continental club than Maastricht foresaw. And, left outside, it will have the prospect of steadily becoming weaker relative to the EU countries. The history of the British economy when it "enjoyed" economic policy independence suggests that freedom from the EMU's discipline will be a false, unproductive freedom.[2]

These prospects seem clear enough so that, eventually, reason will dictate the U.K.'s recommitment to the European Union. Britain's tardy ratification of the Maastricht Treaty in July 1993 at least kept this option open.

This question is one of the few regarding the development of European unity where the United States can once again play a role. The traditional safe haven for British particularism has been the special relationship with the United States. If, as I believe, a divided European Union is not in our basic interests—if, furthermore, our future military commitment in Europe will be at best limited—we should make it clear to the U.K. that we can and will no longer play the role for it that we did in the 1950s and 1960s. We should let Britain know that there is no future in its being more old-school Atlanticist than the United States is. President Clinton did make it clear enough in his first years in office that the special relationship was over, but he did so in such a way as to deprive himself of influence over Britain's decisions regarding Europe, assuming he wanted to have such influence. But the time may come again when the U.S. can positively influence British policy.

This would require a broader view than we have sometimes taken. The American contribution to the troubles of the European Community in September 1992 was to add fuel to the fire of ill-judged British criticism of Germany and of the workings of the EMS. We have to recognize that we have more at stake than the modest effect on the American economy of the level of German interest rates.[3]

Whether or not we act in such a farsighted way, the U.K. is likely to make the right choice if it rationally examines the alternatives open to it. The political drama is far from over; the "Euroskeptics" within the Conservative party, cheered on by ex-Prime Minister Margaret Thatcher, are strong. On the other hand, the Labour party, which for a generation was the truly Euro-skeptical party, has come to see virtues in the European Union. And the game is not over among the Conservatives. To give an example, in June 1994, Chancellor of the Exchequer Kenneth Clarke stated his personal commitment to a single European currency. He argued that the U.K. must be in a position to join EMU if the occasion arises.[4] And the British public at that point seemed quite sure that there would be a single currency shared by at least three EU member-states by 2000.[5]

In any event, the sort of European Union that is developing is one that is likely to be different from the Maastricht model. It could be more palatable to countries like the U.K. and Denmark; their reservations have had an impact on European thinking. The idea of a multispeed Europe (to use only one of the images for the same phenomenon) has gained currency. British Foreign Secretary Douglas Hurd said in the spring of 1994 that the European Union would be a flexible grouping, following a "multi-track, multi-speed, even multi-layered approach, which will increasingly be the wave of the future. It threatens no one."[6]

Or not quite. In 1994 some fear developed in France that Germany was losing its old devotion to an integrated, federal Europe; the process was dangerous because it would liberate German power rather than yoking it to the European wagon.[7] Enlargement of the

EU to the east also created problems for the French because, at least for some years, enlargement would almost compel flexible commitments.

Later in the spring of 1994, Alain Lamassoure, the French minister for European Affairs, called for a "new founding contract" to be drawn up in 1996. It would provide that only those countries that committed themselves to going ahead on all of the subjects covered by Maastricht—economic and monetary union, a common foreign and security policy, cooperation on immigration, police, and judicial matters—would have the right to vote on these subjects. Those who did commit themselves would agree to press ahead in these areas. Once this new contract was signed, but only then, the European Union would be opened to new members. Lamassoure said his initiative would make sense only if Germany and France were among the "new founders." Germany's reaction seems to have been somewhat skeptical. For some Germans, "variable geometry" was already established at Maastricht, and the idea of formalized second-class status for Eastern Europe was not appealing.[8]

To say, as Hurd did, that the European Union is likely to be "multi-speed" is to state the obvious. But it also leaves open fundamental questions about the basic approach the European Union should take. Quite aside from the question of their desire to participate, it is clear that not all members of the EU will meet the convergence requirements to enter the EMU, even by January 1999. This is true even if some of the requirements are given a relatively liberal reading.[9] On the other hand, the British view that the EU's institutions and programs should become like an à la carte menu, with countries picking and choosing which bits to participate in, is not the only reading of "multi-speed."

Heavier guns than Lamassoure were fired at the idea of an à la carte EU—guns that pushed the alternative vision of a hard core of countries which would accept the goal of a more perfect union and which would proceed at their own pace, without allowing those who chose not to do so or who could not do so, to slow the process or even to have a voice in the process.

One of the guns was the German Christian Democratic party, which at the beginning of September 1994 published a paper entitled "Reflections on European Policy," which incorporated these ideas. Undiplomatically, it named the members of the hard core: France, Germany, and the three Benelux states. The other gun was French Prime Minister Edouard Balladur, who almost simultaneously gave an interview in which he advocated a Europe of concentric circles, with the innermost circle pushing ahead to a single currency, common laws, and a common foreign and defense policy. The next ring would be occupied by countries which could not or would not go so far, like the U.K., Spain, and Italy, whose EU obligations would remain at more or less their current level. The outer circle would include countries like the prospective entrants from Central and Eastern Europe, from whom less could be expected for some years to come. Balladur, unlike the Germans, did not name the countries in the inner circle.[10]

The German proposals hardly drew unanimous applause within the EU. The Italian government stated that they were "unacceptable." Spain said it would try to be part of the hard core, but the Netherlands, though named as one of that elite group, was critical. British Prime Minister John Major reiterated the British position, saying that the creation of tiers or circles within Europe could lead to "dangerous divisions" and that Europe needed greater flexibility, allowing each state to choose the integration projects in which it wanted to participate. But late in September, the European Parliament adopted overwhelmingly a resolution on a "multispeed Europe" which rejected "an à la carte Europe in which any member is entitled to dissociate itself from any Community policy" and stated that "if a small minority of states attempted to block all progress during the 1996 intergovernmental conference (IGC), ways would have to be found of allowing states which want to pursue their efforts to achieve European integration to still do so."[11]

Indeed, while the other states in the EU might worry about Franco-German dominance, and some might regret the marginalization of the U.K. (self-inflicted though that might be), the German-French approach probably appealed more to the majority of the governments of the EU than did the British approach. The approach promised a clearer, more predictable, shape for the EU (though it might be difficult to put into practice), and it would be a better basis for political unity than the British approach.

By mid-1995, with the intergovernmental conference to review the Maastricht Treaty drawing near, this issue became more urgent.[12] The British government adopted a defensive, conservative position, arguing for only minimal changes in the European Union's structure. Prime Minister Major put particular emphasis on retention of the veto.[13]

The Germans maintained their essential insistence on a politically more integrated Europe. In yet another set of papers, circulated in June 1995, the Christian Democrats (this time with Chancellor Helmut Kohl an active participant) abandoned their discriminatory organizational detail and concentrated on substance. Their most significant proposal was to make all European Union foreign policy decisions, except those with direct military implications, subject to majority voting, doing away with national vetoes in this most sensitive area. Dissenters or abstainers could opt out but not stop a majority in matters involving military strategy or possible use of troops. The Christian Democrats also proposed that the 1996 intergovernmental conference fix a date for the merger of the Western European Union with the European Union.[14]

The German approach, obviously fundamentally different from that of the British, drew a mixed reaction from France's new president, Jacques Chirac. Chirac came to office with the reputation of being much less Europeanist than his two immediate predecessors, Valéry Giscard d'Estaing and François Mitterrand; and even the latter had made no secret of his reservations about Germany's federalist thrust.[15] The shared adversity of having large troop contingents in Bosnia had pushed Britain and France closer together. After a mid-June meeting with Prime Minister Major, Chirac noted France's "common approach" with Britain on institutional reform, including majority voting. While the Franco-German axis was "essential for Europe to move forward," it was "necessary, but not sufficient. . . . We will not build Europe without Britain," Chirac said.[16]

The U.K. has at many points hoped to reverse the alliances within the EU by forming a bloc with France. However, despite the sympathetic response France has sometimes made, the end result has always been that France cleaves to her partner on the Rhine. In addition to all the historic reasons for this choice, France now will have to weigh the facts that Britain is opposed to EMU, which continues to be a prime goal of French policy, and that the German price for

EMU is greater political integration in the EU. I suspect that France will ultimately pay the German price (while trying, probably with success, to lower it).

Britain then will be faced with the choice of being left out or signing on to EMU and whatever political integration comes with it. If it chooses to stay out, history may judge its current leaders guilty of the same poor judgment and chauvinism Winston Churchill displayed in his comment when the European Coal and Steel Community (the lineal predecessor of the EU) was founded in 1951: "I love France and Belgium but we must not allow ourselves to be pulled down to that level."[17]

The EU's intergovernmental conference of 1996 could make the most important decisions for the future of European integration since the historic sessions of the 1950s. Its agenda could easily extend its labors into 1997. That has the not-incidental advantage, for many Continental countries, of allowing time for a new British government to take office. Continental observers believe—and hope—that Labor will form the next British government. The Conservatives, in power since 1979 and forced to hold elections no later than the spring of 1997, have ceased to be Britain's European party; their policy is increasingly that idiosyncratic mix of laissez-faire economics and political nationalism associated with Margaret Thatcher (even if the party forced her from office in 1990). The Labour party, especially since Tony Blair became its leader in the summer of 1994, has turned its back on its anti-European past. Labour finds the Continent's social market economy, or Rhenish capitalism, attractive.

The prelude to the intergovernmental conference is proving to be a real debate about the basics of the European Union, unlike the preparations for the Maastricht Treaty, which resembled nothing so much as a bureaucratic star-chamber proceeding. But even if that debate produces institutional innovation in the EU, the intergovernmental conference will not be the last word on the constituting of a real union of Europe; even the Germans are not proposing a truly federal Europe, yet.

The European Union is, and will continue to be, handicapped in speaking to the rest of the world (and to its own citizens) by the lack of a single leader. The idea of a single president for the EU has been ventilated, and it has attracted some support, including that of the former president of the European Commission, Jacques Delors. This by itself would not be a magical solution either for the problem of how to provide direction to an EU that may soon have twenty members or for the melding of many disparate foreign and security policies into one, but it might help.[18]

The commission's report, *European Security Policy in the Run-up to 2000,* made the more modest proposal of creating a body like the European Commission with responsibility for the EU's foreign and defense policies, to be headed by a prominent politician with powers similar to those of the president of the commission.[19] While the German Christian Democrats' proposals of September 1995 echoed much of the commission's report, they shrank from advancing this recommendation, writing only of the creation of a foreign and security policy secretariat responsible for analysis and planning.

The process of European unification may take longer, and be more complicated, than seemed likely at the beginning of the 1990s. But the institutional debate that began in the summer of 1994 is a healthy sign, and, given continued German leadership, should produce some forward movement. While its precise paths and forms remain uncertain, European unification still remains the future for which we should prepare our policies.

CHAPTER 11

CAN WE FORGE A NEW ALLIANCE?

THE NEED FOR A NEW RELATIONSHIP WITH EUROPE

The previous chapters must leave little doubt about my belief that the United States should attempt to create a new relationship with Europe. Over the last forty-six years, the Atlantic Alliance has provided the sustaining framework within which other American relationships with Europe have lived and generally flourished. A new relationship, while having a security component, will have to find strength elsewhere.[1]

In the world of the 1990s it is difficult to identify a military threat to the countries of the Atlantic Alliance, whether external or internal. It remains to be seen whether Russia in the long run will become a normal democratic state, as loath as other democratic states to use military force. Whether a balance of power can be maintained in East Asia is equally unknowable. Some lesser rogue states could develop the power to threaten us. But for the moment, and indeed for the medium term, we face no threat even mildly comparable to the one with which we lived for more than forty years.

On the other hand, while it would be going too far to say that the countries of the alliance face a common economic threat, they share a sense that Japan is a menacing competitor. They also perceive that the challenges to their societies are predominantly economic. While many of these challenges are essentially internal, transatlantic economic differences are possible, and may be likely, in the absence of the mitigating circumstances of the Cold War—the shared sense of danger that produced comity within the alliance.

Furthermore, the international economic institutions of early postwar creation are in need of reform, in terms both of governance and scope. The Europe of Economic and Monetary Union (EMU) and the European Currency Unit (ECU) does not fit smoothly into these dollar-centered, U.S.-dominated international monetary arrangements. The Uruguay Round was a great success, but it did not produce the last word in international trade regimes. And another such round is not likely to take place in the foreseeable future.

Difficult though the problems of the international economy, and of economic relations between Europe and America, may be, they are not at crisis level. In this, they resemble the security situation. There is a terrible tendency, in our present-obsessed system of government, to avoid even thinking about problems until they are unavoidable—in fact, until they verge on being overripe.[2] But ignoring the need for change, emphasizing instead the need to maintain the old familiar relationships, from NATO on down, is likely to produce a situation in which NATO will lose its vital spirit, leaving economic disputes to grow, untempered by security concerns. At that point, the United States might be tempted to retreat from the world, back to the Western Hemisphere. The alternative is to forge a new alliance based on economics, on transatlantic integration, if one dare utter the word.

THE REALITY OF TRANSATLANTIC INTEGRATION

The British government's reluctance to accept the "F-word" — *federalism*—in European Union decisions and documents suggests what the reaction would be if one were to suggest some sort of "Federal Union" between the European Union and the United States. Such an idea is simply not on the agenda, certainly not in the United States, and almost as certainly in Europe. Even an *approach* to a transatlantic federation would have to depend on a much higher degree of community between the two sides of the North Atlantic than exists now or prospectively.

The European Union itself, of course, evolved from beginnings that were humdrum and technical. None of the efforts to march straight toward an objective of political union had any effect until a strong foundation of functional integration was laid.

There is a nonpolitical reality of de facto integration of our economies that is too easily ignored by those, theoreticians or practitioners, who adopt a purely political approach to international relations. As Stephen Woolcock has written, "Transatlantic trade and investment relations operate on two planes, political and corporate. On the corporate plane trade and above all investment continue to grow, with the result that economic interdependence increases. . . . The political plane, by contrast, is characterized by some shrill language and mutual recrimination."[3]

Lawrence Summers, the Clinton administration's undersecretary of the Treasury for Monetary Affairs, has made a similar point, arguing that "some would have the U.S. and other industrial democracies . . . pursue policies directed at containing threats posed by foreign commercial rivals in an effort to preserve something called economic security. In my view this is a profoundly misguided vision. It fails to recognize the fundamental difference between prosperity and power. Power can be gained only at someone else's expense. Prosperity can be shared."[4]

The interpenetration of the European and American economies is very deep, "unmatched by any other inter-regional relationship in the world."[5] While Asia now exceeds Europe as a market for U.S. exports, two-way trade across the Atlantic is enormous—well over $100 billion in each direction.

Europe is the largest investor in the U.S., accounting for fifty-nine percent of total foreign direct investment, compared to Asia's twenty-six percent. European direct investments in the U.S. amounted to $249 billion in 1992. Europe is the dominant location for U.S. foreign investment (forty-nine percent of the total, compared to sixteen percent in all Asia; only five percent in Japan). U.S. direct investments in Europe, whose book value was $240 billion in 1992, have sales revenues of $800 billion. Almost fifteen percent of products sold in Europe are made by U.S. companies, either in Europe or in the U.S. Thirteen percent of the products sold in the U.S. are European in origin. While European affiliates employ over 2.9 million workers in the U.S., our affiliates in the EU employ over 2.4 million workers. In 1992 Europe was the source of twenty-seven and a half percent of the worldwide revenues of the sixteen biggest U.S. corporations that break down their revenues geographically. There are massive technology flows and numerous strategic alliances between European and American firms.[6]

The business interests that exist across national boundaries within the nations of the Atlantic area might not prevail against strong nationalist forces. One analyst holds that only in the United States do global corporations act as if they realize that they have a natural stake in a rules-based multilateral trade and investment system.[7] But in the current, relatively calm and not particularly nationalist atmosphere, such transnational interests can have substantial weight in national decision-making.

There is, nevertheless, reason to fear that the economic—and eventually the political—paths of Europe and America will increasingly diverge for want of a shared sense of purpose, and under the pressure of domestic interests that will not be as inhibited by security concerns as they once were. It is important to act before the great divide widens and deepens—important not only because international relations, economic and political, will be affected but also because the economies of Europe and America need scope and stimulus.[8]

FORMALIZING TRANSATLANTIC INTEGRATION

A number of examples are suggestive of how de facto integration might be preserved and deepened through international agreement. Among these are the North American Free Trade Area (NAFTA), the European Economic Area, and the efforts in both the Uruguay Round and its predecessor, the Tokyo Round, to develop—apart from the main menu of tariff liberalization—sectoral understandings with less than universal membership. There are many humbler examples, where technically oriented negotiators from the private and the public sectors have cooperated to develop understandings to regulate given areas of international economic life.[9] The unifying element of these various examples is an effort to go beyond traditional trade liberalization to the collective regulation or facilitation of other aspects of international economic intercourse.

Significantly, earlier suggestions for moving in this direction as between the countries of the Atlantic world, principally the United States and the European Community, came not from wild-eyed utopians but from some very experienced commercial diplomats. Joseph Greenwald, once our ambassador to the European Community, wrote:

> There is a third option for U.S. negotiating objectives. It might be called a regional approach as opposed to the global or national approach. The United States might try to negotiate an EFTA-type deal with the Com-

munity. It could be a formal, institutionalized, comprehensive trade and investment agreement, including dispute settlement provisions on the model of the U.S.-Canada Free Trade Agreement. . . . The Community might be amenable to a bilateral agreement that would go beyond trade and economic matters to include political and security issues.[10]

While not arguing specifically for a U.S.-EC arrangement, Sylvia Ostry, once Canada's senior international economic official, has suggested that the economic integration within the Atlantic world might be reflected in plurilateral regulation of trade and investment within that area (or, perhaps, within a metaphoric Atlantic world that includes Japan: the Organization for Economic Cooperation and Development group).[11]

More recently Robert Hormats, for years a senior American foreign economic policymaker and now an investment banker, wrote:

Political tolerance would be in short supply for another global trade negotiation soon after the seven-year Uruguay Round. . . . A successor round of global negotiations . . . will not likely occur until the next century, if ever. In the meantime, many of the issues the Uruguay Round left unresolved—environmental regulations, investment rules, intellectual property protection and access for suppliers of services—lend themselves better to bilateral and regional settlements, where direct reciprocity between countries is a more compelling motivator and lowest common denominator resolutions are more avoidable.[12]

Other practical people have raised their voices in favor of a special arrangement with the European Union. A political agenda lies behind some of these statements. Lane Kirkland, president of the AFL-CIO, called for a North *Atlantic* Free Trade Area as an alternative to the North *American* Free Trade Area then under negotiation. He argued that a North Atlantic pact would bring greater economic benefits without hurting American workers. He also, less predictably, said a "North Atlantic agreement would anchor the United States in Europe. . . . Permanent U.S. cooperation with Europe—

economic rather than military—would reinforce the common democratic values that are at the root of the . . . alliance."[13] Clyde Prestowitz, well-known for his critical view of Japan's trade practices, has argued that U.S. preoccupation with Asian export markets should not detract from efforts to develop new ties with Europe, which is economically important and which shares most strongly U.S. views regarding the future of the world economic order.[14]

RESISTANCE FROM AMERICA

The arguments for attempting to create a North Atlantic trade and investment zone, along the lines of NAFTA and the European Economic Area, are quite strong. So is the probable resistance.

That resistance would have several roots. Over time, any system tends to become ossified. Vested interests grow in strength in stable and peaceful political settings.[15] Of the world's major countries, none has been more blessed, or cursed, by stability than the United States. Our resistance to change is enhanced by our constitutional system, which is designed to prevent wrong actions, not to facilitate reforms that might have a positive effect. The result, as noted earlier, is that, despite a two-hundred-year lead, we run the risk of being overtaken and passed by the European Union in terms of the creation of a truly unified market for goods, services, capital, and even labor. The same institutional lethargy also makes it difficult to break out of our self-imposed national backwardness by opening our markets to our friends and competitors in Europe, even though the transitional pains and costs would be minimal.[16]

A related but not identical problem is that of sovereignty. The progressive surrender of sovereignty by the countries of the European Union has been made easier by the fate most of them shared in World War II: having been defeated. Nothing tarnishes sovereignty like defeat. It is no accident that the most reluctant European integrator, the United Kingdom, was victorious in World War II. The United States not only has no memory of defeat; it has become used to bestriding this planet. This sense of dominance has not been quenched by our relative loss of power, for the implosion of our principal adversary has left us—if only for the moment—in a unique position in the world.

We are also used to playing a truly global role; we have derived a certain prideful pleasure from accusing the Europeans of having at best a regional vision. For all of our stress on the Atlantic Alliance, the United States has operated most forcefully elsewhere. All of our post-1945 wars and skirmishes have been outside Europe. Both the apostles of a rather high-minded internationalism and those who wish to continue our global interventionism would be uncomfortable with a strong focus on Europe. But a closer relationship with Europe need not and should not mean raising barriers to the rest of the world (although one could hope that it would lead to a greater sense of priorities in our foreign policy).

Especially in the early part of his term, President Clinton's foreign policy statements were often classic examples of the high-minded, Wilsonian approach I refer to. Speaking to the UN General Assembly in September 1993, Clinton said: "our overriding purpose must be to expand and strengthen the world's community of market-based democracies . . . for our dream is of a day when the opinions and energies of every person in the world will be given full expression in a world of thriving democracies that cooperate with each other and live in peace."[17]

However, as time passed, the Clinton administration seemed more willing, at least in rhetoric, to accord Europe differentiated status. Clinton's reluctance, expressed at the margins of the January 1994 NATO Summit, "to draw a new line through Europe" by allowing Central European nations, but not Russia, into NATO might suggest opposition to a special arrangement with the European Union.[18] But when Clinton visited Europe in July 1994, he made a point of holding a U.S.-EU summit with German Chancellor Kohl (chairman of the European Council) and EU Commission President Delors. And Clinton had, in connection with the June 1994 D-Day celebrations, declared himself in favor of a "united and strong" Europe, adding that a weak Europe was not in the interests of the United States, economically, politically, or militarily. He and people around him talked of "deepening the transatlantic community," sometimes about the need to build a new one, involving a strong bilateral relationship between the U.S. and an EU expanding eastward under German leadership.[19]

By the beginning of June 1995 Secretary of State Warren Christopher, who had once criticized the foreign policy he inherited as being overly Eurocentric, said that the transatlantic relationship "cannot be sustained by nostalgia. Every generation must renew the partnership by adapting it to meet the challenges of its time." He suggested a U.S.-European partnership was vital to lead the world on crucial issues: "Our nations, working together, have the unique capacity to provide global leadership."[20]

Resistance to a North Atlantic initiative might also come from those who think the United States should give priority to relations with East Asia. At another time, in another place, President Clinton seemed to be among these, when he proposed a "Pacific Community" in a meeting with Asian heads of government in 1993.[21] Asian dynamism impresses and stimulates Americans,[22] but a leading American economist has predicted that the rapid growth rates of the newly industrialized nations of East Asia will soon slow down, as Japan's already has.[23] There is real doubt as to whether the East Asian nations feel that they are a community,[24] and there is even more doubt that there is a sense of community between them and the United States which is in any way comparable to transatlantic sentiments.[25] Furthermore, in contrast to the case with Europe, trade constitutes the bulk of the U.S.-Asian relationship, and it produces a steady stream of conflicts between the two sides of the Pacific.

Finally, there are bureaucratic problems. Those in our government who take an interest in relations with Europe are very largely children of NATO, devoted to a particular view of the relationship and most reluctant to accede to a different emphasis. International economic specialists are far less resistant to such change, but, given the way our government is organized, they generally have little influence on "high policy." And even if they could gain support within the administration for a new grand initiative toward Europe, the numerous, and conflicting, forces within the American political system which have historically aborted many international economic initiatives would come into play.[26]

What is missing from this inventory is resistance from the American public in general. As reported earlier in this book, the evidence is that while the American public is primarily interested in domestic problems, it endorses engagement abroad in selected cases. Americans consider Europe to be more important than Asia, and they have warmer feelings toward European countries than they do for most others. The majority of Americans favor maintaining our commitment to NATO and are prepared to see American troops defend Western Europe—in contrast to their opposition to military intervention in most other parts of the world. Finally, Americans do not see Western Europe as an economic threat.[27] If the American public is prepared *not* to resist a new initiative toward any part of the world, it would be one that involves Western Europe.

RESISTANCE FROM EUROPE

These grounds for American resistance have their counterparts in Europe. Some, at least, in the United States have for years been aware of the need to refound the transatlantic relationship. But until quite recently the attention given to this problem in Western Europe was marginal at best. What attracted—and nearly exhausted—attention was the diptych of Western European integration and Western European relations with the recovered eastern half of Europe.[28] A maintenance approach was taken to transatlantic relations: an occasional effort by Helmut Kohl or Jacques Delors to satisfy U.S. demands in the Uruguay Round; some ritualistic words about allegiance to NATO and a desire that the U.S. remain militarily committed to and in Western Europe.[29] The prevailing attitude was that transatlantic issues were not urgent and could be put on the back burner. By the time attention is paid to them, it could be too late.

An early warning of this possibility was the disillusionment regarding Western Europe that developed in Washington in 1991–1992. One senior American official[30] felt the major cause of this disillusionment was the European Community's failure to respond to the openings for a new U.S.-European relationship given it by Bush and Baker in 1989–1990, most notably in James Baker's Berlin speech of December 1989, in which he proposed achieving, "whether in treaty or some other form, a significantly strengthened set of institutional and consultative links" between the U.S. and the EC.[31]

The U.S.-EC understanding of November 1990, which combined a statement of shared principles with a sort of memorandum of understanding regarding meetings between the U.S. and the EC, does not seem to have been enough to put the relationship on a new footing. Much more had been hoped for by Baker and his confidant, Undersecretary Robert Zoellick, when they seized on what they thought was a real opening provided by German Foreign Minister

Hans Dietrich Genscher to arrive at an institutional or legal link between the EC and the U.S. The unexciting and hardly revolutionary declaration—"more cosmetic than substantive"—was the best that could be negotiated. While the fault lay largely with the European side, the U.S. helped limit the achievement by leaving the initiative to the Europeans, and then by developing cold feet itself about a "treaty."[32] If one report can be believed, this transatlantic declaration had by 1993 become such a dead letter that President Clinton's national security advisor admitted he had never heard of it.[33]

The European Community also failed to take advantage of the opportunity to complete the Uruguay Round in the closing months of the Bush administration.[34]

In 1993 the EC began discussing ways to revive the dialogue with the United States, but quietly, and in modest terms. The EC Commission and the member-states in early 1993 circulated drafts calling for efforts by the EC and the U.S., building upon the 1990 document, to develop joint political and security responses.[35] Even after President Clinton's July 1994 trip to Berlin for a U.S.-EU summit, the *Financial Times* could justly comment that nearly five years after Secretary of State Baker's call in that same city for new institutional links between the European Community (as it then was) and the U.S., work on building a new transatlantic community had hardly begun.[36]

Whereas in the United States the resistance to a transatlantic free trade area is largely political, in the EU there might be relatively greater resistance from economic interests. Neither European agriculture nor certain cozened high technology industries would take pleasure in a freer competition from American producers than they already have been subjected to as a result of the Uruguay Round.

The Vision and Leadership Gap

The last time that Europe and America were compelled to address the fundamentals of their transatlantic relationship was the late 1940s. Today the leaders as well as the general public on both sides of the Atlantic seem, by comparison, unaware of the importance of that relationship. Stanley Hoffmann says of Europe: "What is lacking currently is elites and leaders with a daring vision. The convergence of Monnet, Schuman, Adenauer and de Gasperi was exceptional. . . . A less grandiose but uplifting convergence around the vision of '1992' brought together Delors, Thatcher, Kohl, and Mitterrand."[37] By mid-1995, only Kohl was still in office. While he is vigorously playing the role not only of German but also of European leader, it is widely believed that he will leave office no later than the end of this parliament in 1998.

In the United States the interest and receptivity of American leaders regarding Europe declined sharply in the late 1960s. "Whereas Monnet and other key European officials had easy access to Eisenhower, Dulles, and Kennedy, they found it difficult to establish informal relations with their successors. . . . Their passing from the governmental scene symbolized the arrival of a younger generation of American statesmen who felt less committed to building the kind of world that their predecessors had imagined in the wake of . . . World War II."[38]

Yet there are some glimmerings of hope. The interest taken in relations with the EC by Secretary of State Baker, and the recent statements of support for the EU and transatlantic cooperation by President Clinton and some around him, suggest a more positive interest in Europe and the European Union on the part of U.S. leaders than has been seen for a generation. And as time goes on, one has to hope that the failure of European and the United States to cooperate effectively on several post-Cold War issues—of which the most conspicuous has been Yugoslavia— will have a chastening effect and produce receptivity to an effort to reknit the Atlantic world.

LEADERSHIP: THE EUROPEANS TO THE RESCUE?

When I began writing this book, I felt quite strongly that if a lead were to be taken in transforming the Atlantic Alliance, it would come from the United States. After all, in the formative late 1940s, it had been the United States that led; and while later transatlantic projects and decisions were of lesser magnitude, they too were almost invariably the results of American initiatives. Several Americans, Henry Kissinger being the most conspicuous, did begin speaking and writing on the subject. Robert Zoellick— who, as undersecretary of state, was eager in 1990 to establish a legal basis for U.S.-EC relations— chaired a study group which in 1993 called for elevation and formalization of the relationship.[39] But in the first half of 1995, Europe has awakened, and quite suddenly European politicians and high officials took up the transformation of the transatlantic relationship as an important subject.

The EU Commission's ambassador in Washington, Andreas van Agt, a little ahead of the game, made speeches in late 1994 urging consideration of a transatlantic free trade area. Van Agt saw such a free trade area as having mainly a political significance: it would help the transatlantic partnership "at a time when problems between the US and Europe are mounting (Bosnia, Iran, how to deal with Japan) and doubts are surfacing about the value and viability of our NATO alliance."[40]

The real opening of the discussion, however, was at the Wehrkunde meeting in Munich in early February of 1995. There, the French foreign minister and the German and U.K. defense ministers all brought up the idea of a transatlantic pact. Several speakers called for continued U.S. leadership in the current alliance, but also for a simultaneous search for what French Foreign Minister Alain Juppé called a "new transatlantic charter." German Defense Minister Volker Rühe said, "the American-European partnership must become a comprehensive, problem-solving community. The old transatlantic bargain, whereby protection was provided [by the Americans] in return for influence, must evolve into a new, wider transatlantic contract to handle the entire spectrum of political, economic, and military-strategic issues." It was also suggested, however, that this new partnership should be between equals. NATO had been a "Mormon marriage," with the U.S. a benevolent patriarch lording it over a bevy of grateful European consorts. What now was needed was a modern marriage between two equal partners.[41]

Once the theme was set, many joined the chorus. Jacques Santer, president of the EU Commission, called for a "genuine transatlantic pact." An investment pact might be the first step; the goal, a transatlantic single market. The Transatlantic Policy Network, a coalition of European parliamentarians and multinationals, called for a new political treaty between the U.S. and the EU. France was said to be determined to use the discussion going on in NATO on the criteria for new members to force a radical redefinition of the mission and future of the organization.[42] French officials reportedly were arguing within NATO that its expansion would require a complete rewriting of the North Atlantic Treaty, with the European Union signing the new Atlantic Charter as an equal partner with the United States. While Germany evidently did not advocate wholesale revision of the treaty, Germany's Rühe, during an early March visit to Washington, called for some treaty changes and "a new trans-Atlantic Covenant" that would enlarge the political role of the EU within NATO. Finally, when British Prime Minister Major came to see President Clinton at the beginning of April, he raised the idea of a transatlantic free trade agreement.[43]

The official American response was relatively sparse, and tepid. In February Undersecretary of Commerce for International Trade Jeffrey Garten—speaking in the context of the joint sponsorship by his department and the EU Commission of a U.S.-European business effort to develop a long-term vision for the transatlantic relationship—raised the possibility of a free trade agreement between the U.S. and the European Union. Immediately after John Major's April visit to Washington, Assistant Secretary of State Richard Holbrooke revealed that discussions of a transatlantic free trade agreement had been going on within the Clinton administration for at least six months. The U.S. had already discussed the idea with its European allies; the talks were very preliminary but would continue: "It's a good idea whose time hasn't quite come yet." Holbrooke went on to say that a transatlantic free trade pact "will be part of the future intense dialogue on the future of Europe."[44]

Some notable American private citizens did respond loudly and clearly. At a dinner for John Major during his visit to Washington, AFL-CIO President Lane Kirkland expressed support for expanding the European Union westward. Henry Kissinger, addressing a London conference on "Britain and the World," said the special relationship between the United States and Britain should give way to a special relationship between the United States and Europe; he proposed a North Atlantic free trade group to give that relationship an economic foundation.[45]

Kissinger's premise, as stated in a subsequent article, was that "NATO expansion requires a decision, not a study. Nevertheless, by itself it will not create a new sense of Atlantic community. Security can no longer be the principal unifying bond of the Atlantic nations because, fortunately, there no longer exists a unifying threat." He argued that "the time has come to put into effect a North Atlantic

Free Trade Area. . . . The conditions are propitious. . . . Prime Minister John Major of Great Britain and Foreign Minister Klaus Kinkel of Germany have expressed their interest in such a project. A major American initiative would be received as was Gen. George Marshall's speech for European recovery and would almost surely produce a creative response. . . ."[46]

While he cannot be credited with a major initiative, Secretary of State Warren Christopher did make the first high-level official American response to the European chorus in a speech in Madrid at the beginning of June 1995. He praised the idea of establishing a transatlantic free trade area and outlined a vision for tighter transatlantic ties that would be based not just on security concerns and NATO but also on heightened political and economic cooperation. Christopher qualified his endorsement of a free trade area by saying it must neither undermine multilateral trade liberalization nor disadvantage less developed nations. Emphasizing that he spoke for President Clinton, he called on the European Union to open talks aimed at drawing up, by the end of 1995, a wide-ranging agenda for developing security, economic, and political relations in the twenty-first century. "We must not take this relationship for granted," Christopher said; "it is our responsibility to build the partnership that will ensure that, by working together, our next fifty years will be as great as the last."[47]

WHY DID EUROPE SPEAK OUT? WHY WAS THE AMERICAN RESPONSE TEPID?

Adversity caused Europe to raise and push the issue of the transatlantic relationship. Some in Europe also saw an opportunity.

At the beginning of the 1990s, coming off the heady years in which the single market took form, and with a sense that it had a new freedom of action as a result of the end of the Cold War, the European Community was afflicted by grandiosity. But the next few years were not happy ones for the (rebaptized) European Union. Much went wrong, and hoped-for progress was not made, particularly after the Maastricht Summit of 1991.

The weakness of European political and military capabilities—first revealed in the relatively benign (for Europe) context of the Gulf War and demonstrated in the European reaction to the conflict in Bosnia—and the snail-like progress the EU made to remedy these weaknesses, led most Europeans, even the French, to realize how much they depended on the United States. The trend to increasing nationalism in Russia after the autumn of 1993 only increased Europeans' sense of vulnerability. The sluggishness and declining competitiveness of the (still very rich) European economies, and the periodic turbulence to which they were subjected by the fluctuations of the dollar, also provided evidence of a different sort of dependence on the United States.

At the same time, the United States was perceived to be slipping away from its European connections. It not only withdrew troops from Europe; it seemed to be paying less attention to Europe. When the United States did address itself to a European issue relating to Russia, such as expansion of NATO, it frequently seemed to speak over the heads of its erstwhile allies in Western Europe and talk directly to Moscow.

There was fear that the United States no longer had much interest in traditional relationships, that its commitments abroad would be decided without reference to the past. The American imagination might fasten on Asia, a more exciting (if challenging) area, rather than on Europe—at least to the extent that the U.S. paid any attention at all to the world beyond the oceans.

It is natural that a Europe which to some degree is at the mercy of U.S. decisions in both the military and economic spheres should want to affect those decisions.[48] And Europe, after experiencing the contrast just in this century between internal warfare and peaceful stability, should also want to preserve the United States as permanent balancer of its power relationship.

While Europe's worries were and are about security, in the broadest sense, most of the Europeans who spoke of creating something new in the transatlantic partnership talked in terms of economics: a free trade area. There are two explanations for this emphasis. It was felt that, with the decline in the military threat, some new basis for the U.S. commitment to Europe had to be developed. Second the EU is still essentially an economic organization. At this stage in its development, it has little to offer in the political and military areas, but its economic clout is substantial.

While some saw problems, and tried to resolve them, others saw opportunities, and tried to exploit them. The French emphasis on reconstructing NATO to become a U.S.-EU alliance is the prime case in point.

The tepid U.S. response was the product of the change in American attitudes toward Europe (and the world in general) which the Europeans perceived. American politics turned domestic in 1992 and continued so through 1995. The Clinton administration paid attention to foreign problems when it had to, or when, as in the case of international economics, there was a direct connection to domestic well-being. The government's rhetoric was multilateralist, its behavior generally unilateralist. The middle ground of participating in, and leading, alliances was given little stress. The Republicans, while rejecting the multilateralist rhetoric, did not otherwise offer an alternative.

In these circumstances, the resistance to doing anything new or far-reaching with Europe, while hardly overwhelming, long prevailed. However, the Clinton administration was, to an extent, the captive of its own speeches. After initially making noises about diminishing the Eurocentrism of the past, the president and his officials began to emphasize America's interest in the transatlantic partnership. When the European calls for a new look at that partnership became loud and insistent enough, Washington had, at the least, to say it would join in the examination. That is what Warren Christopher did in June 1995.

WHAT IS ON OFFER?

The European proposals have been stronger on desire and will than on detail.[49] However, at least three different possible forms of a new transatlantic partnership have been proposed:

1. A transatlantic free trade area. This was originally thought of as an EU-U.S. free trade area; more recently it has been taken to mean an EU-NAFTA agreement. This is the formula favored by Germany. It has the advantage, for both sides, of being a familiar device. Agriculture would probably be the major sticking point in negotiating such a free trade area; free trade in agriculture might have to be introduced over a much longer time span than for industrial products (on which EU and U.S. tariffs are already low).

2. A transatlantic "economic space." This scheme, proposed by Sweden, is inspired by the European Economic Area. It would not touch tariffs but seek to remove nontariff barriers to trade in manu-

factures and services. This proposal would avoid thorny problems like agriculture but include what is increasingly seen as the most significant sort of barrier to international economic interaction.

3. A new transatlantic charter or treaty. This is favored by those who want a "great leap forward," probably including the French. The content of this charter or treaty is not clearly spelled out, but what would seem to differentiate it from the first two formulas is that it would explicitly cover security. That, in turn, differentiates it in terms of short-term possibility: while the European Union already has the power to negotiate on a wide range of economic issues, it will not have clear powers, or even ideas, about security, at least until after the 1996 intergovernmental conference to review the Maastricht Treaty.

How Should the U.S. Respond?

The United States should act quickly, while it still benefits from Europe's sense of need, the history of the alliance, and nostalgia; while it has more to offer than it may have later; and before some schism develops, after which the recomposition of the relationship will be much more difficult.

The key to the future of the relationship, important though the security aspect is, lies in reconstructing U.S.-EU economic relations, transforming them from an adversarial to a cooperative, if not an integrationist, mode. In terms of the menu of possibilities just listed, the U.S. should seek both a free trade area and an economic zone; that is, it should aim for a form of economic integration like that of the European Economic Area, covering trade in goods and services and creating an open market for investment and business activity.

Trade is important. In the words of an *Economist* editorial, "progress on trade would surely help to cement the North Atlantic alliance. . . . Economics and security should go hand in hand, and the European Union, whatever its shortcomings, shows that economic co-operation can lead on to a much more elaborate and cohesive joint undertaking."[50] But there is more to U.S.-European relations than trade. Trade has been disturbed by conflicting macro-economic policies; an economic area would certainly benefit from, and may in fact require, more effective transatlantic policy coordination. And the time has come for a reform of the Bretton Woods institutions. At this point, a graceful invitation to the European Union to share the leadership and management of these international economic institutions would mean something. If we wait too long, we may lose the leadership position we can now offer to share.

Finally, the United States should be prepared to concede what is in its own interest and agree to a reconfiguration of NATO, which would turn it essentially into a U.S.-EU pact. It can offer a reworked, or re-understood, military alliance with Western Europe. This arrangement need no longer involve the stationing of American troops in Western Europe. Perhaps some air and naval units might remain, and we could continue for a while to make up for European deficiencies in logistics, communications, and intelligence.[51] It could also involve additional pre-positioning of supplies, making the commitment of the United States to come to the aid of its European allies more credible and more feasible. These changes would be consistent with the North Atlantic Treaty, though they would produce a different NATO, and a different American role within NATO. They would take something that I view as inevitable—the final drawdown of American ground forces from Europe—and turn it into something positive, by giving Europe an equal voice in the alliance.

Europe, however, must demonstrate, to itself and to the United States, two things before this transformation is made. First, Europe has to be able to assume the greater part of its own defense. Second, the new transatlantic partnership should be an alliance with worldwide scope; the participants should be prepared to act together, not just in defense of their own territory but in pursuance of common interests outside it. This effort will involve more significant political consultation within the new partnership—the new alliance—than there has ever been up to now, either between the U.S. and the EU, or within NATO.

The specific form these new understandings might take is secondary, though not unimportant. It would be best to be precise, to spell out the obligations of the two sides. But whether this is done by a combination of agreements—for example, by a new single market agreement with the EU combined with some revision of the North Atlantic Treaty, or by placing some sort of broad transatlantic charter over everything—is not a vital concern.

What is important is to remember the advantages we want to reap from these arrangements. We want, in my judgment, to create a transatlantic relationship in which economic issues are dealt with as essentially internal matters, a transatlantic relationship that will look out on the rest of the world and deal with it, in political and security affairs, in a coordinated manner. Europe—the Europe of the European Union, which will soon comprehend most of the states to the west of the former Soviet Union—is a natural partner because of the compatibility of our cultures and political systems, in a way that the other great powers of the world—Russia, China, even Japan—are not. And the European Union, though it has been passing through one of its periodic fits of pessimism, remains one of the world's great centers of power. As Kissinger has put it, the importance of the Atlantic relationship for the future lies "in its decisive role in helping America cope with the foreseeable evolution of the twenty-first century."[52]

TIMING

Both the European Union and the United States will be preoccupied in 1996: the EU by the intergovernmental conference, the U.S. by the presidential elections. While preparatory work, and even some minor agreements, are possible, fundamental decisions must await 1997, at least.

The idea of a new transatlantic partnership has now been advanced, mainly by the Europeans. And however tepid the U.S. response, it appears agreed that the idea should be fleshed out. But taking decisions and making them acceptable to the public on both sides of the Atlantic will require imagination and will.

Waiting until 1997 may make these latter two commodities more available than they are now. If the EU manages to navigate through its intergovernmental conference and come out with a European Union that is definitely on the way to having a common foreign and security policy, it will be more prepared to deal with its external relations. And it will be an entity which is more worth dealing with.

The United States may, over this same period, go through a process similar to what Europe has gone through in arriving at its proposals for a new transatlantic relationship. The U.S. may realize that it needs Europe; that Europe is the best partner available to it in dealing with a world which elsewhere presents problems and dangers.

The benefits from such decisions are not just there for the reaping. The ideas have been sown, but their policy fruits need to be coaxed to maturity. The public—in America and, I believe, in Europe—would not resist; but leadership of a sort we have not seen in recent years will be required.

CONCLUSION

A new alliance between the United States and the European Union is but a piece of the New World Order. It is not even the whole story of U.S. relations with Europe, though the European Union is swelling to include countries to the north, the south, and, especially, the east. It is an attempt to deal now with a manageable problem, as opposed to seeking utopia tomorrow.

A re-based relationship between Western Europe and the United States would, at the least, do something for the broader question of European order. By providing a new basis for cooperation between the countries on the two sides of the Atlantic, the life of the alliance, which has been and is seen as a stabilizing element in Europe, would be extended. This, in turn, would give time and space for the Organization for Security and Cooperation in Europe to develop, possibly making use of the alliance as its "secular arm" until it can take on more responsibilities itself.

A permanent alliance between the EU and the United States, founded upon a degree of economic integration that would with time make a transatlantic separation more and more difficult, would also provide the hegemonic leadership which may be necessary to avoid a rerun of the global strife of the last century. This alliance could also facilitate the refoundation of the international economic institutions, which for more than twenty years have been in a difficult interstitial state between U.S. dominance and shared management.

It would, finally, respond to America's need for a partner in the world—a partnership based on something more than a temporary assessment of the balance of interests, an enduring relationship that is now advocated even by that hardened realist, Henry Kissinger.[53] Europe's need for reassurance has made it turn again to us. Our own need for help in coping with a world which we cannot ignore, and in which strong and compatible friends and allies are hard to come by, should make us answer by transforming the old alliance, creating a new alliance for the twenty-first century.

NOTES

INTRODUCTION

1. Secretary of State John Foster Dulles to the American Embassy in Belgium, 26 Jan. 1956, in *Foreign Relations of the United States, 1955–57* (Washington: Government Printing Office, 1986), 4:399.

2. W. R. Smyser writes that the post-1989 European state system might be described as the "Europe of Berlin," but he argues that the new Germany is democratic and responsible, and not bent on aggression. See Smyser, "Dateline Berlin: Germany's New Vision," *Foreign Policy*, no. 97 (Winter 1994–95): 140, 149.

3. Stanley Hoffmann, "The Crisis of Liberal Internationalism," *Foreign Policy*, no. 98 (Spring 1995): 176.

CHAPTER 1—THE OLD ORDER PASSES

1. Vyacheslav M. Molotov, speech of 2 July 1947, cited in *Documents on American Foreign Relations, Vol. IX, January 1–December 31, 1947*, ed. Raymond Dennett and Robert K. Turner (Boston: Princeton University Press for World Peace Foundation, 1949), 184–87.

2. Democratic freedoms in the West were subject, of course, to the constraints imposed by the two "enforcer" states, the USSR and the U.S. See Karl-Heinz Kamp, "The Folly of Rapid NATO Expansion," *Foreign Policy*, no. 98 (Spring 1995): 123.

3. A. W. DePorte, *Europe between the Superpowers: The Enduring Balance*, 2d ed. (New Haven: Yale University Press, 1986), ix.

4. The INF treaty signed by Reagan and Gorbachev in December 1987, which provided for the elimination of intermediate-range missiles by both sides, formalized an understanding in principle reached by the two leaders at their Reykjavik summit in October 1986. This was the end of a story that had begun in the late 1970s as a result of Western European worries about the deployment by the Soviets of a new class of missiles, the SS-20s, and also about the

credibility of the U.S. nuclear commitment to Europe. Installation of new U.S. missiles in Europe was an answer to both concerns. Mutual elimination of intermediate-range missiles solved the problem of the SS-20s but reopened the decoupling issue. See Jonathan Dean, "Military Security in Europe," *Foreign Affairs* 66, no. 1 (Fall 1987): 25–26; and Lynn E. Davis, "Lessons of the INF Treaty," *Foreign Affairs* 66, no. 4 (Spring 1988): 720–21.

5. Raymond L. Garthoff, *Détente and Confrontation: American-Soviet Relations from Nixon to Reagan* (Washington: Brookings Institution, 1985), 1029.

6. W. R. Smyser, "Dateline Berlin: Germany's New Vision," *Foreign Policy,* no. 97 (Winter 1994–95): 148.

7. Garthoff, *Détente and Confrontation,* 500.

8. See Christopher Cviic, *Remaking the Balkans* (New York: Council on Foreign Relations Press, 1991), and Emmanuel Todd, *L'invention de l'Europe* (Paris: Seuil, 1990). Samuel P. Huntington calls this, the "eastern boundary of Western Christianity in the year 1500," the "most significant dividing line in Europe." See Huntington, "The Clash of Civilizations," *Foreign Affairs* 72, no. 3 (Summer 1993): 30.

9. As Gregory Treverton put it, "When communism fell first in Poland and Hungary, the United States responded with only half a B-2 bomber's worth of aid to these two countries. . . ." See Treverton, "America's Stakes and Choices in Europe," *Survival* 34, no. 3 (Autumn 1992): 128–29. American businessmen showed more enthusiasm. In the year ending in September 1992 American investments in Eastern Europe boomed, with 219 acquisitions and start-ups, a figure which was 30 percent of all foreign-investment deals monitored and 29 percent of the $28 billion-value of such transactions. As a result, the U.S. moved ahead of Germany as the largest investor in the region. See Gene Koresh, "Yankees Go East—On a Scale That's 'Startling,'" *Business Week,* 18 Jan. 1993, 26.

The United States did play a leadership role with regard to the former Soviet Union, but even so, the European Union countries provided more aid. Of the $94.4 billion in Western aid received by the USSR or the Commonwealth of Independent States since 1989 (and through 1993), $60.5 billion came from EU nations, only $12 billion from the U.S. See Martin Walker, "Financing Russia's Future," *Europe,* Feb. 1994, 6–8. Smyser notes that Germany alone, with a much smaller national economy than the United States, provided $52 billion in aid to Russia and the other successor states to the USSR between 1989 and 1993, and $25 billion to the states of Central and Eastern Europe. Germany was, of course, second to the U.S. in private investment. See "Dateline Berlin: Germany's New Vision," 146.

10. Kamp, "The Folly of Rapid NATO Expansion," 120.

11. Foreign direct investment (FDI) in Eastern Europe and the former Soviet Union, in which the American private sector took the lead, was small compared to the overall challenge. According to an Economic Commission for Europe report, at the end of 1993, FDI per capita in Eastern Europe, the European states of the Commonwealth of Independent States, and the Baltic states, was $43. In Eastern Europe it was higher but still small: $99 per capita. While per capita FDI was relatively large in Hungary ($242) and the Czech Republic ($556), it is useful to compare flows of direct investment into all of Eastern Europe with the amount going to Mexico. Foreign direct investment in Eastern Europe was just under $4 billion in 1993 and $1.3 billion in the first half of 1994. Mexico alone received $3.3 billion in the first six months of 1994. See Francis Williams, "West Urged to Step Up Aid to Eastern Europe," *Financial Times,* 6 Dec. 1994, 6.

12. "Skepticism on Central Europe Trade Zone," *New York Times,* 28 Sept. 1992, D2.

CHAPTER 2 — THE TRANSFORMATION
OF OLD RELATIONSHIPS

1. Sometimes the European—or at least the French—response was not so tolerant. The French, well into the 1990s, were hostile to the possibility of NATO's broadening its competence to include politics. French President François Mitterrand stormed out of NATO's Rome summit of November 1991, furious at the idea that NATO was to develop a more political role in relations with the East. He remarked ironically, "I did not know it had a political role. I am surprised that it has a new one." Cited in Anand Menon, "From Independence to Cooperation: France, NATO, and European Security," *International Affairs* 71, no. 1 (Jan. 1995): 23.

2. Richard G. Lugar, "NATO: Out of Area or Out of Business," speech to Overseas Writers Club, Washington, D.C., 24 June 1993,

cited in Jonathan Dean, *Ending Europe's Wars* (New York: Twentieth Century Fund Press, 1994), 342-43. This argument—that if the U.S. commitment to NATO is to survive, NATO must go out of area—is discussed at length in Paul R. S. Gebhard, "The United States and European Security," *Adelphi Paper* 286 (Feb. 1994); and David Gompert and Richard Kugler, "Free-Rider Redux," *Foreign Affairs* 74, no. 1 (Jan.–Feb. 1995): 7–12.

3. See, for example, Gebhard, "United States and European Security," and Gompert and Kugler, "Free Rider Redux."

4. A rush to disengage had not, well into the 1990s, shown up in American opinion polling. The latest in a series of polls taken over the last twenty years for the Chicago Council on Foreign Relations shows, if anything, the reverse. With the end of the Cold War and of the USSR, a sharp decline in American support for NATO might have been expected, but leadership support for maintaining the current level of support for NATO, which dropped dramatically between 1986 and 1990, rebounded from thirty-five percent in 1990 to fifty-seven percent in late 1994. The general public's commitment to NATO has remained largely unchanged, with fifty-six percent in favor of keeping it unchanged, as of late 1994. See John E. Rielly, "The Public Mood at Mid-Decade," *Foreign Policy*, no. 98 (Spring 1995): 77, 89.

5. Suzanne Wilking, "L'Italia e gli italiani secondo i tedeschi," *Relazioni Internazionali*, no. 21 (March 1993): 77–78, 82.

6. Nicholas Ridley's remarks are contained in an interview published in the 12 July 1990 issue of the *Spectator* (8–10). He also described France as Germany's "poodle." Ridley was forced to resign his post as secretary of state for Trade and Industry in the Thatcher government. See obituary, "Lord Ridley, 64, Outspoken Tory Who Served on Thatcher Cabinet," *New York Times,* 6 Mar. 1993, 10. Ridley was close to Mrs. Thatcher; her delay in firing him may suggest she did not perceive the interview as cause for dismissal. See Louise Richardson, "British State Strategies," in *After the Cold War: International Institutions and State Strategies in Europe, 1989–1991,* ed. Robert O. Keohane, Joseph S. Nye, and Stanley Hoffmann (Cambridge: Harvard University Press, 1993), 152. Mrs. Thatcher's memoirs are, strangely, almost silent on Ridley's resignation.

7. See Timothy Garton Ash, "Germany's Choice," *Foreign Affairs* 73, no. 4 (July–Aug. 1994): 71.

8. Josef Joffe, "After Bipolarity: Germany and European Security," *Adelphi Paper* 285 (Feb. 1994): 40.

9. Prof. Catherine Kelleher called attention to the correlation of these events in a lecture at the MIT Center for International Studies on 18 March 1992.

10. W. R. Smyser, "Dateline Berlin: Germany's New Vision," *Foreign Policy,* no. 97 (Winter 1994–95): 152.

11. This is another point made by Prof. Kelleher in her 18 March 1992 lecture.

12. In "After Bipolarity: Germany and European Security" (38–39), Joffe gives a long list of foreign policy options the new Germany seeks to keep open.

13. The language of the German Basic Law had been interpreted to mean that German forces could not be used for missions abroad. The German Constitutional Court decided that German forces can be used for peacekeeping and peacemaking missions outside the NATO area, if the deployment is under the auspices of an international organization such as the UN or NATO and is approved by the Bundestag. See Craig Whitney, "Court Permits German Troops a Foreign Role," *New York Times,* 13 July 1994, A1; "Unbound," *Economist,* 16 July 1994, 45; and Smyser, "Dateline Berlin: Germany's New Vision," 143.

14. Consideration of the comparison between France and Germany—one with nuclear weapons but relatively weak, one without such weapons but strong—might, incidentally, lead Americans to reflect on how adequate a basis for international political strength our own military prowess will be.

15. Dominique Moïsi and Michael Mertes, "Europe's Map, Compass, and Horizon," *Foreign Affairs* 74, no. 1 (Jan.–Feb. 1995): 131.

16. Patrick E. Tyler, "Pentagon Imagines New Enemies to Fight in Post-Cold-War Era," *New York Times,* 17 Feb. 1992, A1.

17. Smyser, "Dateline Berlin: Germany's New Vision," 140, 155–56.

CHAPTER 3 — WESTERN EUROPE ON THE ROAD TO INTEGRATION

1. Elke Thiel, "Changing Patterns of Monetary Interdependence," in *The Dynamics of European Integration,* ed. William

Wallace (New York: Pinter for the Royal Institute of International Affairs, 1990), 70–71.

2. Charles A. Coombs, *The Arena of International Finance* (New York: John Wiley and Sons, 1976), 84–85.

3. Susan Strange, *International Monetary Relations,* vol. 2 of *International Economic Relations of the Western World 1959–1971,* ed. Andrew Shonfield (New York: Oxford University Press for the Royal Institute of International Affairs, 1976), 129–33.

4. Strange, *International Monetary Relations,* 330.

5. Elke Thiel, "Changing Patterns of Monetary Interdependence," 71.

6. In the mid-1960s de Gaulle waged a campaign against supranationalism in the form of majority voting, withdrawing French representation from key EC meetings. France resumed its participation only when the others conceded, in the misnamed Luxembourg Compromise of 1966, which established unanimity as the general rule.

7. Lord (Peter) Carrington, cited in David G. Haglund, *Alliance within the Alliance? Franco-German Military Cooperation and the European Pillar of Defense* (Boulder: Westview Press, 1991), 43.

8. Stanley Hoffmann, "The European Community and 1992," *Foreign Affairs* 68, no. 4 (Fall 1989): 31.

9. Lord (Arthur) Cockfield, the chief architect of the Single Market as a member of the EC Commission, suggests that Mrs. Thatcher's support was based on ignorance. See reviews of Cockfield's book, *The European Union: Creating the European Market* (New York: John Wiley, 1994), in the *Economist,* 18 June 1994, 99; and the *Financial Times,* 30 June 1994, 16. For Margaret Thatcher's view, see her *The Downing Street Years* (New York: HarperCollins, 1993), esp. 547 and 555–57.

10. Haglund, *Alliance within the Alliance,* 63; Kenneth Waltz, *Theory of International Politics* (Reading, MA: Addison-Wesley, 1979), 134–38.

11. David Marsh, "Bundesbank to Criticise Kohl's Maastricht Deal," *Financial Times,* 29 Jan. 1992, 1.

12. Many states have chosen to keep their currencies closely linked to the deutsche mark, which means their monetary policies are still essentially determined by the Bundesbank.

13. David Buchan, "A Long March towards Euroarmy," *Financial Times,* 18 Oct. 1991, 23.

14. Paul Lewis, "Germany Tells the U.N. It Wants a Permanent Seat on the Council," *New York Times,* 24 Sept. 1992, A1; Paul Lewis, "Germany Refines Bid for U.N. Role," *New York Times,* 30 Sept. 1993, A8.

15. Julia Preston, "Italian Crusade: Parity to a Fault," *Washington Post,* 4 June 1995, A23.

16. Haglund, *Alliance within the Alliance,* 8.

17. *Alliance within the Alliance,* 74–5.

18. Edward Mortimer writes that the British government's conclusion from the Iraq war was that the EC should not be too ambitious. In the rest of Europe, while it was agreed that the Gulf crisis revealed "Europe's incapacity for joint action," the conclusion drawn was that this "showed precisely how urgent it was to introduce tighter, more systematic procedures for cooperation in foreign and security policy." Edward Mortimer, "European Security after the Cold War," *Adelphi Paper* 271 (Summer 1992): 54.

19. Greece was accused in the European Court of Justice of violating the Maastricht Treaty. See Gillian Tett, "Greece Set for Legal Fight over Macedonia," *Financial Times,* 14 Apr. 1994, 16; and William N. Dunn, "Macedonia: Europe's Finger in the Dike," *Christian Science Monitor,* 9 May 1994, 19. The court rejected the EU Commission's request for an emergency injunction ordering the Greek government to end the blockade. See Lionel Barber and Kerin Hope, "Legal Move on Greek Embargo Fails," *Financial Times,* 30 June 1994, 3; and "Athènes peut poursuivre le blocus de la Macédoine," *Le Monde* (Paris), 1 July 1994, 6. Greece was able to maintain the blockade by claiming that Macedonia was a threat to its national security. See Misha Glenny, "Heading Off War in the Southern Balkans," *Foreign Affairs* 74, no. 3 (May–June 1995): 104; and James Pettifer, "Macedonia: Still the Apple of Discord," *World Today* 51, no. 3 (Mar. 1995): 57.

A less significant, more evanescent flare-up of old-style nationalism occurred when in May 1994 the right-wing government of Silvio Berlusconi came to power in Italy. It blocked consideration of Slovenia's application for association with the EU over the issue of compensation for ethnic Italians who lost property when Slovenia, then part of Yugoslavia, was awarded Italian territory in 1945. In March 1995, after the fall of the Berlusconi government, Italy withdrew its veto. See Edoardo Gardumi, "MSI e Martino allarmano la Slovenia," *L'Unità* (Rome), 28 May 1994, 7; "Le climat se détend entre la Slovénie et l'Italie," *Le Monde,* 7 Mar. 1995, 5; and Anton Bebler, "Slovenia and Europe," *World Today* 51, no. 5 (May 1995): 98–99.

20. In December 1994, the CSCE was renamed the Organization for Security and Cooperation in Europe.

21. Jacques Delors, analyzing the errors made with regard to Yugoslavia, has written that "it was clear that economic arguments, however sound, would not persuade the players to abandon entrenched positions." See Delors, "European Unification and European Security," *Adelphi Paper* 284 (Jan. 1994): 5.

22. Noel Malcolm, "The Case against 'Europe,'" *Foreign Affairs* 74, no. 2 (Mar.–Apr. 1995): 68. Another British writer on Yugoslavia, Misha Glenny, writes of the "clownish efforts of the European Union" in the southern Balkans, the "EU's inability to conduct subtle and effective diplomacy," and the "chaotic, failed diplomacy of the EU." His standard of comparison is the United States (though not for its Bosnia policy). See Glenny, "Heading Off War in the Southern Balkans," 102, 104.

23. See "Battle Lines over Defense," *Economist,* 4 Feb. 1995, 45.

24. Ian Davidson, "WEU to Play More Important Role in European Defense," *Financial Times,* 11 Dec. 1990, 3. The WEU grew to ten members in November 1992 with the accession of Greece. See *Strategic Survey 1993–1994* (London: Brassey's for the International Institute of Strategic Studies, 1994), 115.

25. Cited in "A Euro Jigsaw Puzzle for George Bush to Solve," *Economist,* 30 Mar. 1991, 23–24. This message from the United States to its European allies was drafted by a senior State Department official but probably prompted by the National Security Council. When it provoked irritation verging on outrage (even the British government thought it overdone), it became known in Washington as the "Bartholomew letter" (as if it were a personal message from Undersecretary of State for Security Affairs Reginald Bartholomew). The episode is reminiscent of the flap caused by a monitory letter sent in 1985 by then Assistant Secre-

tary of State Richard Burt, when the WEU was being revived.

26. In the European Army discussions, Germany first proposed a national corps; the French insisted that a European division must contain at least two nations' forces. The compromise reached, with the aid of General Dwight Eisenhower, was a mixed corps made up of national divisions. See Edward Fursdon, *The European Defense Community: A History* (New York: St. Martin's Press, 1980), 123–24.

Chapter 4 — NATO: Triumph and Tragedy

1. Charles M. Spofford, foreword to Harold van Buren Cleveland, *The Atlantic Idea and Its European Rivals* (New York: McGraw-Hill, 1966), xiii. Henry Kissinger has recently expressed a quite different point of view. He criticizes the tendency of the Clinton administration to talk either in global terms or in terms of a "Pacific Community." The latter, he says, does not exist, whereas a community of values does exist between the United States and Europe—by which he clearly means Western Europe. If we cannot preserve an alliance with that like-minded area, we shall be left alone in the world and condemned to pursue a purely *Realpolitik* policy uncongenial to American traditions. See Kissinger, *Diplomacy* (New York: Simon and Schuster, 1994), 810–11, 819, 826, 828, 831. In my view, Kissinger is right in this, but the links between Western European countries are even closer than the transatlantic connection.

2. John Lewis Gaddis, "Toward the Post-Cold War World," *Foreign Affairs* 70, no. 2 (Spring 1991): 116.

3. *Strategic Survey 1993–1994* (London: Brassey's for the International Institute for Strategic Studies, 1994), 117. For the text of the NATO PfP decision, see paragraphs 13–16 of the "Declaration of the Heads of State and Government Participating in the Meeting of the North Atlantic Council Held at NATO Headquarters, Brussels, 10–11 January 1994," published in *Survival* 36, no. 1 (Spring 1994): 162–67. The PfP was aimed at states that had been part of the former Soviet bolc, but some other European non-NATO countries have decided to participate.

4. The Visegrad states are the Czech Republic, Hungary, Poland, and Slovakia.

5. Roger Cohen, "Yeltsin Opposes Extension of NATO to Eastern Europe," *New York Times,* 2 Oct. 1993, 4.

6. See Renée de Nevers, "Russia's Strategic Renovation," *Adelphi Paper* 289 (July 1994): 66; Jonathan Dean, *Ending Europe's Wars: The Continuing Search for Peace and Security* (New York: Twentieth Century Fund Press, 1994), 344–45; *Strategic Survey 1993–1994*, 117; and Istvan Szonyiu, "Security Challenges: The Case of Hungary" (Paper delivered at conference on "The Interaction of the EU and NATO," Rome, 21–22 Jan. 1994), 9.

7. Bruce Clark, "Russia Warns on Pace of Nato Expansion into East Europe," *Financial Times,* 23 June 1994, 18.

8. Bruce Clark and Laura Silber, "Russia Warns NATO on Eastern Expansion, *Financial Times,* 2 Dec. 1994, 1; Elaine Sciolino, "Conflict in the Balkans: In Brussels, U.S. and NATO Say Dispute on Bosnia War Is Resolved," *New York Times,* 2 Dec. 1994, A14; Daniel Williams, "Russian Minister Balks at NATO's Expansion Plans," *Washington Post,* 2 Dec. 1994, A33.

9. Daniel Williams, "Yeltsin, Clinton Clash over NATO's Role," *Washington Post,* 6 Dec. 1994, A1; Bruce Clark and Virginia Marsh, "Yeltsin Hits at Nato Plan to Expand Eastwards," *Financial Times,* 6 Dec. 1994, 1; Elaine Sciolino, "Yeltsin Says NATO Is Trying to Split Continent Again," *New York Times,* 6 Dec. 1994, A1.

10. Other factors contributed to the strain, most notably Western distress at and criticism of the Russian suppression of the rebellion in Chechnya.

11. Ann Devroy and Fred Hiatt, "U.S., Russia Cite Discord at Summit," *Washington Post,* 11 May 1995; Chrystia Freeland and Bruce Clark, "Summit Fails to Narrow Gap over Nato," *Financial Times,* 11 May 1995, 2. The formal dialogue between NATO and Russia began on 31 May 1995. Kozyrev did not fail to note that "hasty resolution" of the NATO expansion issue could threaten Russian-NATO relations and Russia's involvement in the PfP. See Michael Dobbs, "NATO Has Initial Talks with Russia," *Washington Post,* 1 June 1995, A1; and "A Russian Grunt," *Economist,* 3 June 1995, 45.

12. The Visegrad countries—the Czech Republic, Hungary, Poland, and Slovakia—are not only the most ardent suitors of membership in NATO but also the most attractive candidates under consideration by NATO for membership. Albania, Bulgaria, Romania, and Slovenia (but not the other countries of the former Yugo-

slavia) are interested in membership. (While they are not part of Eastern Europe in this sense, it is worth noting that the Baltic states, formerly part of the Soviet Union, are also interested.)

13. *Strategic Survey 1993–1994,* 9–10.

14. For example, in his intervention to the opening meeting of the NACC, Secretary of State James Baker said, "the NACC could play a role in controlling crises in Europe. It might, for example, serve as a forum for communicating NATO crisis responses to liaison states, as well as give liaison states access to NATO when necessary." Cited in *U.S. Department of State Dispatch* 2, no. 51 (23 Dec. 1991): 903–4. Kissinger suggests giving the PfP's functions to the CSCE (and rebaptizing the latter the PfP). See *Diplomacy,* 825.

15. Manfred Woerner, cited in Richard Weitz, "Pursuing Military Security," in *After the Cold War: International Institutions and State Strategies in Europe, 1989–1991,* ed. Robert O. Keohane, Joseph S. Nye, and Stanley Hoffmann (Cambridge: Harvard University Press, 1993), 344–45. Woerner, appointed secretary general of NATO in 1988, died in office in August 1994.

16. Edward Fursdon, *The European Defense Community: A History* (New York: St. Martin's Press, 1980), 123–24.

17. Quentin Peel, "Kohl Reveals Vision of European Defense Identity," *Financial Times,* 7 Nov. 1991, 3.

18. Manfred Woerner, cited in Jude Webber, "NATO Chief Rules Out Role for a New European Force," *Boston Globe,* 22 Oct. 1991, 19.

19. After saying "Our premise is that the American role in the defense and the affairs of Europe will not be made superfluous by European union," President George Bush departed from his prepared remarks to add: "If our premise is wrong, if, my friends, your ultimate aim is to provide individually for your own defense, the time to tell us is today." This statement produced European assurances of support for the presence of U.S. forces in Europe. See Alan Cowell, "Bush Challenges Partners in NATO over Role of U.S.," *New York Times,* 8 Nov. 1991, A1. However, the summit failed to sort out the relationship between NATO, the WEU, and the EC. See the following articles in *Financial Times*: Robert Mauthner and Lionel Barber, "US Seeks EC Defense Pledge," 8 Nov. 1991, 1; Mauthner and Barber, "Nato Fails to Agree to Future Defence Framework,"

9–10 Nov. 1991, 24; Ian Davidson, "An Innovative Bit of Theatre," 11 Nov. 1991, 32; and "Nato's Role in Europe," 11 Nov. 1991, 14.

20. Woerner is quoted, and van Eekelen's views are cited, in *Strategic Survey 1993–1994*, 115.

21. Alain Juppé, cited in Anand Menon, "From Independence to Cooperation: France, NATO, and European Security," *International Affairs* 71, no. 1 (Jan. 1995): 29.

22. Paul R. S. Gebhard, "The United States and European Security," *Adelphi Paper* 286 (Feb. 1994): 21–23.

23. For a plan for a U.S. force in Europe of 75,000, including some relatively small ground-combat units, see Don M. Snider, "US Military Forces in Europe: How Low Can We Go?" *Survival* 34, no. 4 (Winter 1992–93): 24–39.

24. Alan Riding, "Foreigners Hope Clinton Keeps Policy," *New York Times*, 5 Nov. 1992, B10. Even before the Clinton administration had time to develop and implement its new defense policy, U.S. strength in Europe had been significantly reduced—from 324,000 before the fall of the Berlin Wall to 187,000 in early March 1993. NATO Secretary General Woerner greeted the 100,000 troop target with "satisfaction": "The new Administration . . . has no intention of going below that number, at least not before 1996. And 1996 is far away." Quoted in "U.S. Affirms Plan for a 40% Troop Cut in Europe," *New York Times*, 30 Mar. 1993, A5. See also "Les Etats-Unis vont évacuer vingt-huit nouvelles bases militaires en Europe," *Le Monde*, 14–15 Mar. 1993, 20.

25. Stationing troops in Europe added ten percent to the basic operating cost, as of 1992. Japan and Korea, on the other hand, are covering all added costs; it may, indeed, be cheaper to base U.S. forces in those countries than in the U.S. See Gebhard, "The United States and European Security," esp. 3, 14, 47, 49–52, 58–60.

26. For a similar judgment, see Sidney Blumenthal and James Chace, "Memo to the Democrats," *New York Times Magazine*, 23 Feb. 1992, 33; and "Why Not a French-German Army?" *New York Times*, 21 Oct. 1991, A16.

27. The January 1994 NATO Summit Declaration says: "We give our full support to the development of a European Security and Defence Identity. . . . The emergence of a European Security and Defence Identity will strengthen the European pillar of the Alliance while reinforcing the transatlantic link and will enable European

allies to take greater responsibility for their common security and defence." See paragraph 4, "Declaration of . . . 10–11 January 1994," in *Survival* 36, no. 1 (Spring 1994): 163.

CHAPTER 5 — CAN EUROPEAN SECURITY BE BASED ON THE OSCE?

1. "A Club for All Europe," *Economist,* 17 Nov. 1990, 20. For rather the same idea, expressed less aphoristically, see Charles L. Glaser, "Why NATO Is Still Best: Future Security Arrangements for Europe," *International Security* 18, no. 1 (Summer 1993): 5–51, esp. 28–29.

2. In December of 1994, the name was changed from the Conference on Security and Cooperation in Europe to the Organization for Security and Cooperation in Europe.

3. As Gregory Treverton put it, the CSCE "has turned out to be an artefact of the Cold War; it was useful when the purpose was formally reassuring communist leaders about the sanctity of their borders, while informally subverting them through humanitarian and other East-West contacts." See Treverton, "America's Stakes and Choices in Europe," *Survival* 34, no. 3 (Autumn 1992): 123–24.

4. Jonathan Dean, *Ending Europe's Wars: The Continuing Search for Peace and Security* (New York: Twentieth Century Fund Press, 1994), 214–15.

5. Frederick Kempe, "Eastern European Nations Edging Closer to NATO," *Wall Street Journal,* 15 Feb. 1991, A9.

6. Hans Dietrich Genscher, cited in Robert Mauthner, "CSCE Agrees Procedure for Dealing with Crises," *Financial Times,* 21 June 1991, 2.

7. Robert Mauthner, "CSCE Officials Seek Ways to Defuse Crisis," *Financial Times,* 3 July 1991, 2; Robert Mauthner and Ariane Genillard, "CSCE Calls for Immediate End to Hostilities," *Financial Times,* 4 July 1991, 2; and Mauthner and Genillard, "Moscow Joins Belgrade to Block CSCE Mission," *Financial Times,* 5 July 1991, 2.

8. "War in Europe," *Economist,* 6 July 1991, 13.

9. Judy Dempsey, "CSCE Does Its Best to Rise to the Occasion," *Financial Times,* 8 Aug. 1991, 2; Judy Dempsey and David Gardner, "Genscher Says Yugoslav Peace Talks Must Start," *Financial Times,* 15 Aug. 1991, 2.

10. Eliasson is quoted in Richard Weitz, "The CSCE and the Yugoslav Conflict," *RFE/RL Research Report,* 31 Jan. 1992, 25–26.

11. Douglas Hurd, cited in John Lloyd and Mark Nicholson, "West Calls for Intervention Powers in East Europe," *Financial Times,* 11 Sept. 1991, 20.

12. Russia had already taken over the USSR seat, and the three Baltic republics had already been admitted; at this point, only chaotic Georgia remained outside the spreading CSCE tent.

13. Thomas L. Friedman, "10 Former Soviet Republics Join Human Rights Group," *New York Times,* 31 Jan. 1992, A9.

14. Robert Mauthner, "CSCE to Gain Ten New Members," *Financial Times,* 30 Jan. 1992, 2.

15. Vaclav Havel, cited in Thomas L. Friedman, "10 Former Soviet Republics Join Human Rights Group," A9.

16. Friedman, "10 Former Soviet Republics Join Human Rights Group," A9.

17. Genscher, cited in Ariane Genillard, "Stronger Security Role Urged for CSCE," *Financial Times,* 31 Jan. 1992, 3.

18. "Les pays membres de la CSCE décident de modifier la règle de l'unanimité dans des cas 'très graves,'" *Le Monde,* 1 Feb. 1992, 6.

19. John Kornblum, chief U.S. delegate to the 1992 CSCE review conference, said in a television broadcast that "the US would probably find it useful if Nato was one of the agencies for providing troops for the CSCE." Cited in Robert Mauthner, "US Says CSCE Could Use NATO Force," *Financial Times,* 26 Feb. 1992, 2.

20. Edward Mortimer, "Europe's Security Surplus," *Financial Times,* 3 Mar. 1992, 11.

21. Cited in Craig R. Whitney (*New York Times*), "NATO Offers Its Help in Trouble Spots," *International Herald Tribune,* 5 June 1992, 1. See also Robert Mauthner, "Nato Agrees to Peacekeeping Role in Europe," *Financial Times,* 5 June 1992, 4.

22. Robert Mauthner, "WEU Prepares to Strap on Some Weapons," *Financial Times,* 19 June 1992, 2. See also Craig R. Whitney, "WEU Seeks to Tighten Embargo of Serbia," *International Herald Tribune,* 20–21 June 1992, 2.

23. See extensive reporting in the press of 9–11 July 1992.

24. Robert Mauthner and Judy Dempsey, "West to Send Air-sea Force on Serbian Sanctions Patrol," *Financial Times*, 11 July 1992, 1.

25. Craig R. Whitney, "Belgrade Suspended by European Security Group," *New York Times*, 9 July 1992, A13; Francine Kiefer, "CSCE Seeks to Streamline Its Organization in Bid for More-Decisive Role," *Christian Science Monitor*, 9 July 1992, 1; Mauthner and Dempsey, "West to Send Air-sea Force on Serbian Sanctions Patrol," 1.

26. See "Into the Bosnian Quagmire," *Independent*, 11 July 1992, 14; "Stabilising Europe," *Financial Times*, 9 July 1992, 20; and "Watch This Space," *Economist*, 18 July 1992, 49.

27. Claire Tréan, "Le Sommet d'Helsinki a révélé la peur des Occidentaux d'être entraînés dans le conflit," *Le Monde*, 12–13 July 1992, 3.

28. For a similar judgment—the "CSCE should really have organized the conference held . . . at the initiative of . . . [French Prime Minister Edouard] Balladur"—see Dean, *Ending Europe's Wars*, 236. On the Balladur Plan, see *Strategic Survey 1993–1994* (London: Brassey's for the International Institute for Strategic Studies, 1994), 112; David Buchan, "New French Pact Aims to Avoid 'Second Yugoslavia,'" *Financial Times*, 10 June 1993, 2. Despite some watering down by the time a meeting to pursue the Balladur idea was held in Paris in May 1994, the proposal was met with skepticism by participants and observers, be they Russian, Central European, or American. See "Bilan mitigé pour la conférence sur la stabilité en Europe," *Le Monde*, 29–30 May 1994, 5; Sophie Shihab and Yves-Michel Riols, "La Russie réserve un accueil mitigé au Pacte de stabilité en Europe," *Le Monde*, 28 May 1994, 3; Anthony Robinson and David Buchan, "Russia Rejects French Initiative," *Financial Times*, 27 May 1994, 2; and Stéphane Marchand, "Washington: 'Initiative bienvenue,'" *Le Figaro*, 27 May 1994, B-3. The concluding session of Balladur's Conference on Stability in Europe met in March 1995; attended by fifty-two of the members of the OSCE, it ended this long detour from the OSCE: participants agreed to deposit some one hundred bilateral and regional treaties with the OSCE, which was to monitor their implementation. See "Stability in Europe," *Financial Times*, 21 Mar. 1995, 15; and David Buchan, "France

Pushes for Bilaterals," *Financial Times*, 17 Mar. 1995, 3. This could propel the OSCE toward becoming a regional peacemaker. See "Whose Stability Pact?" *Economist*, 18 Mar. 1995, 55.

29. John Lloyd and Bruce Clark, "Russia, US Square Off over Security," *Financial Times*, 28 Nov. 1994, 2; Jane Perlez, "Unease at European Security Parley," *New York Times*, 5 Dec. 1994, A13; Bruce Clark and Virginia Marsh, "CSCE Agrees to Karabakh Peace Operation," *Financial Times*, 7 Dec. 1994, 2; "Europe's Post-post-cold-war Defences Wobble into Action," *Economist*, 10 Dec. 1994, 45–46; "Allies Again?" *Economist*, 6 May 1995, 13–14; Chrystia Freeland and Bruce Clark, "Summit Fails to Narrow Gap over Nato," *Financial Times*, 11 May 1995, 2. The "Western" view of the CSCE includes that of the Czech president, Vaclav Havel: the CSCE should not stand in the way of the association with NATO and the EU of states that were previously in the Soviet sphere of influence, but it can be an important vehicle for bringing East and West closer together and can, as well, be an instrument for conflict prevention through preventive diplomacy and for peacekeeping. See Havel, "A New European Order?" *New York Review of Books*, 2 Mar. 1995, 43–44.

30. See Richard Ullman's *Securing Europe* (Princeton: Princeton University Press, 1991), esp. 63–82 and 138–53.

31. See Dean, *Ending Europe's Wars*, 238–39.

32. Douglas Jehl, "Clinton Urging NATO Attacks to Deter Serbs," *New York Times*, 21 Apr. 1994, A1; Alexander MacLeod, "Russia and West Join Efforts to Find Peace Deal for Bosnia," *Christian Science Monitor*, 27 Apr. 1994, 1.

33. Henry Kissinger, *Diplomacy* (New York: Simon and Schuster, 1994), 825.

34. Havel, "A New European Order?" 43–44.

35. Mortimer, "Europe's Security Surplus," 11.

36. The WEU's role in the Gulf War cannot be described as operational, and the dispatch of a small WEU flotilla to the Adriatic in July 1992 hardly was a demonstration of significant operational capability. (It was convenient that the area of operation was so close to Italy, which was ready to provide support.) Even with the creation of a "planning cell" to focus on peacekeeping, humanitarian aid, and crisis management, the WEU falls far short of NATO's capability. See Lionel Barber and Kerin Hope, "Greece Welcomed into

Revived WEU," *Financial Times,* 20 Nov. 1992, 2; and "The Defence of Europe: It Can't Be Done Alone," *Economist,* 25 Feb. 1995, 19–21.

CHAPTER 6 — THE EUROPEAN UNION AS AN EMERGING ECONOMIC SUPERPOWER

1. Gerard Curzon, *Multilateral Commercial Diplomacy* (London: Michael Joseph, 1965), 98–105; Gary Clyde Hufbauer, ed., *Europe 1992: An American Perspective* (Washington: Brookings Institution, 1990), 3–5.

2. John E. Rielly, "The Public Mood at Mid-Decade," *Foreign Policy,* no. 98 (Spring 1995): 84, 87.

3. See C. Michael Aho, "'Fortress Europe': Will the EU Isolate Itself from North America and Asia?" *Columbia Journal of World Business* 29 (Fall 1994): 32–39. For the views of a British free trade advocate suspicious of EU protectionism, see Martin Wolf, *The Resistible Appeal of Fortress Europe* (Washington: Center for Policy Studies and American Enterprise Institute, 1994).

4. To be sure, worker participation was already the rule in Germany and some other European countries. But the Vredeling proposal would have extended it to other countries, e.g., the U.K., which, in the absence of EC legislation, would not have required it. Furthermore, there was fear that the home operations of American firms would be open to scrutiny as a result of worker participation in Europe.

5. In September 1994 the EU Commission issued a directive requiring all companies employing at least 1,000 workers within the EU and 150 in two or more member states to create an information and consultative committee for its employees throughout Europe. When in March 1995 American-based Ingersoll-Rand decided to comply, it angered other American companies with European operations, even though the September 1994 directive fell far short of the Vredeling and other proposals of the early 1980s to put workers on boards, in imitation of the German co-determination provisions. See Robert Taylor, "US Group Breaks Ranks on Works Councils," *Financial Times,* 29 Mar. 1995, 2.

6. See Philip H. Trezise, ed., *The European Monetary System: Its Promise and Prospects* (Washington: Brookings Institution, 1979), esp. the contributions of Ralph Bryant, Robert Solomon, Benjamin

J. Cohen, and William Fellner.

7. See Robert Triffin, "The American Response to the European Monetary System," in *The European Monetary System,* ed. Trezise, 68–69.

8. The contrast between European progress toward, and American backwardness with regard to, economic integration is discussed in Michael Prowse, "EC Ahead in Trade Stakes," *Financial Times,* 28 Oct. 1991, 32. On banking legislation, see Keith Bradsher, "Bank Bill Is Cleared for Vote: Measure to Allow Interstate Branches," *New York Times,* 26 July 1994, D1; "American Banks Outward Bound," *Economist,* 30 July 1994, 70; and "The Struggle to Reform America's Banking System," *Economist,* 6 Aug. 1994, 59–60.

9. The European Economic Area Treaty was signed in May 1992. Only eighteen nations (the twelve members of the EC and six of the seven members of the European Free Trade Area) wound up taking part in the EEA, because Switzerland rejected the EEA in a December 1992 referendum.

10. John T. Woolley, "Policy Credibility and European Monetary Institutions," in *Euro-Politics: Institutions and Policymaking in the "New" European Community,* ed. Alberta M. Sbragia (Washington: Brookings Institution, 1992), 166–68.

11. "Policy Credibility and European Monetary Institutions," 174. Tommaso Padoa-Schioppa puts it similarly: the EU cannot simultaneously enjoy a single market for goods and service, complete capital liberalization, fixed exchange rates, and national monetary policy autonomy. One of these has to give; since the first three lead to gains in efficiency and savings in transaction costs, he urges the submergence of national monetary policy autonomy in a monetary union. Cited in Wayne Sandholtz, "Monetary Politics and Maastricht," *International Organization* 47, no. 1 (Winter 1993): 20.

12. Karl Otto Pohl, cited in Woolley, "Policy Credibility and European Monetary Institutions," 175.

13. Cited by Quentin Peel, "German Nerves at Loss of D-mark," *Financial Times,* 12 Dec. 1991, 3. In early 1995, German Finance Minister Theo Waigel supported recent assertions by the Bundesbank that the German electorate, skeptical about a single European currency, would find it difficult to accept one called the "ECU." (The

European Currency Unit (ECU) has lost a third of its value against the deutsche mark over the last twenty years.) See David Marsh, "Waigel Fuels Anti-Ecu Sentiment," *Financial Times,* 19 Feb. 1995, 2. Names that are more Germanic than "ECU," such as "franken," have been suggested for the single currency; see "European Monetary Union: Fazed," *Economist,* 3 June 1995, 69.

14. Dominique Moïsi and Michael Mertes, "Europe's Map, Compass, and Horizon," *Foreign Affairs* 74, no. 1 (Jan.–Feb. 1995): 131.

15. The mechanism was preserved in attenuated form by expanding the permitting zone of fluctuation around the central rate from plus-or-minus 2.25 percent to 15 percent.

16. The Spanish peseta and the Portuguese escudo were devalued on 6 March 1995. The French franc has had periodic difficulties. However, other currencies, in the "D-mark" bloc—such as the Dutch guilder, the Belgian franc, and the Austrian schilling—have remained very tightly linked to the deutsche mark. See "A Funny New Emu," *Economist,* 4 Mar. 1995, 49–50; and a number of articles in the *Financial Times* of 7 March 1995, esp. Peter Norman and Lionel Barber, "A Test for the ERM, a Warning for the Emu"; and Tom Burns and Peter Wise, "Madrid Puts on a Brave Face," both on p. 2.

17. Woolley, "Policy Credibility and European Monetary Institutions," 158.

18. "Multi-speed Move to Union," *Financial Times,* 12 Dec. 1991, 14.

19. Wynne Godley had a point, as Hillenbrand notes, in asking whether an economic union with a single currency managed by an EU central bank can really function in the absence of any central political management or commensurate political institutions: without a federal government. See Martin J. Hillenbrand, "An Assessment of the EC Future," *Annals of the American Academy of Political and Social Sciences,* no. 531 (January 1994): 171. Hans Tietmeyer, who became president of the Bundesbank in 1993, said in a June 1994 interview that monetary union needed firm foundations, not only economic but also political: "In my view there must also be political conditions. That means a clear will to move in political solidarity. . . . In the long run, monetary union cannot and will not

survive without being embedded in a broad political, common environment." Cited in Richard Lambert, Christopher Parkes, and Quentin Peel, "Stability in a Storm-tossed World," *Financial Times,* 29 June 1994, 17.

20. True to form, ever ostrich-like, the U.S. Treasury essentially ignored the intra-European negotiations leading up to the Maastricht Treaty. See Mark M. Nelson, "Transatlantic Travails," *Foreign Policy,* no. 92 (Fall 1993): 82–83.

21. Study of the Directorate General for Economic and Financial Affairs, published as "One Market, One Money," *European Economy,* no. 44 (Oct. 1990): 11.

22. Daniel Gros and Niels Thygesen, "The Institutional Approach to Monetary Union in Europe," *Economic Journal* 100 (Sept. 1990): 927. The Commission study quoted in note 21, above, says, "With the ECU becoming a major international currency, there will be advantages for the Community as banks and enterprises conduct more of their international business in their own currency; moreover, the monetary authorities will be able to economize in external reserves and achieve some international seigniorage gains."

23. See Christopher Taylor, "EMU: The State of Play," *World Today* 51, no. 4 (Apr. 1995): 77–78.

24. "European Monetary Union: Fazed," *Economist,* 3 June 1995, 69.

25. Former Bundesbank President Pohl would have gone further: "Those countries which are willing and able to establish a currency union with a strong central bank and single currency should do so, not in 1997 or 1999 [as in the Maastricht Treaty] but in the near future." Pohl acknowledged that his proposal would amount to a "two-speed Europe"—which already existed. Germany, France, Benelux, Austria, and Switzerland were, in Pohl's judgment, already in a position to form a currency union. He also said that the September 1992 crisis strengthened the case for a single European central bank; continuation of the current German-led EMS would be more and more difficult as other countries' willingness to follow the Bundesbank's lead waned. See "Pohl Backs Union of Strong Currencies," *Financial Times,* 24 Sept. 1992, 3.

Pohl's successor at the Bundesbank, Helmut Schlesinger, poured cold water on the idea of a "mini" monetary union. See "Franc Fortified," *Economist,* 3 Apr. 1993, 72. But Schlesinger's successor, Hans Tietmeyer, has said, "I do not think it likely that monetary union will be possible with all the present or future members from the beginning." Cited in Richard Lambert, Christopher Parkes, and Quentin Peel, "Tietmeyer Stresses Need for Political Consensus," *Financial Times,* 29 June 1994, 1. Part of the generally favorable decision of the German Constitutional Court regarding the Maastricht Treaty could be a barrier to a monetary union of a subset of EU countries. See Michel Aglietta and Jean Pisani-Ferry, "Post-Collapse of the ERM: What Rules for the Game?" *International Economic Insights* 5, no. 1 (Jan.–Feb. 1994): 45–47.

26. On political and business elites, see Dick Leonard, "Eye on the EU," *Europe,* Dec.–Jan. 1993–94, 4; David Marsh, "An Elusive Corporate Consensus," *Financial Times,* 24 Feb. 1994, 10; Edgar S. Woolard, Jr. (Dupont's chief executive), "Europe Must Sharpen Competitive Edge," *Financial Times,* 12 July 1994, 15; and Helmut Werner (president of Mercedes-Benz), "Why Europe Needs a Single Currency," *Financial Times,* 26 May 1995, 13. On general attitudes, see Sandholtz, "Monetary Politics," esp. 26; and Richard C. Eichenberg and Russell J. Dalton, "Europeans and the European Community: The Dynamics of Public Support for European Integration," *International Organization* 47, no. 4 (Autumn 1993): 507–34. The *Economist* ("European Monetary Union: Fazed") states that in 1991 two-thirds of EU citizens thought there would be a single currency by the end of the century. By June 1994 fifty-one percent did. Significantly, in Germany, only a minority did.

In a poll conducted in Britain and Germany in November 1994 a large majority in each country favored a referendum on the introduction of a single currency by the EU. When asked how they would vote on such a referendum, only thirty-three percent in Britain and twenty-four percent in Germany said they would support a single currency. A majority in each country would oppose it. See David Marsh, "Poll Shows Support for Vote on EU Single Currency," *Financial Times,* 5 Dec. 1994, 1.

27. Christopher Taylor, "EMU: The State of Play," 78; Martin Wolf, "Does Emu Entail Political Union?" *Financial Times,* 20 Feb. 1995, 20.

CHAPTER 7 — THE "EUROPEAN UNION": POLITICAL UNION OR OVERREACH?

1. French Foreign Minister Robert Schuman told Dean Acheson in the autumn of 1951 that he had a political community in reserve "wider than the ECSC [European Coal and Steel Community] and the EDC [European Defense Community]" and that German Chancellor Konrad Adenauer and Italian Prime Minister Alcide De Gasperi were both pressing for one. De Gasperi also proposed that the future EDC Assembly draft a European constitution as a basis for negotiation by the governments. See François Duchêne, *Jean Monnet: The First Statesman of Interdependence* (New York: W. W. Norton, 1994), 234.

2. Robert Schuman, cited in Noel Malcolm, "The Case against 'Europe,'" *Foreign Affairs* 74, no. 2 (Mar.–Apr. 1995): 55. See also Duchêne's biography of Jean Monnet.

3. Walter Russell Mead, "Memo for a New Europe," review of *Jean Monnet: The First Statesman of Interdependence*, by François Duchêne, *Washington Post Book World*, 1 Jan. 1995, 7.

4. There is a continuum, from foreign policy to security policy to defense policy to defense, with the sensitivity of the issues—both within Europe and between Europe and the United States—growing from one step to another. See Anand Menon, Anthony Forster, and William Wallace, "A Common European Defence?" *Survival* 34, no. 3 (Autumn 1992): 99–100.

5. In the discussions leading up to the Maastricht Treaty, the British government resisted extension of qualified majority voting to the defense area with the argument that troops could not be sent to be killed by intergovernmental majorities. See Menon, Forster, and Wallace, "A Common European Defence?" 109.

6. For the complete text of the 19 April 1990 letter from Kohl and Mitterrand to the Irish government (which held the presidency of the EC) from which this quotation is drawn, see Finn Laursen and Sophie Vanhoonacker, eds., *The Intergovernmental Conference on Political Union* (Dordrecht, Netherlands: Martinus Nijhoff, 1992), 276.

7. David Bruce, cited in Dean Acheson, *Present at the Creation* (New York: W. W. Norton, 1969), 557.

8. Jean De Ruyt, *European Political Cooperation: Toward a Unified European Foreign Policy* (Washington: Atlantic Council of the United States, 1989), 14.

9. Ian Davidson, "WEU to Play More Important Role in European Defense," *Financial Times,* 11 Dec. 1990, 3.

10. Reason eventually prevailed. It was agreed in June 1993, at the first joint meeting of the WEU and NATO Councils, to merge the WEU force with the NATO units, under NATO command. See *Strategic Survey 1993–1994,* 114; and Trevor Taylor, "Western European Security and Defence Cooperation: Maastricht and Beyond," *International Affairs* 70, no. 1 (Jan. 1994): 6.

11. See Council of the European Communities, *Treaty on European Union* (Luxembourg: Office for Official Publications of the European Communities, 1992), ARTICLE J.4, and the "Declaration on Western European Union," annexed to the final Act of the Treaty and published with it. For a convenient textual source, see Richard Corbett, *The Treaty of Maastricht: From Conception to Ratification; A Comprehensive Reference Guide* (Harlow, U.K.: Longman Affairs, 1993), 431, 478–80. Also see "A Step towards 'Ever Closer Union,'" *Financial Times,* 12 Dec. 1991, 5; "Multi-speed Move to Union," *Financial Times,* 12 Dec. 1991, 14; Robert Mauthner, "Common Policy Relies on WEU," *Financial Times,* 12 Dec. 1991, 2; and Finn Laursen and Sophie Vanhoonacker, eds., *The Intergovernmental Conference on Political Union* (Dordrecht, Netherlands: Martinus Nijhoff, 1992).

12. "The Deal Is Done," *Economist,* 14 Dec. 1991, 52.

13. *Treaty on European Union,* ART. J (see Corbett, *Treaty of Maastricht,* 429–32); "A Step towards 'Ever Closer Union,'" *Financial Times,* 6.

14. Britain and Italy developed in the course of 1991 a rare tactical alliance against France and Germany regarding European defense, producing a paper in October 1991—a little ahead of the Franco-German proposals for a French-German based European force—which sought to avoid undermining NATO by emphasizing a European force that would act *outside* Europe. See George Brock and Michael Binyon, "Britain Accepts EC Goal of a United Policy on Defence," *Times* [London], 5 Oct. 1991, 7. The text of the "Anglo-Italian Declaration on Security and Defense" is in Laursen and Vanhoonacker, eds., *The Intergovernmental Conference on Political Union,* 413–14. See also John W. Holmes, "Italian Foreign Policy in a Changing Europe," in *Italian Politics,* vol. 8, ed. Gianfranco

Pasquino and Stephen Hellman (New York: Pinter, 1993), 165–77, esp. 168–70.

15. Quentin Peel, "Bonn Presses Euro Force Plan," *Financial Times*, 6 Feb. 1992, 1.

16. Hella Pick, "Britain Signals Doubts on Bonn-Paris Joint Force Plan," *Guardian* (London), 14 Feb. 1992, 8.

17. My sources are American diplomats whose names cannot be cited; a German diplomat, equally unnameable, commented that the alleged sensitivity of Americans to the Franco-German corps proposal seemed, based on congressional contacts, to be limited to the administration. One compensation, from a European point of view, was that the United States took a slightly more favorable view of the Western European Union, as more controllable and less dangerous than bilateral Franco-German machinations.

18. Alan Riding, "France Moves to Take Bigger Part in Defining New Role for NATO, *New York Times*, 30 Sept. 1992, A3; David Buchan and David White, "Joxe Urges Bigger French Role in Nato," *Financial Times*, 30 Sept. 1992, 3; "Joxe in Box," *Economist*, 3 Oct. 1992, 56. While Joxe ruled out a return to NATO's integrated military command, his statements both about the corps and about a change in France's empty seat approach to NATO military discussions were significant shifts in the French position. Joxe and the Ministry of Defense had been unhappy with France's isolated position, conscious both of the weaknesses of an autonomous French defense and of the advantages of cooperation with NATO. If Joxe felt free to say as much as he did, Mitterrand must have taken him off the leash.

19. This is the first case of French agreement to place French forces under NATO's operational command since de Gaulle pulled France out of the NATO's military structure in 1966. See Daniel Vernet, "Nouveau pas de Paris vers l'OTAN," *Le Monde*, 12 Mar. 1993, 1; and David Buchan, "Nato Blessing for the Eurocorps," *Financial Times*, 22 Jan. 1993, 2.

20. Jacques Delors, "European Integration and Security," *Survival* 32, no. 2 (Mar.–Apr. 1991): 99–109. Three years later, Delors wrote of the insufficiency of economic arguments in the face of the Yugoslav conflict and the need it demonstrated for a European "strategic planning and analysis capability." See his "European Unifica-

tion and European Security," *Adelphi Paper* 284 (Jan. 1994): 4–5.

21. Corbett, *The Treaty of Maastrich,* 385–86.

22. See, for example, Robert Mauthner, "Common Policy Relies on WEU," *Financial Times,* 12 Dec. 1991, 2.

23. Trevor Taylor, "A European Defense Entity: European Institutions and Defense," in *Europe in the Western Alliance: Towards a European Defense Entity?* ed. Jonathan Alford and Kenneth Hunt (New York: St. Martin's Press, 1988), 213.

24. Edith Cresson, cited in Michael Meimeth, "France Gets Closer to NATO," *World Today* 50, no. 4 (May 1994): 84.

25. Such a dialogue would perhaps not be entirely welcome to NATO members other than the U.S. and the EU: Canada, Iceland, Norway, and Turkey. At least one main motive for the Norwegian government's unsuccessful effort in 1994 to persuade its citizens to join the EU was its sense of the importance of being in on European political discussions. In the case of Turkey, the EU has suggested another way out, by offering it "full participation" but not membership in the WEU. See Robert Mauthner and David Gardner, "Defense Identity Takes Shape," *Financial Times,* 11 Dec. 1991, 2.

In fact, on the basis of a meeting of the WEU Council held parallel with the Maastricht Summit, not only Turkey but also Norway and Iceland have been granted associate membership in the WEU (and Denmark and Ireland are WEU observers). See the second declaration on WEU attached to the Maastricht Treaty; Arthur den Hartog, "Greece and European Political Union," in Laursen and Vanhoonacker, eds., *Intergovernmental Conference,* 95; *Strategic Survey 1993–1994,* 115; and Bruce Clark, "Old Enemies Make Tricky Friends," *Financial Times,* 9 June 1994, 15.

26. NATO agreed to limited activity in the former Yugoslavia in the early part of 1993. In February 1994 NATO threatened air strikes, and late that month, in the first combat action in the alliance's history, two NATO planes shot down four Serb planes. In succeeding months there were several other, collectively ineffectual, NATO air actions in the former Yugoslavia.

27. The Iraq crisis and the more recent Yugoslav tragedy are evidence that even when the EU can reach agreement at the rhetorical level, it still lacks the capability to *act* in a manner appropriate to such a challenge.

28. For a discussion of this and related subjects, see John W. Holmes, "U.S. Policy Options," in *Maelstrom: The United States, Southern Europe, and the Challenges of the Mediterranean,* ed. John W. Holmes (Cambridge, MA: World Peace Foundation, 1995), 213–35.

29. Perhaps the NATO initiative can be seen as the political-military complement to the EU's economic programs, but that still means the EU is not growing into an international political player. The EU seems to be slow in acting in the Middle East, partly because of French ambivalence about letting other countries involve themselves in what France still regards as "its" area, especially in Algeria. Thus, the French government early in February turned down a proposal by President Mitterrand for an EU-sponsored peace conference on Algeria. It is ironic—given the history of French relations with NATO—that also in February, France agreed to the NATO initiative. See Lionel Barber and Bernard Gray, "Nato Moves to Head Off Islamic Security Threat," *Financial Times,* 9 Feb. 1995, 1.

30. However, it was decided in December 1992 to wind up the IEPG and, as the Western European Armaments Group, incorporate it into the WEU. See Trevor Taylor, "Western European Security and Defence Cooperation," 4.

31. Combined Lockheed-Martin Marietta defense sales are about $17 billion. British Aerospace's 1993 defense sales were $5.86 billion. See "A Eurogun Is a Tricky Thing," *Economist,* 8 Apr. 1995, 53–54; and Yves Boyer, "Technologies, défense et relations transatlantiques," *Politique Etrangère,* no. 4 (Winter 1994–95): 1009.

32. See "Attack the Frontiers" and "A Eurogun Is a Tricky Thing," *Economist,* 8 Apr. 1995, 18 and 53 respectively.

33. Boyer, "Technologies, défense et relations transatlantiques," 1009–10.

34. "Attack the frontiers," *Economist,* 8 April 1995, 18, 20.

35. Lionel Barber, "EU Must End 'Rudderless' Foreign Policy," *Financial Times,* 28 Jan. 1995, 2; "Battle Lines over Defence," *Economist,* 4 Feb. 1995, 45–46.

36. A purely French-German armaments procurement agency was scheduled to begin operation in 1995. In February 1995 the U.K. countered, suggesting the creation of a European project office to run international weapons programs; if successful, it could evolve

into a European defense procurement agency. In March the U.K. was invited to join the Franco-German agency as a founder member. See Boyer, "Technologies, défense, et relations transatlantiques," 1009–10; Bernard Gray, "UK Floats Plan for European Weapons Agency," *Financial Times*, 27 Feb. 1995, 16; and Gray, "UK Invited to Join Planned Franco-German Arms Group," *Financial Times*, 28 Mar. 1995, 1.

37. "Attack the frontiers," 18.

38. Eisenhower was commissioned to answer this question during the EDC debate and confirmed the German view that units should be of one nationality through the division level, being integrated at the corps level (the French argued for integration at the division level). See Edward Fursdon, *The European Defense Community: A History* (New York: St. Martin's Press, 1980), 123–24. This is the choice recently made by NATO in restructuring its integrated forces.

39. Anand Menon, "From Independence to Cooperation: France, NATO, and European Security," *International Affairs* 71, no. 1 (Jan. 1995): 23.

40. Mitterrand's 1992 and 1991 statements are quoted in "La force d'Euro-frappe?" *Economist*, 18 Jan. 1992, 48. Delors's statement is quoted in Jacques Amatric, "La France suggère à ses partenaires une 'doctrine' nucléaire pour l'Europe, *Le Monde*, 12–13 January 1992, 1. See also Ian Davidson, "France Signals Reversal of Nuclear Weapons Doctrine," *Financial Times*, 11–12 January 1992, 1.

41. That these were Mitterrand's thoughts is the interpretation in "La force d'Euro-frappe?" 48.

42. Amalric, "La France suggère à ses partenaires d'étudier une 'doctrine' nucléaire pour l'Europe." Amalric also argued that the very nature of the French force was outdated by the disappearance of the Soviet threat.

43. David Buchan, "France Offers Talks with UK on Nuclear Weapons," *Financial Times*, 2 Oct. 1992, 2; "France-OTAN: le dogme en question," *Le Monde*, 4–5 Oct. 1992, 1.

44. Nicholas K. J. Whitney, "British Nuclear Policy after the Cold War," *Survival* 36, no. 4 (Winter 1994–95): 107.

45. Menon, "From Independence to Cooperation: France, NATO, and European Security," 27.

46. Alain Lamassoure, cited in David Buchan, "Nuclear Cover Urged for EU," *Financial Times,* 22 Dec. 1994, 2.

47. French Defense White Paper, February 1994, cited in David S. Yost, "Nuclear Debates in France," *Survival* 36, no. 4 (Winter 1994–95): 126.

48. Whitney, "British Nuclear Policy," 110. Neorealists expect Germany to acquire its own nuclear capability (and some think it would be a good thing). See for example Kenneth N. Waltz, "The Emerging Structure of International Politics," *International Security* 18, no. 2 (Fall 1993): 44–79, esp. 66. For a persuasive argument that Germany will postpone such choices, see Timothy Garton Ash, "Germany's Choice," *Foreign Affairs* 73, no. 4 (July–Aug. 1994): 65–81.

49. Hillary Barnes, "WEU Row Fuels Danish Debate on EC Treaties," *Financial Times,* 21 Feb. 1992, 3. The positive majority in the second Danish referendum of 18 May 1993 was achieved after the European Council decided in December 1992 to grant Denmark an exemption from the treaty in the area of defense policy (as well as monetary policy, European citizenship, and judicial and police affairs). See Mathias Jopp, "The Strategic Implications of European Integration," *Adelphi Paper* 290 (July 1994): 19.

50. Quentin Peel, "Franco-German Defence Proposal Comes under Attack," *Financial Times,* 10 Feb. 1992, 5. Richard Perle, an American participant, took a similar line.

51. In the words of Anand Menon, "France proved unwilling to make practical concessions to European cooperation that went beyond gesture politics." See Menon, "From Independence to Cooperation: France, NATO, and European Security," 23.

52. See "La maîtrise de l'arme nucléaire doit rester totalement entre les mains françaises," *Le Monde,* 14 Jan. 1992, 12. On the other hand, Mitterrand's statements drew this response from Jean François-Poncet, foreign minister under Giscard d'Estaing: "It is clear that at the end of the road of European solidarity there must be nuclear solidarity." See Amalric, "La France suggère . . . une 'doctrine nucléaire' pour l'Europe," 1.

53. See Jopp, "Strategic Implications of European Integration," esp. 29 and 47, concerning the meager contribution of the WEU to the Yugoslav crisis.

54. "The Defence of Europe: It Can't Be Done Alone," *Economist,* 25 Feb. 1995, 20.

55. *Strategic Survey 1993–1994,* 116.

56. Norway, another EFTA member (not a neutral, but a member of NATO), applied as well; negotiations with it also concluded in March 1994. However, the Norwegian voters rejected membership in a November 1994 referendum. (Norway's citizens had rejected EC membership once before, in 1972.)

57. David Gardner, "Oslo Begins High-stakes Game with EC," *Financial Times,* 6 Apr. 1993, 2; Gardner, "New Applicants to Give Up the Neutrality Habit," *Financial Times,* 2 Feb. 1993, 2. Austria, Sweden, and Finland acquired observer status in the WEU upon acceding to the EU (the other two EU members with observer status are Ireland and Denmark). In February 1995 Austria joined NATO's Partnership for Peace program.

58. "A Sea of Change," *Economist,* 14 Mar. 1992, 55.

59. The East Central European nations to which the EU first offered association agreements are the Czech Republic, Bulgaria, Hungary, Poland, Romania, and Slovakia. Albania has a cooperation agreement (a rung down)—as do (as of early 1995) Belarus, Kirghizstan, Moldova, Russia, and the Ukraine.

60. Steel, textiles, and agricultural products—the exports in which the East European states are most competitive—are subject to limitations.

61. Judy Batt, "The Political Transformation of East Central Europe," in *Redefining Europe: New Patterns of Conflict and Cooperation,* ed. Hugh Miall (New York: Pinter, 1994), 45.

62. As a result of the Maastricht negotiations, all members of the European Union are eligible for membership in the WEU, with its strong mutual defense provision. See Trevor Taylor, "Western European Security and Defence Cooperation," 3. The defense of a non-NATO WEU member by the other WEU members, most of which are members of NATO, could in turn trigger NATO's mutual assistance provision, posing a critical problem for non-EU members of NATO, like the U.S.

63. The agreements were signed on 12 June 1995. Slovenia (the only remaining state currently under EU consideration for an association agreement) hoped to sign its agreement later in June. See

"Baltic States Sign EU Accords," *Financial Times,* 13 June 1995, 2; and Dominique Moïsi and Michael Mertes, "Europe's Map, Compass, and Horizon," *Foreign Affairs* 74, no. 1 (Jan.–Feb. 1995): 125–26.

64. Moïsi and Mertes, "Europe's Map, Compass, and Horizon," 127.

65. Christopher Parkes, "Hungarians and Czechs Set Their Eyes on 2000," *Financial Times*, 12 Dec. 1994, 2.

66. Jacques Santer, in "Santer Backs EU Expansion to East," *Financial Times*, 13 Dec. 1994, 2.

67. Part of Greece's price for the conclusion of the EU-Turkey customs union in March 1995 was the EU's agreement to begin accession negotiations with Cyprus (and Malta) within six months after the end of the 1996 intergovernmental conference. However, Cyprus's admission to the EU depends upon a settlement of the conflict between Greek and Turkish Cypriots that broke out in 1974. See Philippe Lemaitre, "L'Europe conclut une union douanière avec la Turquie," *Le Monde,* 8 Mar. 1995, 2.

68. Turkey is a particularly difficult case. It very much wants to enter the EU, and it is already a member of NATO. There is a serious question of how to collocate Turkey, to find some sort of European framework for it, so not to leave it vulnerable to pressure to "go Islamic." Yet the resistance of the current EU member states to Turkey's entry is evident. While Turkey, like some other applicants, has been handled by having consideration of its application postponed, there is a difference. The eventual EU attitude toward some other present or potential applicants will be positive, but it would take a revolution in attitudes for Turkey—which is regarded as "non-European" or Islamic—to be accepted. Turkey makes its own prospects worse by human rights violations, especially involving the Kurds. A useful step but hardly a definitive solution, the customs union between the EU and Turkey—agreed to in March 1995—was conditional upon Turkey's improving its human rights performance before the effective date of the pact, 1 January 1996. See Lemaitre, "L'Europe conclut une union douanière avec la Turquie"; Nicole Pope, "Ankara se félicite de l'accord de Bruxelles," *Le Monde,* 8 Mar. 1995, 2; John Barham, "Treaty Sends Turkey Westwards," *Financial Times,* 7 Mar. 1995, 4; and "Turkey Can Be Part of Europe," *Economist,* 1 Apr. 1995, 13–14.

69. On the need to find a new confederal framework for the former Yugoslavia, see Flora Lewis, "Reassembling Yugoslavia," *Foreign Policy,* no. 98 (Spring 1995): 132–44.

70. In March 1993 the EC offered Russia the prospect of an eventual free trade agreement. An EU-Russian "partnership agreement" was signed in June 1994; it offers the prospect of a free trade area at the turn of the century, but there is no sign this is the prelude to Russian membership of the EU. See David Gardner, "Brussels Explains Trade Plan for Moscow," *Financial Times,* 25 Mar. 1993, 2; and Lionel Barber, "Yeltsin Signs Plan to Bring Russia Back into Europe," *Financial Times,* 25–26 June 1994, 2.

71. Michael Rühle and Nicholas Williams, "NATO Enlargement and the European Union," *World Today* 51, no. 5 (May 1995): 87. Michael Stürmer notes that "it is not clear that the Russians appreciate the intimate connection between the WEU and Nato. Through their overlapping membership and mutual security guarantees, WEU members are in practice covered by the Nato defence umbrella." Stürmer also argues (correctly in my view) that "it would be far-fetched to bring them [the Baltic republics] into Nato's fold, not least for reasons of history, geo-political strategy and credibility. While they should be given every sign of friendship, this should stop short of full membership of the EU because of its implications for the WEU." See Stürmer, "The Need for a Grand Design," *Financial Times,* 13 June 1995, 16.

72. On Russia's military capability, see Benjamin S. Lambeth, "Russia's Wounded Military, *Foreign Affairs* 74, no. 2 (Mar.–Apr. 1995): 86–98.

73. Clinton argued at the January 1994 NATO Summit that the alliance could not "draw a new line between East and West" that might foreclose "the best possible future for Europe, which is a democracy everywhere, . . . people cooperating everywhere for mutual security." Cited in Henry Kissinger, *Diplomacy* (New York: Simon and Schuster, 1994), 824.

74. The opening shot was Ronald D. Asmus, Richard L. Kugler, and F. Stephen Larrabee, "Building a New NATO," *Foreign Affairs* 72, no. 4 (Sept.–Oct. 1993): 28–40. They refined their argument in "NATO Expansion: The Next Steps," *Survival* 37, no. 1 (Spring 1995): 7–33. For references to most of the statements on the subject, see Michael E. Brown, "The Flawed Logic of NATO Ex-

pansion," *Survival* 37, no. 1 (Spring 1995): 34–52. Two articles subsequent to Brown's survey are Michael Mandelbaum, "Preserving the Peace: The Case against NATO Expansion," *Foreign Affairs* 74, no. 3 (May–June 1995): 9–13; and Karl-Heinz Kamp, "The Folly of Rapid NATO Expansion," *Foreign Policy,* no. 98 (Spring 1995): 116–31.

75. The statement is taken from the communiqué of the summit, as cited in Rühle and Williams, "NATO Enlargement and the European Union," 88.

76. Barry James, "Poll Reveals Concern about EC Security," *International Herald Tribune,* 15 Mar. 1993, 1.

77. Menon, Forster, and Wallace, "A Common European Defence?" 108.

78. Raymond Vernon, personal communication, 26 December 1992. For a pre-Maastricht discussion of the European Community's deficiently democratic processes, see Shirley Williams, "Sovereignty and Accountability in the European Community," in *The New European Community: Decision-making and Institutional Change,* ed. Robert O. Keohane and Stanley Hoffmann (Boulder: Westview Press, 1991), 155–76.

79. Delors, cited in Howard LaFranchi, "EC Seen Falling Short in Economic, Foreign Policy," *Christian Science Monitor,* 7 Apr. 1993, 8.

80. Moïsi and Mertes, "Europe's Map, Compass, and Horizon," 124. Part of the explanation is European economic recovery, often associated with a rebound in the EU's fortunes. This correlation is charted in Graham Bishop, "EMU Is Still Alive," *Financial Times,* 7 Mar. 1994, 22; and Peter Norman, "Debate on EMU Timing Hots Up," *Financial Times,* 28 Nov. 1994, 18. Western Europe's economies, after doing poorly in 1991–1993, began recovering in 1994 and were strong in 1995, with the recovery predicted to continue through 1996.

CHAPTER 8 — U.S. INTERESTS

1. See, for example, Stephen M. Walt, "U.S. Grand Strategy for the 1990s: The Case for Finite Containment," in *U.S. National Security Strategy for the 1990s,* ed. Daniel J. Kaufman, David S. Clark, and Kevin P. Sheehan (Baltimore: Johns Hopkins University Press, 1991), 136–66.

2. Senator Bob Dole, leader of the Republican majority in the

Senate, in early 1995 gave a similar definition of U.S. interests. His list began with "preventing the domination of Europe by a single power" and "maintaining a balance of power in East Asia." He correctly added "preserving access to natural resources, especially in the energy heartland of the Persian Gulf." For him, America's other three core interests are maintaining security and stability in our hemisphere, strengthening international free trade and U.S. access to markets, and protecting American citizens and property overseas. See Bob Dole, "Shaping America's Global Future," *Foreign Policy,* no. 98 (Spring 1995): 35.

3. George F. Kennan, *Memoirs: 1925–1950* (Boston: Little, Brown, 1967), 359.

4. While these are the core interests of the United States, it is a fact that many of our military adventures of the postwar period have, especially in retrospect, little connection with these interests. And saying oil is important to the world and the United States does not mean that actions like our military intervention against Saddam Hussein are the only, or the best, way of dealing with the oil security problem.

5. As Kissinger puts it, "Geopolitically, American is an island off the shores of . . . Eurasia, whose resources and population far exceed those of the United States. The domination by a single power of either of Eurasia's principal spheres—Europe or Asia—remains a good definition of strategic danger for America, Cold War or no Cold War." See Henry Kissinger, *Diplomacy* (New York: Simon and Schuster, 1994), 813.

6. Patrick E. Tyler, "U.S. Strategy Plan Calls for Insuring No Rivals Develop," *New York Times,* 8 Mar. 1992, sec. 1, p. 1.

7. Evidently the paper was not agreed to by either the U.S. State Department or the National Security Advisor.

8. Council of the North Atlantic Treaty Organization, cited in *Documents on American Foreign Relations, Vol. XII, January 1–December 31, 1950,* ed. Raymond Dennett and Robert K. Turner (Boston: Princeton University Press for World Peace Foundation, 1951), 213.

9. *Documents on American Foreign Relations, Vol. XII,* 215.

10. See Benjamin S. Lambeth, "Russia's Wounded Military, *Foreign Affairs* 74, no. 2 (Mar.–Apr. 1995): 86–98.

11. Philip Zelikow puts it rather similarly: except for the Ukraine

and the Baltic States, U.S. stakes in the former USSR are at the moment limited. See Zelikow, "Beyond Boris Yeltsin," *Foreign Affairs* 73, no. 1 (Jan.–Feb. 1994): 51–52.

12. Graham Allison and Robert Blackwill, "America's Stake in the Soviet Future," *Foreign Affairs* 70, no. 3 (Summer 1991): 78.

13. Allison and Blackwill also argued that "Soviet conventional forces—from three to four million soldiers and the largest weapons arsenal in the world—will still be capable of threatening Europe in the absence of an American guarantee" (see "America's Stake," 85). By 1995 Russian armed forces had shrunk to perhaps 1.5 million (see Fred Hiatt, "Russian House Votes Longer Draft Term," *Washington Post*, 8 Apr. 1995, A21). A high proportion are officers and many—perhaps most—units are incapable of military operations, and its military airlift capability is limited. As Benjamin Lambeth has written, "Today it is unlikely that Russia, with its decimated and poorly supported conventional forces, could mount a large scale cross-border operation against a well-equipped opponent. Its logistics system has been stretched to the breaking point just to sustain some 40,000 troops bogged down in Chechnya. See Lambeth, "Russia's Wounded Military," 90. See also Michael E. Brown, "The Flawed Logic of NATO Expansion," *Survival* 37, no. 1 (Spring 1995): 36.

14. See "Why Aid to Russia?" *Washington Post*, 28 May 1995, C6.

15. See Zbigniew Brzezinski, "The Premature Partnership," *Foreign Affairs* 73, no. 2 (Mar.–Apr. 1994): 67–82.

16. In early 1992 it was reported that the Pentagon had, to justify a substantial active force, come up with a list of "illustrative" threats, one of which is an invasion of Lithuania through Poland by a Russian-Belarus coalition; the Defense Department scenario was said to call for a massive NATO response, including a U.S. contribution of seven divisions. Distressing though such an invasion would be, especially because of the detail of armed movement through Poland, one wonders not only how realistic a basis there was for the Pentagon's scenario but also why the Pentagon so quickly assumed that a NATO response would be called for. See Patrick E. Tyler, "Pentagon Imagines New Enemies to Fight in Post-Cold-War Era," *New York Times*, 17 Feb. 1992, A1; and Tyler, "War in 1990's? Doubt on Hill," *New York Times*, 18 Feb. 1992, A1.

On the matter of Brzezinski's prescription of a U.S. policy of pursuing geopolitical pluralism within the ex-USSR, Philip H. Gordon responds that it is chimerical to believe in the possibilities of geopolitical independence of the non-Russian former Soviet republics and that it is equally implausible the U.S. would intervene on their side. See Gordon, "Who Will Guard the Russians?" *Foreign Affairs* 73, no. 3 (May–June 1994): 177–78.

17. From a speech by John Quincy Adams on 4 July 1823, during and referring to the movements for South American and Greek independence; cited in George F. Kennan, "On American Principles," *Foreign Affairs* 74, no. 2 (Mar.–Apr. 1995): 118.

18. Both the West and Russia may have exaggerated the significance of Chechnya as a precedent. Chechnya resisted the tsarist empire for half of the nineteenth century. It is one of only four non-Russian republics in the Russian Federation where the local ethnic group includes more than fifty percent of the population, and none of the others could go it alone. See "Make Peace in Chechnya," *Economist,* 10 June 1995, 14. It is encouraging that Russia in the spring of 1995 consented to OSCE mediation. See "OSCE to Mediate Chechen Talks," *Washington Post,* 23 May 1995, A10.

19. Lee Hockstader, "Moscow Says It May Use Force to Protect Russians in Ex-Soviet States," *Washington Post,* 19 Apr. 1995, A28; John Thornhill, "Kozyrev Remarks on Use of Force Fuel Fears in Ex-Soviet States," *Financial Times,* 21 Apr. 1995, 2; "The Bear's Jaws," *Economist,* 22 Apr. 1955, 54.

20. According to a poll conducted in late 1994, only twenty percent of the American public and twenty-one percent of American leaders would favor the use of U.S. troops if Russia invaded the Ukraine. See John E. Rielly, "The Public Mood at Mid-Decade," *Foreign Policy,* no. 98 (Spring 1995): 88, 90.

21. Matthew Kaminski, "Belarus Heads Back to Russian Fold," *Financial Times,* 16 May 1995, 3; Margaret Shapiro, "Belarus Voters Support Resumed Ties to Russia," *Washington Post,* 16 May 1995, A14.

22. Regarding the Ukraine, see Eugene B. Rumer, "Eurasia Letter: Will Ukraine Return to Russia?" *Foreign Policy,* no. 96 (Fall 1994): 129–44.

23. Fareed Zakaria, "Offer Russia a Peace of Vienna," *New York Times,* 9 May 1995, A27.

24. The G-7 summits have involved the seven leading industrialized nations of the western world: the U.S., Japan, Germany, France, the U.K., Italy, and Canada.

25. See Michael Dobbs and R. Jeffrey Smith, "U.S. Offers Assurances on NATO," *Washington Post,* 7 May 1995, A1. Clinton was trying to deal with Moscow's complaints that the effect of NATO expansion would be to draw new lines in Europe.

26. In February 1995 Secretary of Defense William Perry said that some Soviet bloc states would "never qualify for NATO membership" (cited in Dobbs and Smith, "U.S. Offers Assurances on NATO"). He certainly meant to include Russia among those states.

27. William Perry, interview on the "Diane Rehm Show," WAMU, Washington, D.C., 9 May 1995. Perry's reference to a "new Russia" implies a fundamentally changed—a stable, thoroughly democratic, and Western—Russia.

28. Zbigniew Brzezinski, "A Plan for Europe," *Foreign Affairs* 74, no. 1 (Jan.–Feb. 1995): 35.

29. Richard Holbrooke, "America, a European Power," *Foreign Affairs* 74, no. 2 (Mar.–Apr. 1995): 50–51. In March 1995 EU foreign ministers urged that NATO sign a nonaggression pact with Russia. See Tom Buerkle, "EU Urges NATO and Moscow to Make Treaty," *International Herald Tribune,* 20 Mar. 1995, 1; and Lionel Barber, "EU May Back Nato-Russia Pact," *Financial Times,* 20 Mar. 1995, 1.

30. Brzezinski, "A Plan for Europe," 35–36. As noted in chaps. 4 and 5 above, Clinton made a gesture toward using the OSCE as a venue for security consultations in his May 1995 meeting with Yeltsin, but evidently without making substantial progress.

31. Zakaria, "Offer Russia a Peace of Vienna," A27; Jane M. O. Sharp, "Tasks for NATO I: Move East and Revise the CFE," *World Today* 51, no. 4 (Apr. 1995): 67–70; Richard A. Falkenrath, "The CFE Flank Dispute, *International Security* 19, no. 4 (Spring 1995): 118–44.

32. Michael Rühle and Nicholas Williams, "NATO Enlargement and the European Union," *World Today* 51, no. 5 (May 1995): 88.

33. Rumer, "Will Ukraine Return to Russia?" 142–44.

34. See Karl-Heinz Kamp, "The Folly of Rapid NATO Expansion," *Foreign Policy,* no. 98 (Spring 1995): 122–23, 126; Michael

Mandelbaum, "Preserving the Peace: The Case Against NATO Expansion," *Foreign Affairs* 74, no. 3 (May–June 1995): 9–13 9–10; and Brown, "The Flawed Logic of NATO Expansion," 37–38.

35. For somewhat similar thoughts, see Robert Jervis, "The Future of World Politics: Will It Resemble the Past?" *International Security* 16, no. 3 (Winter 1991–92): 72.

36. A. J. P. Taylor, discussing the subdivision of the South Slavs into separate nations as the Ottoman Empire came to an end, wrote that the Turks' creation of an independent Bulgarian Church in 1870 "split [the Bulgarians] from the Serbs and thus inaugurated the disunity between the South Slavs which has persisted from that day to this. Yet on the basis of religion and political background, Bulgarians and Serbs were far more akin than Serbs, Croats, and Slovenes, between whom union has been successfully accomplished." See Taylor, *The Struggle for Mastery in Europe* (Oxford: Oxford University Press, 1954), 241. Aside from the uncharacteristically optimistic last phrase, Taylor's discussion was prophetic as well as historical.

37. Jacques Delors, "European Unification and European Security," *Adelphi Paper* 284 (Jan. 1994): 5.

38. These countries did, of course, contribute troops to UNPROFOR, the UN's "peacekeeping" force. And NATO did eventually provide support to that force.

39. The United States has displayed concern for the impact on its interests if the war in the former Yugoslavia spreads elsewhere—in particular, if such spread might provoke a general Balkan war involving Greece and Turkey, which are American allies and members of NATO. We have uttered warnings to Serbia about conditions in Kosovo and, more materially, stationed about five hundred troops in Macedonia as a deterrent to the war's spreading southward (and, presumably, a trip wire for more massive military invention should it do so). The EU has been less active in these regards. See Misha Glenny, "Heading Off War in the Southern Balkans," *Foreign Affairs* 74, no. 3 (May–June 1995): 98–108

40. A. J. P. Taylor, *The Struggle for Mastery in Europe*, 234.

41. I have expressed at greater length my view that the United States should not intervene in the former Yugoslavia. See John W. Holmes, "The US Is Half Right On Yugoslavia," *Christian Science Monitor,* 22 June 1992, 19. U.S. aircraft have, of course, participated in NATO air strikes in support of UNPROFOR.

42. For a thorough report on the influence of Central and Eastern European ethnic groups on American politics and policy, see Dick Kirschten, "Ethnics Resurging," *National Journal,* 25 Feb. 1995, 484–87.

43. Pat Towell, "House Votes to Sharply Rein In U.S. Peacekeeping Expenses," *Congressional Quarterly Weekly Report,* 18 Feb. 1995, 538.

44. See chap. 4, above. The pejorative catch phrase for opposition to NATO enlargement is "giving Russia a veto."

45. Evidence on public attitudes does not demonstrate more willingness to take military risks for the Visegrad states than for Bosnia. Americans have consistently opposed U.S. military involvement in Bosnia, where few think the U.S. has vital interests at stake. (There has been public support for our participation in peacekeeping, except when it was clear this risked American lives, and for our helping extract UN troops and hostages, but a varying response to the idea of U.S. air strikes, as opposed to committing land forces.) In a poll conducted in late 1994, thirty-two percent of the public favored the use of U.S. troops if Russia invaded Poland; fifty percent were opposed. These figures are similar to those in polls on U.S. military involvement in Bosnia. This contrasts with plurality approval (forty-two percent in favor) of expansion of NATO to include Poland, Hungary, and the Czech Republic. The American public is clearly increasingly averse to foreign military intervention in general, but it does make exceptions. There was strong popular support for the intervention in the Persian Gulf, and the public appears willing, in the majority, to support U.S. troops in the defense of Western Europe against Russia, and Saudi Arabia against Iraq. Public opinion seems largely to be based on a concept of national interest, and only thirty-one percent of the American public, in the late 1994 poll, felt the U.S. has a vital interest in Poland. See Andrew Kohut and Robert Toth, "Arms and the People," *Foreign Affairs* 73, no. 6 (Nov.–Dec. 1994): 47–61; Rielly, "Public Mood at Mid-Decade," 76—90; and a *Newsweek* poll summarized on "ABC World News Saturday," 3 June 1995.

46. Kamp, "The Folly of Rapid NATO Expansion," 119.

47. In late 1994, economic competition from Japan was regarded as a critical threat to the U.S. by sixty-two percent of the American

public; only twenty-seven percent so viewed economic competition from Europe. See Rielly, "Public Mood at Mid-Decade," 87.

48. On the these questions of the Middle East and the Mediterranean, see John W. Holmes, ed., *Maelstrom: The United States, Southern Europe, and the Challenges of the Mediterranean* (Cambridge, MA: World Peace Foundation, 1995).

49. Kissinger, *Diplomacy*, 826.

CHAPTER 9—WHAT ARE OUR OPTIONS?

1. See Michael Howard, "A European Perspective on the Reagan Years," *Foreign Affairs* 66, no. 3 (America and the World 1987/88): 478–93, esp. 479–80.

2. Europeans being what they are, this attitude is mixed with a fear that the United States will look too much to its own concerns and ignore the old Continent. There was a flare-up of this fear in February 1993, when some Europeans worried that the Clinton administration was at best uninterested in—at worst, negatively inclined toward—Europe. Chancellor Helmut Kohl, speaking at the annual Wehrkunde conference in Munich in early February, seemed to express this concern when he called on the United States to maintain its commitments in Europe: "It is imperative that the U.S., mindful of the lessons from history this century, continue to play its central role in matters of European security." Cited in Edward Mortimer and Quentin Peel, "US Reassures Allies over Commitment to Nato," *Financial Times,* 8 Feb. 1993, 12.

3. John E. Rielly, "The Public Mood at Mid-Decade," *Foreign Policy,* no. 98 (Spring 1995): 76–90. The most profound shift in foreign policy attitudes revealed by the polling reported in this article is a decline in American support for several humanitarian foreign-policy goals. At its lowest level in two decades is the public's endorsement of our protecting weaker countries against foreign aggression, our promoting and protecting human rights in other countries, and our helping to improve the living standards of less developed countries. See Rielly, "The Public Mood," 81.

4. For a statement of one prominent Republican's views, see Bob Dole's "Shaping America's Global Future," *Foreign Policy,* no. 98 (Spring 1995): 29–43. It should be noted that the House passed

in June 1995 a Defense Authorization bill ordering a cutback of American forces in Europe from 100,000 to 25,000 unless Europe contributed more to their maintenance costs. This is not the first time Congress has made a threat of this sort, of course. See chap. 4, above, for discussion of the cost of keeping troops in Europe, compared to that of keeping troops in Asia: Japan and Korea already do what the House wanted Europe to do.

5. See Michael Clough, "Grass-Roots Policymaking: Say Good-Bye to the 'Wise Men,'" *Foreign Affairs* 73, no. 1 (Jan.–Feb. 1994): 2–7; and Mark M. Nelson, "Transatlantic Travails," *Foreign Policy,* no. 92 (Fall 1993): 75–77. Secretary of State Warren Christopher has said, "I think we're somewhat too much European-centered sometimes" (interview by Robert MacNeil on the "MacNeil-Lehrer News Hour," PBS, 1 June 1993). Too much of Washington, in Christopher's opinion, has too long had a "Eurocentric attitude"; they should remember that "Western Europe is no longer the dominant area of the world . . ." (cited in Ann Devroy and R. Jeffrey Smith, "Clinton Seeks Foreign Policy Bearings in Post Cold War Fog," *Washington Post,* 17 Oct. 1993, A1).

6. To say there are three options is to treat options as ideal models; a more finely grained approach could produce a slightly greater number of choices. For a somewhat similar approach, also describing three options (reasserting U.S. leadership, selective engagement and cooperative introversion, and disengagement and confrontational introversion), see Phil Williams, Paul Hammond, and Michael Brenner, "Atlantis Lost, Paradise Regained? The United States and Western Europe after the Cold War," *International Affairs* 69, no. 1 (Jan. 1993): 1–17.

7. The views here summarized are, in order, those of Hannes Adomeit, "Russia: Partner or Risk Factor in European Security," *Adelphi Paper* 285 (Feb. 1994): 15–33, esp. 32; Philip Zelikow, "Beyond Boris Yeltsin," *Foreign Affairs* 73, no. 1 (Jan.–Feb. 1994): 55; and Zbigniew Brzezinski, "The Premature Partnership," *Foreign Affairs* 73, no. 2 (Mar.–Apr. 1994): 68, 79–82.

8. Evidently Mr. Quayle was not correctly quoted.

9. William Diebold, "Political Implications of U.S.-E.C. Economic Conflicts (III): American Trade Policy and Western Europe," *Government and Opposition* 22, no. 3 (Summer 1987): 286; quoted

in Sylvia Ostry, *Governments and Corporations in a Shrinking World: Trade and Innovation Policies in the United States, Europe, and Japan* (New York: Council on Foreign Relations Press, 1990), 26.

10. Robert O. Paxton, "De Gaulle and His Myth," review of *De Gaulle,* by Jean Lacouture, *New York Review of Books,* 23 Apr. 1992, 19.

11. The argument that U.S. willingness to engage in Yugoslavia would lead to the death of NATO was raised in European interviews in July 1992, particularly in Paris.

12. Michael Wines, "Clinton Says Foreign Policy Must Focus on the Economy," *New York Times,* 6 July 1994, A10. Ironically, most of the foreign policy issues that had demanded Clinton's attention—Somalia, Bosnia, North Korea, and Haiti—were essentially political and not very amenable to economic remedies.

13. Robert Zoellick, under secretary of state in the Bush administration, attributes part of the blame for America's failure to engage with the EC, and specifically with Delors, to the fact that the senior figures of the administration—Bush, James Baker, and Brent Scowcroft—were all problem-solvers rather than strategists. See Charles Grant, *Delors: Inside the House that Jacques Built* (London: Nicholas Brealey, 1994), 167.

14. In early 1993 some leading European politicians—French Prime Minister Bérégovoy and ex-Prime Minister Barre, and German Chancellor Kohl—saw in the currency speculation that was straining the EMS the hand of the United States (operating with the help of Britain), working to destroy the system because it might threaten American economic hegemony: the mirror image of American fears of the creation of an overweening European bloc. Eventually the polemic ended, with the Bundesbank's lowering its interest rates (German monetary policy was the real economic problem) and the Clinton administration's displaying a somewhat more positive attitude toward Europe (reducing the underlying nervousness about American intentions). See "War of Attrition,"*Economist,* 9 Jan. 1993, 66–68; and Joseph Fitchett and Carl Gewirtz, "A Plot to Derail Europe's Monetary System? Charges Surface of US.-Led Turmoil to Protect American Economic Clout," *International Herald Tribune,* 3 Feb. 1993, 3. It is probably an indication of somewhat better U.S.-Western European relations that

the sharp decline in the dollar vis-à-vis the major European curren-cies (and the yen) in March 1995 did not provoke the same kind of response. There was certainly criticism of the U.S. for not doing its duty and keeping the dollar stable, and irritation that Europe's re-covery was being shaded by a loss of competitiveness due to the dollar's fall. But there was not the same spinning of theories of a U.S. anti-European plot.

15. For a fair, if unkind, sorting out of the many different strains in the Clinton foreign policy, see Richard Haass, "Paradigm Lost," *Foreign Policy* 74, no. 1 (Jan.–Feb. 1995): 43–58.

16. Henry Kissinger has written: "Theoretically it is possible for the United States to conduct its policy purely on the basis of na-tional interest, not unlike what Great Britain in the 19th century termed the policy of 'splendid isolation.' This would require a care-ful assessment of rewards and penalties for each region of the world and a balancing of them to produce actions most compatible with America's national interest. . . . But in fact the United States lacks a tradition of a foreign policy based entirely on the national interest. . . . A country founded by peoples . . . who believed in the universal application of the values of their society cannot simply abandon the Wilsonianism that has dominated 20th-century Ameri-can foreign policy." See Kissinger, "For U.S. Leadership, a Moment Missed," *Washington Post,* 12 May 1995, A25.

17. As the *Economist* editorialized, "Mr. Clinton has never been happy in . . . [his role as commander-in-chief]. It is not simply a matter of his youthful opposition to the war in Vietnam. . . . It is a visceral discomfort with the application of American power in the world, even at the level of moral suasion, and even in concert with allies." See "The O'Grady Syndrome: How Bill Clinton Missed His Best Chance Yet to be Commander-in-chief," *Economist,* 17 June 1995, 15.

18. The United States had a taste of this new European strength and unity in March 1995, when the EU foreign ministers produced a recommendation that NATO and Russia enter into a nonaggres-sion pact. The U.S. has traditionally been apprehensive about a Eu-ropean caucus deciding on positions to take within NATO, partly because such agreed positions cannot be negotiated. For the EU min-isters, however, it was a way of telling the U.S. that it could not by itself handle the issue of NATO enlargement. See Tom Buerkle, "EU

Urges NATO and Moscow to Make Treaty," *International Herald Tribune,* 20 Mar. 1995, 1; and Lionel Barber, "EU May Back NATO-Russia Pact," *Financial Times,* 20 Mar. 1995, 1. The *Wall Street Journal* fulminated against the EU's effrontery in "NATO Abolished," 21 Mar. 1995, A20.

19. See for example John W. Holmes, "Don't Reverse US Alliances," *Christian Science Monitor,* 21 Aug. 1992, 18. There are hints of the Eastern alternative in Stephen J. Flanagan, "NATO and Central and Eastern Europe: From Liaison to Security Partnership," *Washington Quarterly* 15, no. 2 (Spring 1992): 141–51.

20. See Treverton, "America's Stakes and Choices in Europe," 134–35.

Chapter 10—But What If Europe Breaks Apart?

1. In the words of Roy Denman, "Britain has been divided about Europe since the war. Its learning curve has been nonexistent." See Denman, "This Sceptered, Smug, Shortsighted Isle," *New York Times,* 18 Jan. 1995, A21. Denman, originally a British official, was the EC Commission's representative in Washington, 1982–1989.

2. When Geoffrey Home resigned from Mrs. Thatcher's cabinet in November 1990, he argued that if the U.K. failed to play a full role in the EC, it would be relegated to second-class status in Europe, for European integration would continue whether or not the U.K. participated. See Louise Richardson, "British State Strategies," in *After the Cold War,* ed. Robert O. Keohane, Joseph S. Nye, Stanley Hoffman (Cambridge: Harvard University Press, 1993), 167.

3. See John W. Holmes, "A New Special Relationship for Britain," *International Herald Tribune,* 2 Feb. 1993, 6.

4. Kenneth Clarke, cited in Philip Stephens and David Owen, "Euro-sceptics Enraged by Clarke Speech." *Financial Times,* 30 June 1994, 11.

5. In a European poll conducted in May 1994, sixty-four percent of British respondents felt this way (the EU average was forty-seven percent). See David Marsh, "Euro-poll Blow for Single Currency," *Financial Times,* 1 June 1994, 1; and Marsh, "Voters Divided on EU's Important Issues," *Financial Times,* 1 June 1994, 4. However, when asked a different question in November 1994 — whether they would support a single currency if given the opportunity to vote in a referendum—only thirty-three percent answered

yes. See David Marsh, "Poll Shows Support for Vote on EU Single Currency," *Financial Times*, 5 Dec. 1994, 1.

6. Douglas Hurd, cited in Ian Davidson, "It's Not on the Menu: Mr. Hurd's Portrayal of an à la Carte Europe Is Deceptive," *Financial Times*, 18 May 1994, 12.

7. Though they have emerged from their Gaullist phase, the French themselves are hardly to be described as European federalists. But they prefer that the Germans be federalists.

8. See Alain Lamassoure, "Europe 96: pour un nouveau contrat fondateur," *Le Monde*, 31 May 1994, 4; Tom Buerkle, "France Wants Core of Members to Pursue Selected EU Goals," *International Herald Tribune*, 31 May 1994, 1; and Michael Binyon, et al., "Bonn-Paris Joint Strategy for Europe," *Times*, 31 May 1994, 1.

9. Ireland has already benefited from such a liberal reading. Its ratio of debt to GDP (Gross Domestic Product) is well above the Maastricht limit of sixty percent and is unlikely to reach that level in just a few years. The EU Commission suggested, at the end of June 1994, that Ireland be given a green light on this score because its debt ratio is declining. See Peter Norman, "Brussels Move to Exempt Ireland from Debt Rules," *Financial Times*, 4 July 1994, 1. Germany has made it clear that it will not let the criteria be stretched too far, however.

10. "Europe á la Carte," *Economist*, 10 Sept. 1994, 14–15; "Back to the Drawing-board," *Economist*, 10 Sept. 1994, 21–23; Stephen Kinzer, "German Plan for Phased Union of Europe Provokes Controversy," *New York Times*, 4 Sept. 1994, Sec. 1, p. 11.

11. Cited in "News Digest for September 1994," *Keesing's Record of World Events* 40, no. 9:40203.

12. The intergovernmental conference was agreed to at Maastricht.

13. "European Union: Pale Reflections," *Economist*, 10 June 1995, 45–48.

14. "Germany and the EU: Ever Closer, More Tactfully," *Economist*, 17 June 1995, 56; Lucas Delattre, "Le parti de Helmut Kohl lance de nouvelles propositions sur l'Europe," *Le Monde*, 11–12 June 1995, 2; Lionel Barber, "British Hope to Build New 'French Connection,'" *Financial Times*, 13 June 1995, 3.

15. It might be clearer to call the German approach supranationalist rather than federalist.

16. Jacques Chirac, cited in David Buchan, "Chirac Wants to Broaden EU Co-operation with Britain," *Financial Times,* 12 June 1995, 1.

17. Winston Churchill, cited in "Back to the Drawing-board," 23.

18. Philippe Lemaitre, "Les 'grands' à la recherche d'institutions efficaces," *Le Monde,* 4 June 1994, 6; Philippe Lemaitre and Claire Tréan, "Un entretien avec Jacques Delors," *Le Monde,* 1 June 1994, 1; Fabio Luca Cavazza and Carlo Pelanda, "Maastricht: Before, During, After," *Daedalus* 123, no. 2 (Spring 1994): 77.

19. See chap. 7, above.

CHAPTER 11 — CAN WE FORGE A NEW ALLIANCE?

1. The same thinking underlay James Baker's speech in Berlin, in which he proposed "a strengthened set of institutional and consultative links" between the EC and the United States: "He saw that Nato, even if still essential in an adapted form, could never provide a satisfactory institutional framework for this new transatlantic community. Nato puts too much emphasis on military forces, at a time when military aspects of security are no longer the most immediate or most decisive; and Nato casts the US in more of a dominant role in Europe than it now needs or is willing to play. Europe as such is not represented in Nato." See "Atlantic Dialogue," *Financial Times,* 13 July 1994, 17.

2. In the words of Thomas J. Duesterberg, "What is lacking now, perhaps, is the crisis atmosphere that sometimes, as Hegel stated in a famous epigram ('the Owl of Minerva takes flight only as the shades of night are falling') engenders heroic wisdom and leadership." See Duesterberg, "Prospects for an EU-NAFTA Free Trade Agreement," *Washington Quarterly* 18, no. 2 (Spring 1995): 80.

3. Stephen Woolcock, *Market Access Issues in EC-US Relations: Trading Partners or Trading Blows?* (London: Pinter for the Royal Institute of International Affairs, 1991), 25–26.

4. Lawrence Summers, "Shared Prosperity and the New International Economic Order," speech to the Institute of International Economics, Washington, 20 May 1994; cited in Martin Wolf, "Risks in Making False Analogies," *Financial Times,* 23 May 1994, 20.

5. Duesterberg, "Prospects for an EU-NAFTA Free Trade Agreement," 72.

6. Robin Gaster and Clyde V. Prestowitz, Jr., *Shrinking the Atlantic: Europe and the American Economy* (Washington: North Atlantic Research and Economic Strategy Institute, 1994), ii–iv, 6–7, 26–27, 49; Duesterberg, "Prospects for an EU-NAFTA Free Trade Agreement," 72.

7. Sylvia Ostry, *Governments and Corporations in a Shrinking World: Trade and Innovation Policies in the United States, Europe, and Japan* (New York: Council on Foreign Relations Press, 1990), 2–3.

8. This need for stimulation is particularly true of Europe, whose economy has been losing international competitiveness, whereas the American economy has been holding its own. See Duesterberg, "Prospects for an EU-NAFTA Free Trade Agreement," 74; and Martin Wolf, *The Resistible Appeal of Fortress Europe* (Washington: Center for Policy Studies and American Enterprise Institute, 1994), 53.

9. Much of Raymond Vernon's recent research and writing has been on this subject. For an example, see Raymond Vernon, Debora L. Spar, and Glenn Tobin, *Iron Triangles and Revolving Doors: Cases in U.S. Foreign Economic Policymaking* (New York: Praeger, 1991).

10. Joseph A. Greenwald, "Negotiating Strategy," in *Europe 1992: An American Perspective,* ed. Gary Clyde Hufbauer (Washington: Brookings Institution, 1990), 358–59.

11. See Ostry's *Governments and Corporations in a Shrinking World,* esp. 88–89—a book written before Mexico became a member of the OECD. A discussion coauthored by Ostry and C. Michael Aho makes a similar though not identical suggestion: of the alternatives to renewing and enforcing the existing General Agreement for Treaties and Tariffs (GATT) system, "the least bad may be a revival of the old idea of a 'super GATT,' i.e., plurilateral agreements housed in the GATT that could, over time, embrace the full multilateral agenda and GATT members." See Ostry and Aho, "Regional Trading Blocs: Pragmatic or Problematic Policy?" in *The Global Economy: America's Role in the Decade Ahead,* ed. William Brock and Robert Hormats (New York: W. W. Norton, 1990), 172–73.

12. Robert Hormats, "Making Regionalism Safe," *Foreign Affairs* 73, no. 2 (Mar.–Apr. 1994): 98–99.

13. Lane Kirkland, "A NAFTA, but with Europe," *International Herald Tribune,* 25 May 1993, 4.

14. Prestowitz's views are contained in *Shrinking the Atlantic: Europe and the American Economy,* which he coauthored with the trade consultant Robin Gaster. See also Thomas L. Friedman, "Europe, Not Japan, Is Called America's Frontier for Trade," *New York Times,* 10 June 1994, D1; and Nancy Dunne, "Forge Europe Ties, US Urged," *Financial Times,* 14 June 1994, 4.

15. See Mancur Olson, *The Rise and Decline of Nations* (New Haven: Yale University Press, 1982).

16. For an inventory of the areas of economic resistance to a transatlantic free trade area that are operative in Europe and America (the agriculture and high technology sectors, tariff peaks and tariff preferences, and, in the investment area, rights of establishment and ownership restrictions), see Duesterberg, "Prospects for an EU-NAFTA Free Trade Agreement," 74–75.

17. Bill Clinton, "Confronting the Challenges of a Broader World," *U.S. Department of State Dispatch* 4, no. 39 (27 Sept. 1993): 650.

18. President Clinton, "Partnership for Peace: Building A New Security for the 21st Century," *U.S. Department of State Dispatch* 5, no. 1 (Jan. 1994): 4. See also Henry Kissinger, *Diplomacy* (New York: Simon and Schuster, 1994), 824.

19. "M. Clinton souligne la nécessité d'une Europe 'unie et forte,'" *Le Monde,* 2 June 1994, 1; "Atlantic Dialogue," *Financial Times,* 13 July 1994, 17. See also Clinton's June 7, 1994, address to the French National Assembly, *U.S. Department of State Dispatch* 5, no. 24 (June 13, 1994): 381–83; and David Buchan, "Clinton backing strong Europe." *Financial Times,* 8 June 1994, 2.

20. Warren Christopher, cited in Steven Greenhouse, "Christopher Backs Free Trade with Europe," *New York Times,* 3 June 1995, 3. Christopher's statement about the need to adapt the transatlantic relationship, and not simply to base it on nostalgia, echoed a previous statement by Speaker of the House Newt Gingrich.

21. Clinton made the proposal for a "Pacific Community" at the November meeting with the leaders of the Asia Pacific Economic Cooperation group in Seattle. Nothing very definite emerged. See Kissinger, *Diplomacy,* 826, 828; *Strategic Survey 1993–1994* (London: Brassey's for the International Institute for Strategic Studies, 1994), 173–75; Thomas L. Friedman, "Leaders Seek Strong Pacific

Community: Clinton Preaches Open Markets at Summit," *New York Times,* 21 Nov. 1993, sec. 1, p. 1; and George Graham, "Weary Clinton Sets Sights on Pacific Goals," *Financial Times,* 22 Nov. 1993, 5.

22. Francis Fukuyama, "For the Atlantic Allies Today, a Fraying of the Sense of Moral Community," *International Herald Tribune,* 6 June 1994, 4.

23. Paul Krugman, "The Myth of Asia's Miracle," *Foreign Affairs* 73, no. 6 (Nov.–Dec. 1994): 62–78.

24. See Robert A. Manning and Paula Stern, "The Myth of the Pacific Community," *Foreign Affairs* 73, no. 6 (Nov.–Dec. 1994): 79–93.

25. These points are made forcefully by Kissinger in *Diplomacy,* 818–31. Amusingly, Fukuyama (see note 22, above) says, "Realists like Mr. Kissinger have for long argued that durable alliances ought to be formed on the basis of interest alone, in preference to ideology or sentimentality." Kissinger's argument is rather different in *Diplomacy.*

26. See Raymond Vernon and Debora L. Spar, *Beyond Globalism: Remaking American Foreign Policy* (New York: Free Press, 1989).

27. See John E. Rielly, "The Public Mood at Mid-Decade," *Foreign Policy,* no. 98 (Spring 1995): 76–93.

28. I refer to elite opinion. Visits to Europe and discussions with European analysts have left me with the impression that in many European countries, immigration is the primary foreign policy concern among the general public.

29. In the words of a *Financial Times* editorial, "US presidential visits are still treated as a kind of beauty contest, with each European country striving to demonstrate that its relationship with the US is the most 'special'; and yet EU members seem to find it easier to agree on free trade with Russia than with the US." See "Atlantic Dialogue," *Financial Times,* 13 July 1994, 17.

30. Private interview with the author, Washington, D.C., June 1992.

31. James Baker, "A New Europe and a New Atlanticism," speech to the Berlin Press Club, Berlin, Germany, 12 December 1989, in *American Foreign Policy Current Documents 1989,* ed. Nancy L. Golden and Sherrill Brown Wells (Washington: Department of State, 1990), 302.

32. Kevin Featherstone and Roy H. Ginsburg, *The United States and the European Community in the 1990s: Partners in Transition* (New York: St. Martin's Press, 1993), 32, 90–95.

33. "Cool Winds from the White House," *Economist,* 27 Mar. 1993, 58.

34. The Uruguay Round was substantively completed in December 1993; the results of the negotiation were formally signed in Marrakech in April 1994 and entered into effect in 1995. This happy result was arrived at, however, only after a "perils of Pauline" scenario. The Clinton administration wanted the completion and approval of the North American Free Trade Area agreement to precede the Uruguay Round. NAFTA was more controversial than the Uruguay Round; if it had failed to gain Congressional approval, the Round's prospects would have been darkened.

35. "Europe Wants Better U.S. Ties," *Wall Street Journal,* 8 Apr. 1993, A10. A senior U.S. official told me that he viewed this as springing from the consciousness that something should be done to break out of the quiescent state in which in U.S.-EC relations had been for the preceding year, but that it was a modest holding action. It was clear that until Denmark and the U.K. ratified the Maastricht Treaty, the EC would not be ready to go further, for example to the discussion of a U.S.-EC Treaty.

36. "Atlantic Dialogue," *Financial Times,* 13 July 1994, 17.

37. Stanley Hoffmann, "Europe's Identity Crisis Revisited," *Daedalus* 123, no. 2 (Spring 1994): 21–22.

38. Pascaline Winand, *Eisenhower, Kennedy, and the United States of Europe* (New York: St. Martin's Press, 1993), 366. Winand's book is particularly good on this subject. François Duchêne's biography *Jean Monnet: The First Statesman of Interdependence* (New York: W. W. Norton, 1994) gives exactly the same impression: the end of the close Euro-American connection came in the administration of Lyndon Johnson, with George Ball's departure from office being the symbol of the end of an era—reminiscent, on a minor scale, of the famous "dropping the pilot" cartoon on Bismarck's dismissal.

39. The study group produced a report advocating an Atlantic single market: Mark M. Nelson and G. John Ikenberry, *Atlantic Frontiers: A New Agenda for US-EC Relations* (Washington:

Carnegie Endowment for International Peace, 1993). Gaster and Prestowitz's 1994 study urges that "North America and Europe should open exploratory discussions aimed at broadening and deepening economic relations. . . . These discussions would . . . start the United States and Europe down the path to an economic parallel to NATO. . . . As US and European concerns shift from military security to economic security, it is equally important to develop a similar forum for economic issues, both international and domestic." See *Shrinking the Atlantic,* v and 60–61.

On the other hand, a Chatham House study sees a strong case for transatlantic policy integration but also high barriers to it; competitive cooperation, with as much emphasis on cooperation as possible, seems the best practical prescription. See Michael Smith and Stephen Woolcock, *Redefining the U.S.-EC Relationship* (New York: Royal Institute for International Affairs/Council on Foreign Relations Press, 1993), 99–111. Smith and Woolcock's "update" essay is excellent but more pessimistic than this book about the possibilities of transatlantic harmony; see "Learning to Cooperate: the Clinton Administration and the European Union," *International Affairs* 70, no. 3 (July 1994): 459–76.

40. Andreas van Agt, speech notes, sent to the author under cover of a letter of 23 November 1994. See also "Digest," *Washington Post,* 18 Nov. 1994, B1.

41. Rühe is quoted in Rick Atkinson, "U.S. and Europe Seek Stability but Wrangle over Bosnia," *Washington Post,* 5 Feb. 1995, A29. See also Atkinson, "U.S., Europe: The Gap Is Widening," *Washington Post,* 8 Feb. 1995, A22; and Edward Mortimer, "An Unequal Match," *Financial Times,* 8 Feb. 1995, 12.

42. NATO decided at its December 1994 summit to discuss the issue of membership criteria during 1995.

43. Rühe is quoted in Jim Hoagland, "Reaching Out for NATO," *Washington Post,* 12 Mar. 1995, C7. See also Lionel Barber, "Europe Steps Up Efforts to Strengthen Ties with US," *Financial Times,* 20 Feb. 1995; William Drozdiak, "Europeans Say Weak Dollar Gives U.S. Unfair Trade Advantage," *Washington Post,* 7 Apr. 1995, A31.

44. Garten's statements are reported in Nancy Dunne, "U.S. Touts Idea of Free Trade Deal with EU," *Financial Times,* 9 Feb. 1995, 4; Holbrooke's in "Free Trade Zone under Discussion by U.S., Europe," *Washington Post,* 6 April 1995, A28.

45. Kirkland's statement is reported in "Free Trade Zone under Discussion by U.S., Europe"; Kissinger's in John Darnton, "There'll Always Be an . . . ," *New York Times*, 2 Apr. 1995, sec. 1, p. 9.

46. Henry Kissinger, "For U.S. Leadership, a Moment Missed," *Washington Post*, 12 May 1995, A25.

47. Warren Christopher, cited in Greenhouse, "Christopher Backs Free Trade with Europe," 3. See also David White and Guy de Jonquières, "US Calls for Talks to Improve Links with Europe," *Financial Times*, 3–4 June 1995, 22.

48. The degree to which Europe has been at the mercy of the U.S. in the making of important decisions was evidenced during the Persian Gulf crisis. "On at least two major occasions, which were to have profound consequences for its partners," Philip Robins has written, "the United States took decisions unilaterally. . . . Both the Arab and the European members of the anti-Iraq coalition accepted the limits of action laid down by the United States, underlining the diplomatic hegemony of Washington during this brief moment when there was a 'new world order.' That such critical decisions were made without consultations with the British government, a close and frequently uncritical ally . . . deserves wider debate in Britain." See Robins, "The Gulf War in Perspective," *World Today* 50, no. 7 (July 1994): 139.

49. The following analysis is largely based on Lionel Barber and Guy de Jonquières, "US and Europe Eye Each Other Up," *Financial Times*, 12 May 1995, 2; and de Jonquières, "Sweden Urges End to EU-US Non-tariff Barriers, *Financial Times*, 3 May 1995, 6.

50. "In Need of Fastening," *Economist*, 27 May 1995, 15.

51. As early as the spring of 1989, Brent Scowcroft, Bush's National Security Advisor, reportedly thought it would be not only acceptable but advantageous to the United States to withdraw all ground forces from Western Europe, while leaving some air units, if the Soviets withdrew their troops from Eastern Europe. See Michael R. Beschloss and Strobe Talbott, *At the Highest Levels: The Inside Story of the End of the Cold War* (Boston: Little, Brown, 1993), 37–38. The process of withdrawing the troops of the former Soviet Union once stationed in East and Central Europe was completed in 1994.

52. Kissinger, *Diplomacy*, 826.

53. See *Diplomacy*, 810–11, 819, 826, 831.

INDEX

Acheson, Dean, 65, 176n. 1
Adams, John Quincy, 94, 189n. 17
Adenauer, Konrad, 144, 176n. 1
Adriatic Sea, 46, 67, 170n. 36
AFL-CIO, 139
Aho, C. Michael, 200n. 11
Albania: emigration to Italy, 98;
   and EU, 85, 183n. 59; and
   NATO, 164n. 12
Albright, Madeleine, 35
Algeria, 180n. 29
Amalric, Jacques, 78, 181n. 42
American public opinion: attitude
   toward Central and Eastern
   European countries, 100,
   192nn. 42, 45; based on
   concept of national interest,
   192n. 45; and Chechnya, 94,
   189n. 18; decline in support for
   humanitarian goals, 193n. 3;
   defense of Saudi Arabia against
   Iraq, 192n. 45; defense of
   Western Europe against Russia,
   109, 143, 192n. 45; and EC/
   EU, 52, 192n. 45; Europe rated
   above Asia, 109, 142; favors
   selective engagement, 142;
   Japanese economic competition
   viewed as threat, 192n. 47;
   military intervention to defend
   Ukraine, 95, 189n. 20; and
   NATO, 38, 109, 143, 158n. 4;
   Persian Gulf intervention, 192n.
   45; reaction to Yugoslav
   tragedy, 100, 192n. 45; reduced

awareness of importance of
   transatlantic relationship, 144;
   reduced concern for world and
   for Europe, 109; warm feelings
   toward Europe, 142–43;
   Western Europe not an economic threat, 143
Asia: Clinton meeting with Asian
   heads of government, 142;
   dynamism, 142; larger market
   for U.S. exports than Europe,
   137
Atlantic alliance: American
   leadership, 145; divergences no
   longer inhibited by security
   concerns, 138; economic
   competition from Japan, 135;
   fundamental challenges of
   1990s economy, 135; massive
   change required, 121; no
   identifiable military threat in
   1990s, 135, 147; purposes of,
   1, 121; strained by end of Cold
   War, 21–22, 91; threatened by
   U.S. aversion to military
   involvement, emphasis on
   domestic concerns, 114, 116–
   17, 195n. 11; U.S. failure to
   consult, 205n. 48
Atlantic Charter, 146–47
Atlantic community: cannot be
   created by NATO expansion,
   147; compared to "Pacific
   Community," 163n. 1; real
   community of values and

countries, 97; private investment, 8, 156n. 9;

U.S. relations with China: cultural and political gap, 4; China a key area for U.S. interests, 90

U.S. relations with European Community/European Union, 22, 51; Bush administration speeches in favor of European integration, 111; call for U.S.-EU political treaty, 146; decisive for U.S. in twenty-first century, 153; Declaration on U.S.-EC Relations (1990), 3, 116, 143–44; declining interest of American leaders, post-Kennedy, 145, 203n. 38; division of responsibilities, 9–10, 111–12; EC seeks in 1993 to revive dialogue with U.S., 144, 203n. 35; EC's 1991–92 "maintenance" approach to, 143, 202n. 29; 203n. 34; EU not viewed as critical economic threat in 1990s, 52; European politicians in 1995 advocate transforming the relationship, 145–47; fear of European protectionism, 51–52; impact of Economic and Monetary Union, 59–60; initial opposition to single market program, 54–55; linked to U.S. military commitment, 112–13; Middle East policy, 74, 110–11; not given high priority, 116, 143; permanent alliance, 121; reaction to European Monetary System, 53–54; reconstructing economic relations key to future of relationship, 151; shift to encouragement of European defense cooperation, 81; trade and investment agreement, 138–39; U.S.-EU agreement encompassing political and security

issues, 139; U.S. opposition to worker participation in management proposals, 52–53, 171nn. 4 and 5; U.S. study group calls for formalization of relationship, 145, 203n. 39; U.S. yields lead on Eastern Europe and Yugoslavia to EC, 111–12

U.S. relations with Germany, 17; Germany singled out for special attention, 112; monetary policy, 129; nuclear capability, 90–91; reunification, 14

U.S. relations with Italy, 19

U.S. relations with Japan: cultural and political gap, 4, 102; economic rivalry, 101; Japan a key area for U.S. interests, 90; nuclear capability, 90–91

U.S. relations with Russia, 34, 93, 95, 111; Bush and Clinton administrations' hopes for strategic partnership, 111; Conventional Forces in Europe (CFE) treaty, 34, 96; cultural and political gap, 4; economic assistance, 112; NATO enlargement, 34, 95; OSCE, 34; preventing Russian dominance in former Soviet Union, 94, 111; Russia a key area for U.S. interests, 90; U.S. deterrence and European military presence and Russian developments, 92

U.S. relations with United Kingdom, 128–29, 147

U.S. relations with USSR, 8, 93, 156n. 9; Bush administration's attempt to preserve USSR as major power, 110–11

U.S. relations with Western Europe: alliance, 121, 122; attitude toward Eurocorps, 69, 112, 178n. 17, 182n. 50; attitude toward Western